Reframing Authority

Comparative Research on Iconic and Performative Texts

Series Editor

James W. Watts, Syracuse University.

While humanistic scholarship has focused on the semantic meaning of written, printed, and electronic texts, it has neglected how people perform texts mentally, orally and theatrically and manipulate the material text through aesthetic engagement, ritual display, and physical decoration. This series encourages the twenty-first-century trend of studying the performative and iconic uses of material texts, especially as encouraged by the activities of the Society for Comparative Research on Iconic and Performative Texts (SCRIPT).

Published

Iconic Books and Texts

Edited by James W. Watts

Sensing Sacred Texts

Edited by James W Watts

Forthcoming

How and Why Books Matter: Essays on the Social Function of Iconic Texts

James W. Watts

Reframing Authority:
The Role of Media and Materiality

Edited by
Laura Feldt and Christian Høgel

SHEFFIELD UK BRISTOL CT

Published by Equinox Publishing Ltd.

UK: Office 415, The Workstation, 15 Paternoster Row, Sheffield, S1 2BX
USA: ISD, 70 Enterprise Drive, Bristol, CT 06010

www.equinoxpub.com

Portions of this book were published in Volume 8.3 of the journal *Postscripts*.

ISBN 9781781796801 (ePDF) | ISBN 9781781796788 (hb) | ISBN 9781781796795 (pb)

British Library Cataloguing-in-Publication Data

A catalogue record for this book is available from the British Library.

Library of Congress Cataloging-in-Publication Data

Names: Feldt, Laura, editor.

Title: Reframing authority: The role of media and materiality / edited by Laura Feldt and Christian Høgel.

Description: Bristol : Equinox Publishing Ltd., 2018. | Series: Comparative research on iconic and performative texts | Includes bibliographical references and index.

Identifiers: LCCN 2017049754 (print) | LCCN 2018019400 (ebook)

ISBN 9781781796801 (ePDF) | ISBN 9781781796788 (hb) | ISBN 9781781796795 (pb)

Subjects: LCSH: Authority. | Power (Philosophy) | Mass media–Influence. | Social media. | Materialism.

Classification: LCC BD209 (ebook) | LCC BD209 .R44 2018 (print) | DDC 303.3/6–dc23

LC record available at https://lccn.loc.gov/2017049754

Edited and Typeset by Queenston Publishing, Hamilton Canada.

Printed by Lightning Source Inc. (La Vergne, TN), Lightning Source UK Ltd. (Milton Keynes).

Contents

Section III
Authority, Media and Modern Identity Politics

List of Figures

— 1 —

Reframing Authority—The Role of Media and Materiality

Laura Feldt and Christian Høgel

Introduction

Authority has been a key topic in many studies of history, society, literature, and religion, and it can be defined simply as an exercise of power perceived as legitimate. Authority suggests an uneven relation of influence, the power to motivate and gain obedience, or an ascribed prestige, recognition, or status. The contributions of this book argue that forms of mediation and materiality play key roles in any constitution, contestation, or transformation of authority, and that new understanding of authority can be gained by focusing on how authority is created, contested, or transformed in different historical eras and cultures. In spite of the scholarly attention, authority continues to have an elusive quality, and the argument of this book is that new knowledge can be acquired by focusing on the role of materiality and media, as well as on the changes in constellations of authority historically and cross-culturally.

In most societies, relationships and patterns of authority develop which are demarcated by specific forms of mediation—objects, narratives, practices and occasions. Such relationships and patterns have their history, their starting points, their crises and renewals, and—if contestation becomes too strong—a breakdown. As a concept, authority has a wide area of application, from social, political, and text-bound authority, all meanings which fall within the original Latin *auctoritas*, to more performative and ritualized occasions. Authority differs from power, and it is often pointed out how authority, properly understood, hovers between force, or the threat of violence, on the one hand, and persuasion on the other (Furedi 2013, 1; Lincoln 1994). Our analyses investigate, via an intense attention to forms of mediation and materiality, the fundamentally relational character of authority. As the in-depth historical case studies of this book show, authority is fundamentally dependent upon a range of media and materiality forms—objects, props, paraphernalia, space and spatial practices, visual culture, literary forms, technologies, and bodies. Thus it is also vulnerable and in need of continual maintenance, as struggles against, negotiations of, and transformations within authority constellations demonstrate. Despite oft-mentioned "crises of authority" throughout the twentieth and twenty-first centuries, recent developments and research demonstrate the continuing relevance of analyses of how authority functions.

The contributions of this book argue that forms of mediation and materiality play a crucial and constitutive role in processes of authority formation and transformation. We explore the creation, contestation, and breaking of relationships and patterns of authority, taking forms of mediation and material objects as playing key roles in how authority is established, and the manners in which it may be contested or transformed, broken down or transferred. Authority has been the subject of—and the foundation of—much research. This book offers a new, comparative and cross-disciplinary perspective by focusing on the role of media and materiality in the creation and contestation of authority in a series of studies based in different disciplines of the humanistic and social sciences, different periods of history, and various geographical arenas. The case studies all spring from common research interests that developed within the cross-disciplinary research programme *Authority, Materiality and Media*[1] based at the University of Southern Denmark, to which historians, classicists, medievalists, historians of religion and Middle East experts contributed. In the research programme, we discussed and developed new perspectives for understanding how authority is generated, transformed, and challenged by means of material and aesthetic media, which ultimately led to the analyses presented in this book. First, a few words on the key concepts—authority, materiality, and media—which are at the centre of discussion in this book, about the key themes covered, and finally a presentation of the contributions.

Key concepts: Authority and forms of media and materiality

As sociologist Frank Furedi has put it recently, authority has an elusive quality when studied historically (Furedi 2013, vii). With others, Furedi points to how authority differs from power, and how it is positioned between force, or the threat of violence, on the one hand, and persuasion on the other

1. http://www.sdu.dk/en/om_sdu/institutter_centre/ih/forskning/forskningsprogrammer/autoritet_materialitet_medier Accessed August 1st 2017, 9:59 a.m. Our analyses have benefited greatly from discussions in the larger research group. A special thanks goes to Mikael Aktor for his enthusiastic interest in this field and his many contributions to our discussions.

(Furedi 2013, 1; Lincoln 1994). Furedi's account of the historical developments in the concept of authority is interesting for our collection of historical studies, because Furedi stresses the relational and ever fragile character of authority, as historical struggles against, negotiations of, and challenges to, authority demonstrate (Furedi 2013, 3). With Furedi, we stress the importance of situating studies of authority in history (Furedi 2013, 10), because historical studies of authority show that the meaning and performance of authority has continually been an object of negotiation and struggle, even in societies and eras not marked by any distinct crises of authority, such as has been seen as characteristic of modernity by some thinkers (Arendt 1961).

For the concept of authority, a classical point of departure is of course Weber's theory of domination and his "Typen der Herrschaft" (Weber 1980 [1921], 122–176; Weber 1922), which he sometimes uses interchangeably with "Autorität" (e.g. Weber 1980, 122; Weber 1922; Breuer 2011). Weber's approach to authority has been widely used in sociology and in the study of religions (e.g., Lincoln 1994; Lewis 2012). As Weber recognized, a key problem of authority theories concerns the source which is understood to validate authority, or, in other words, what it is that forms the foundation of authority. This insight led Weber to formulate his theory of the three ideal types of authority—charismatic, traditional, and rational-legal; each based on its own form of legitimation (Weber 1980). Weber, however, did recognize the variety of historical manifestations of these types of authority, their ability to shift and transform in various historical contexts. Charismatic authority—the legitimacy of which derives from the ascribed personal qualities of the leader, e.g., from his or her perceived election by a superhuman being—often comes into play in group sociology, and indeed many new religious movements have been seen as founded on this kind of authority. Charismatic authority has often functioned to overturn or transform other types of dominance (Renger 2015), and as Weber also elaborates, it is not stable and often not consistent. It is usually transformed and succeeded by other forms of authority, a rational-legal bureaucracy, or a reorientation towards structures of traditional authority—what Weber terms "routinization" (Weber 1980). Important for our work is that already Weber argued that charisma is a form of recognition (*Anerkennung*), which may be transferred to rules, techniques, blood or family, and to things via "rituelle Versachligung" (Weber 1922). To study how such a transfer occurs, and to analyse in detail how the forms of media and materiality function in the maintenance and transformation of authority historically, is the ambition of this volume.

More recently, the concept of authority has been developed and approached in terms of specific relational, narrative and discursive practices. Historian of religion Bruce Lincoln's 1994 study is useful in this respect, as he situates his approach to authority in the tradition of Foucault and Bakhtin (and others), and stresses that it is important to "treat authority as an aspect of discourse and... [be] more attentive to its labile dynamics than to its institutional incarnations" (Lincoln 1994, 2).[2] Lincoln suggests that historical studies should focus more on "the capacity to produce consequential speech, quelling doubts and winning the trust of the audiences whom they engage" (Lincoln 1994, 4). This approach sees authority less in terms of an entity, and more in terms of an effect, the capacity to produce that effect, and a shared opinion that an actor has this capacity (Lincoln 1994, 10–11). While Lincoln recognizes the importance of objects, spaces, props and paraphernalia (Lincoln 1994,5), he does not devote much space to the analysis of their functioning in the creation or contestation of authority. However, notably, he does point out how authority is always a matter of performance, and that it can, sometimes, be a matter of pretence. Authority is also effective, when people perform accordingly, when they behave *as if* (Lincoln 1994,4). The influence of Michel Foucault, and his approach to power, is clearly visible in the above approach, especially his insistence that power is much more than an external, repressive force, but also something that produces things, pleasure, forms of knowledge, and discourses (Foucault 1980, 119). According to Foucault, power networks run through the social fabric in subtle ways and affect the body, sexuality, the family, kinship, knowledge, technology, etc. (Larsson 2015; Foucault 1980). Subsequent theories of power, such as Stephen Lukes', also stress the importance of analyses of implicit and less directly visible forms of power, and the relational quality of both power and authority (Larsson 2015). However, none of the existing approaches to the concept of authority focuses explicitly on the role of media and materiality in the construction, maintenance, contestation, or transformation of authority. We stress that discourse and speech are not necessarily to be understood as oppositional to a focus on materiality, media, and objects; social constructivism and discourse analysis have brought crucial insights to the theories of how authority functions. Yet, we find it crucial to add, to analyses of authority, analyses of what materiality, objects, and media *do* in constructions, contestations, and transformations of authority. Not only do we focus on authority as an effect and as performed, but we also wish to analyse the role of media and materiality in its effectiveness. Inspired in various different ways by the media and material turn in the human and social sciences, we analyse how materiality figures, how it is mobilized, in performances of authority, without necessarily posit-

2. "Are" changed to "be" to fit sentence by the authors.

ing an acting, human subject behind it. With inspiration from many different ends of a vast and multi-disciplinary field, ranging from archaeological approaches, spatiality theories, perspectives on narrativity, and the revitalized interest in materiality, the contributions of this book offer analyses which do not approach space, objects or other non-human actors as passive, pre-existing forms of materiality, but which try to take into account their performativity, and the networks and relations that enable the creation, maintenance, or contestation of authority. We have found it important to also bring the concept of mediation into the discussion of authority.

While people sometimes think of media as a modern phenomenon, found in the form of technologies such as radio, tv, films, facebook and twitter, etc., it is important to our approach in this volume to clarify that we here work from the assumption that all communication is mediated—from speech and narrative, to our bodies, writing, dance, images, etc. As suggested by Regis Debray, messages never travel unchanged; sender and receiver are also changed by the message exchanged, just as the message itself is transformed by being circulated. Materiality is, invariably, crucial in processes of mediation, because materiality mediates human relationships to the world (Debray 1996, 44). "Media" are thus neither exclusively modern, nor neutral carriers of content or channels of communication, but can be approached broadly as "content-in-form", which has specific material, physical, sensory, social and technological characteristics or affordances, which can be described and analyzed. In this way, they are closely bound to a material context, from which new communicative means, new symbolic values, and new manners of performance may be drawn. New media often lead to social change over time by constructing new patterns of identity formation, socialization, and hierarchy (Meyrowitz 1994). For these reasons, analyses of the material media through which authority becomes effective and is performed are crucial.

Furedi, as Lincoln and Arendt before him, underlines that authority is a relational concept, suggesting a compelling power to motivate and gain obedience, "without having to argue or threaten the use of force"; that authority is an influence which compels (Furedi 2013, 7–9; Lincoln 1994; Arendt 1961). By taking in new media and materiality perspectives and demonstrating their fruitfulness in a series of case studies, the contributions of this book move towards expanding previous understandings of authority. Working cross-disciplinarily, we find it crucial to discuss how forms of authority are fundamentally dependent upon media and materiality in order to function and stay effective, or be overturned (Law 2003). To this end, we deem it necessary to investigate the forms of authority which literature, objects, images, or particular spaces may be ascribed, the obedience or influence they may command. Inspired by Frank Furedi, this book suggests that it is crucial to provide historical context for transformations of authority (Furedi 2013, vii), as a key way of allowing new understanding to emerge, just as it is very important to continually keep in focus how authority is a fragile accomplishment of social interaction that needs maintenance in order not to crumble, and which is necessarily transformed in the course of its management and maintenance over time. With the case studies of this book, we suggest that material media play key roles in that social accomplishment we call "authority." By focusing on media and materiality, the contributors to this book aim also to offer fresh perspectives on traditional questions related to authority, by working together in a long historical, cross-cultural and cross-disciplinary perspective.

The themes and contributions

In our first section, which is entitled "Authority, Materiality, and Premodern Literary Media," all three contributions discuss questions of authority in relation to ancient and medieval literary media: the material and imagined spaces that are foundational in the construction of authority are discussed, the ways in which ancient and medieval literature was ascribed authority, the networks in which literature circulated, as well as the material foundations of the cultures of production and reception of literature.

Laura Feldt's chapter focuses on the role of literary and spatial media in authority changes in late antique Gaul. Feldt uses theories of social space and media to analyze and discuss how the authority of the desert space, and ascetic practice, was negotiated through the literary medium of Eucherius of Lyon's *Epistula de laude eremi* [In Praise of the Desert], as well as how the authority of the text as a medium is constructed. This analysis then forms the basis for a discussion of religious authority changes in late antique Gaul in a time of large scale societal changes in the aftermath of the Roman empire. In this era, the status of asceticism was a matter of contention and the authority of monks and church leaders was insecure, and here literary media promoting ascetic holy figures, and the ascetic space of the desert, played a decisive role in transformations of authority and in negotiations of the meanings of authoritative texts. Such media were created and used by ascetics, bishops, and theologians as means with which to change forms of religious authority. The authority transformations of the era became consequential for Western European history.

In Christian Høgel's chapter, we move to a focus on what happens to the mediation of textual authority when texts travel across cultural contexts.

Høgel discusses the intricate itineraries of texts and stories along the Silk Road, focusing on the journey of the story of *Barlaam and Josaphat* (as it was known in the West) from Sanskrit India to Norse-writing Norway, and thus this chapter offers a broader, more global view of the networks through which literary media migrated in the medieval era. In studies of such transfers of texts, translation has mainly been seen as a linguistic enterprise, requiring the language skills and certain linguistic strategies of the translators. Høgel argues that the material aspects of this process are also vital, and he opens an important discussion about the material conditions constitutive for textual authority as texts travelled. The transformations of the materiality of texts from stringed palm leaves, to single parchment leaves or rolls, and then to bound codices also had an impact on the structure, presentation and symbolic value of these texts, as Høgel points out. The layout, the place and possibility of illuminations, as well as the portability and physical resilience of the written text all depended on the traditional manners of book production, and these varied immensely over the expanse of the Silk Road. Such texts entered, when translated and re-circulated, into a universe of multiple authority holders, where the translators (understood here in a broad sense) would have to reinvent authoritative presentations of the new text, acting in many ways as vendors of it. Showing how authority was performed in such contexts to various degrees, and in new ways, this chapter demonstrates the relational character of authority.

With Lars Boje Mortensen's chapter, we return to medieval Europe, as well as to forms of spatiality, material as well as imagined. In his chapter, Mortensen discusses authority, materiality, and media in relation to medieval libraries and textual culture in Western Europe in the twelfth and thirteenth centuries. More specifically, he focuses on some aspects of textual retrievability, storage and authority that are both important and relevant for a literary media history, but which have tended to fall out of focus both before and after a material turn in literary studies—possibly because they are located in between a concrete material and a more abstract space of intentionality and ideals. In order to appreciate the elevated status of books and book collections and the material authority they projected in the High Middle Ages, Mortensen suggests that it is necessary first to divest ourselves, with the help of media studies, of ideas generated in nineteenth century Romanticism and in the early modern Republic of Letters, both based on print, about authorship, texts, and the prestigious book collections of nations and aristocrats. In this way, going back to an age of precarious small collections of hand-copied books, we can better assess a dynamic period of book culture in the Middle Ages themselves, namely that of the twelfth and thirteenth centuries. In this watershed period, books were still largely kept, consulted, and studied in ecclesiastical, institutional collections. Mortensen points to the role of an overlooked material aspect of medieval books by calling attention to the authority that was bestowed on texts through the libraries or the book collections to which they, almost invariably, were produced to form a part, and whose precarious retrieval and storage mechanisms formed an important part of the horizon of textual copying and creation. In his discussion of selected examples from the textual culture of the High Middle Ages in Papal (or Latin) Europe, Mortensen touches upon the unintended consequences for both intellectual and religious authority: while a larger body of authoritative texts was created, and a larger group of expert authors and interpreters emerged, this expansion also transformed the locus of textual authority into more complex and abstract forms, gradually opening up new possibilities of contesting the authority of experts and interpreters. This trajectory is accompanied by a dialectic between the growth of material libraries, and the emergence of notions of knowledge understood as an eternal, virtual library.

The second section, "Materiality and Claims to Authority—Ancient and Modern," focuses more closely on questions of how materiality figures in claims to authority and on the maintenance of authority claims in different historical eras. In Jane Hjarl Petersen's chapter, occupational authority comes through in an ancient Roman burial site, mediated through the reliefs and inscription accompanying the graves of a midwife and her physician husband, buried at the Isola Sacra necropolis near Rome. Carefully weighing the messages of identity, meant for present and future visitors to the grave, various aspects of the construction of authority come to life: the role of the household, the social mechanisms of professions, the occupational pride. Mirroring to some extent messages from shop signs, the occupational authority presented on the gravestone speaks to the past, the present and the future, and as such offers a multifaceted authorial voice and a material and visual performance of authority effective in the future life of the monument. The owners of the burial place could include later burial of others, not least themselves, and exclude others. Later unwanted interference in the grave was a common fear, and the performance of authority needed to control this future situation, aiming to reach beyond the life span of the survivor.

In the following chapter, Martin Rheinheimer analyses visual and written materials from the Duchy of Schleswig and northern Friesland from the eighteenth and nineteenth centuries, and discusses some of the interesting changes that the authoritative, Christian doctrine of bodily resurrection underwent in modernity. As Rheinheimer shows, the materials document a growing gap between the authoritative creed and people's beliefs, which cannot be attributed solely to intellectual changes, but which was also highly reliant on changes in material living conditions and medical and hygienic progress. The chapter suggests that the belief in the resurrection of the body was quite firm in the general population even in the eighteenth century—the century of the Enlightenment, but that it faded towards the end of the nineteenth century due to changes in the material life conditions. The sources consist of personal letters, sermons, and visual culture such as church paintings and gravestone images. By means of selected examples, he investigates what the authoritative, religious dogma of belief in the resurrection of the body meant to ordinary people. He traces the causes of this belief, and he discusses why it faded towards the end of the nineteenth century.

Olav Hammer's paper takes us deeper into the discussions about how the authority of a sacred text is continually re-constructed and re-negotiated in the face of opposition and broader, societal changes. The Book of Mormon, first published in 1830, presents a detailed account of the migration of several groups from the ancient Near East to the Americas, and how these groups became the ancestors of the Native Americans. The description of these migrations fits well with common early nineteenth-century beliefs about the origins of the indigenous populations of America, but contradicts in numerous ways the scientific consensus that emerged roughly a century ago. Key Mormon apologists have constructed a range of arguments for the literal truth of the Book of Mormon account, discussing potential connections between the world within the text and material evidence from fields such as archaeology, anthropology, DNA analysis, and paleontology. This apologetic literature asserts the authority of its authors to elucidate both the "true" significance of material objects and material geographical features, and the "real" meaning of relevant Book of Mormon passages. Science and religion come into conflict not only as religious communities expand on their beliefs in the face of societal changes. In the case of the Mormon church, as studied in Hammer's chapter, the institutional implications—and their authorial status—come into play, as (e.g.) Mormon universities produce academic-looking research publications, even if these are not governed by the common academic criteria. Hammer's paper examines the structure of a number of common apologetic arguments and the religious use of materiality in claims to authority.

Hammer's discussion of contemporary, religious authority claims leads us towards our third, and final, section, "Authority, Modern Media, and Identity Politics." This section focuses on modern authority constructions and identity politics, and on how media figure in authority transformations. The section's opening chapter, authored by Anne Magnussen, analyses questions of authority in relations to ethno-racial politics in the late nineteenth and early twentieth century in Texas, with the local newspaper, *The Gonzales Inquirer,* as case material. At the end of the nineteenth century, central Texas went through a series of important social, economic, and demographic changes that in many ways challenged Anglo-Texan dominance. The development involved, on the one hand, a narrative of progress and civilization, and on the other, an increased level of racially and ethnically defined violence. Magnussen's chapter is a study of how the local newspaper, *The Inquirer,* tried to overcome the conflict between the high level of violence and the idea that the Anglo-Texans represented an unquestioned authority. It exemplifies the conflict between authority and violence with a study of the newspaper's coverage of the case against Gregorio Cortéz for the killing of the Gonzales County Sheriff Richard Glover in June 1901. The analysis, based on Hanna Arendt's definition of authority and the concept of narrative as its main methodological tool, brings out the relational character of authority.

Maja Gildin Zuckerman's paper also discusses twentieth century media. Her chapter explores one of the first Danish Jewish congregational magazines, *Jødisk Tidsskrift*, and its opposition to the prevailing assimilation politics of the Danish Jewish leadership. It unfolds the various ways in which the congregational journal manifested its explicit agenda of stirring up the Jewish community. It did so, she argues, in an attempt to forge a new foundation for Danish Jewry that rested on an affirmative and particular Jewishness, and not primarily on Danishness, as had been the case throughout the nineteenth century. Thus, the chapter adds two important perspectives to the discussion of authority, materiality, and media: firstly, it foregrounds relations of authority that had attempted to maintain Jewish silence and invisibility within the broader, Danish society, and it shows how vulnerable such dynamics were in view of material manifestations of opposition; secondly, it expounds how references to the past, and specifically to notions of a communal foundation, can legitimize or contest contemporary assymetrical relations within the community. It thus analyses the role of media in a process of authority transformation.

The subsequent chapter connects to the theme by analyzing the role of media and materiality in a long process of authority transformations in modern Turkey. As shown by Dietrich Jung, Mustafa Kemal Atatürk has been omnipresent in modern Turkish history, not only in political and historical narratives but also in a multiplicity of instances of every-day life. In roles such as statesman, officer, lawyer, teacher, or bohemian, modern Turks have hardly been able to escape permanent encounters with Turkey's iconic "father of the state." Focusing on the role of materiality and media, this chapter borrows its conceptual tools from Max Weber and Michel Foucault. It analyses the process of the modern transformation of Atatürk's charismatic authority into the established structures of political legitimacy in the modern state. Thereby, its theoretical trajectory fuses Weber's thesis of the routinization of charismatic authority with Foucault's perspective of modern governmentality, in particular with the move from governmental technologies of domination toward technologies of the self. The chapter argues that in this move Atatürk's charismatic authority has been transformed into the abstract authority of state institutions. At the same time, Atatürk assumed a key function in the modern subjectivation of the Turks as citizens of the state. These moves have been facilitated through the iconographic manifestation of Atatürk's symbolic power in Turkish everyday life. In the visual omnipresence of Atatürk, the rationalized authority of modern Turkish state institutions materialize and the central point of reference for the self-hermeneutics of the modern Turkish subject becomes visible. The iconographic presence of Atatürk is the material dimension of an authority structure, which reminds us of Bentham's panopticon and thereby illustrates the crucial transformations in modernity from means of domination to technologies of the self.

Finally, Mikael Aktor's chapter focuses the investigation of the role of media and materiality for questions of authority on the contemporary era. He analyses South-Indian Brahmin struggles for a renewal of authority, and shows how the attempts to revitalize traditional forms of authority are mediated not only by the material forms of a traditional lifestyle, but must also take place within the framework of the mediatized and commodified society of contemporary India. Aktor's analysis focuses on a ritual which took place in 2014, on the Indian Independence Day August 15, in Chennai, Tamil Nadu, during which 108 married couples were initiated into the worship known as the Pañcāyatana Pūjā. The ritual, which had almost died out in most parts of India, is a worship of five gods in the aniconic forms of five different stones. The married couples all belonged to the group of Smārta Brahmins, a subgroup of the priestly class in the traditional Hindu society. Aktor examines the background for this event, which is part of a broader re-traditionalization of Brahmin values and lifestyle in Tamil Nadu. For historical reasons the priestly authority of Brahmins has been strongly challenged in Tamil Nadu, and the effects of globalization further add to the weakening of their traditional identity. The revitalization of the traditional lifestyle, however, does not come easily but is supported by several different media forms, from how-to-literature in books and on the internet, to different types of merchandise made available by a willing commodification industry.

In these case studies, we have aimed to highlight the relational character of authority and its fragile nature as a social accomplishment dependent on forms of media and materiality. The case studies have sought to analyse how things, paraphernalia, spaces, narratives, texts and their materiality, newspapers, books, religious merchandise, visual culture and more are crucial for the performance of authority, its maintenance, contestation, and transformation historically. In the contemporary world, reframing our understanding of authority is as important as ever.

References

Arendt, Hannah. 1961. "What is Authority?" In *Between Past and Future: Six Exercises in Political Thought*, edited by H. Arendt, 91–142. London: Penguin.

Breuer, Stefan. 2011. *"Herrschaft" in der Soziologie Max Webers.* Wiesbaden: Harrassowitz.

Debray, Regis. 1996. *Media Manifestos.* New York: Verso.

Foucault, Michel. 1980. *Power/Knowledge: Selected Interviews and Other Writings*, edited by C. Gordon. New York: Pantheon Books.

Furedi, Frank. 2013. *Authority: A Sociological Approach.* Cambridge: Cambridge University Press. https://doi.org/10.1017/CBO9781139026338

Larsson, Göran. 2015. "Power." In *Vocabulary for the Study of Religion*, edited by Kocku von Stuckrad and Robert A. Segal. Leiden: Brill.

Law, John. 2003. "The Manager and His Powers." Published by the Centre for Science Studies, Lancaster University, Lancaster LA1 4YN, UK. http://www.comp.lancs.ac.uk/sociology/papers/Law-Manager-and-his-Powers.pdf

Lewis, James R. 2012. *Cults.* London: Equinox.

Lincoln, Bruce. 1994. *Authority: Construction and Corrosion.* Chicago, IL: University of Chicago Press.

Meyrowitz, Jerome. 1994. "Medium Theory." In *Communication Theory Today*, edited by D. Crowley and D. Mitchell, 50–77. Cambridge: Polity Press.

Renger, Almut-Barbara. 2015. "Authority." In *Vocabulary for the Study of Religion*, edited by R. A. Segal and Kocku von Stuckrad. Online edition. Leiden: Brill.

Weber, Max. 1980 [1921]. *Wirtschaft und Gesellschaft. Grundriss der Verstehenden Soziologie.* Fünfte, revidierte Auflage, besorgt von J. Winckelmann. Studienausgabe. Tübingen: Mohr Siebeck.

Weber, Max. 1922. "Die drei reinen Typen der legitimen Herrschaft. Eine soziologische Studie." In *Preussischen Jahrbüchern* 187: 1–12.

Laura Feldt and Christian Høgel

About the authors

Laura Feldt is Associate Professor of the Study of Religions at the University of Southern Denmark, head of the research programme *Authority, Materiality and Media*, and managing editor of *NVMEN—International Review of the History of Religions* with G. D. Alles. Her research has mainly focused on myth, the fantastic, and monsters in ancient Mesopotamia, The Hebrew Bible and ancient Christianity, as well as on religion and contemporary popular culture. Her current research project is about wilderness mythology, space, and religious identity formation in ancient religions.

Christian Høgel is Professor (wsr) of Byzantine Literature and co-director of the Centre for Medieval Literature at the Department of History, University of Southern Denmark, Odense (www.sdu.dk/cml). He has published on Byzantine hagiography (*Symeon Metaphrastes. Rewriting and Canonization* 2002), Arabic-Greek translation (especially the early Greek translation of the Qur'an), and on the Ciceronian concept of *humanitas* (*The Human and the Humane*, 2015).

I

Authority, Materiality and Premodern Literary Media

— 2 —

Authority, Space, and Literary Media—Eucherius' *Epistula de laude eremi* and Authority Changes in Late Antique Gaul

LAURA FELDT

This paper discusses religious authority changes in late antique Gaul, where spatial and literary media played important roles in how religious authority was maintained, negotiated, and transformed in Western Europe in the aftermath of the Roman empire. The analysis uses theories of social space to analyze and discuss how the authority of the desert space, and ascetic practice, was negotiated through the literary medium of Eucherius of Lyon's *Epistula de laude eremi* [*In Praise of the Desert*], as well as how the authority of the text as a medium is constructed. This analysis then forms the basis for a discussion of religious authority changes in late antique Gaul following the success of ascetics as bishops, and the role of spatial and literary media in this process. In a world of large scale societal changes, literary media promoting ascetic holy figures, and the ascetic space of the desert, played a decisive role in transformations of authority and in negotations of the meanings of authoritative texts. Such media were created and used by ascetics, bishops, and theologians as means with which to change forms of religious authority, in an era in which the status of asceticism was a matter of contention and the authority of monks and church leaders was insecure. The authority transformations of the era became consequential for Western European history.

Introduction

Media such as spaces and literature played important roles in how religious authority was maintained, negotiated, and transformed in the context of Western Europe in the aftermath of the Roman empire. In a world of large scale societal changes, literary media promoting ascetic holy figures, and the ascetic space of the desert, played a decisive role in transformations of authority. Such media were created and used by ascetics, bishops, and theologians as weapons with which to change forms of religious authority, in an era in which the status of asceticism was a matter of contention and the authority of monks and church leaders was insecure. In this paper, I discuss how the religious authority of the desert space, and ascetic practices, were constructed and mediated in and through literary media in late antiquity. My analysis focuses on how the authority of the desert space, and ascetic practice, is negotiated through the literary medium of Eucherius of Lyon's *Epistula de laude eremi*, as well as on how the authority of the text as a medium is constructed. This analysis then forms the basis for a discussion of religious authority changes in late antique Gaul following the success of Lérinian ascetics as bishops, and the role of spatial and literary media in this process. The text at the centre of my analysis and discussion of authority, materiality and media is a letter written by bishop Eucherius of Lyon sometime between 412 and 420, or perhaps as late as 427, in which he discusses the desert and desert mythology in relation to the island of Lérins south of the coast of Gaul, the home of an ascetic community and a centre of learning: *Epistula de laude eremi* (Pepino 2009; Leyser 2006, 1999).[1]

The approach taken here suggests that authority is not only a capacity that persons or institutions may have. Instead, authority is seen as fundamentally relational, and both texts, objects, and spaces can enter into authorizing relations with actors. Authority is also understood as more precarious than sometimes thought, and as a social relation which must be constantly re-asserted and re-negotiated via the use of various forms of media and materiality. If we, with contemporary theorists, see authority as an unequal power relation perceived as natural or legitimate, it follows from this view that this unequal influence between parties needs maintenance in order not to dissipate, i.e., be perceived as unnatural and illegitimate. Here, I am interested in how the desert space is constructed as authoritative in a particular text, as well as in how this particular text attempts to bring across its own authority to its reader, via particular relations to other texts, objects, spaces, and practices.

Approaching authority, space, and ancient literary media

As sociologist Frank Furedi has put it recently, authority has an elusive quality (Furedi 2013, vii). The concept of authority differs from that of power,[2] and it is often pointed out how authority, properly understood, hovers between force, or the threat of violence, on the one hand, and persuasion

1. My interest in and approach to this text derives from a larger, comparative research project on ancient wilderness mythologies, which draws on spatiality theory and discussions in the religion and nature field.

2. An equally difficult, and more comprehensive, concept, but Larsson provides a clear discussion, which shows that with Foucault's and Lukes' theories of power, the overlaps between power and authority are greater than ever (Larsson 2015).

or manipulation on the other (Furedi 2013, 1; Lincoln 1994). Inspired by Furedi's approach, I work here from the assumption that authority can be understood as relational and fragile, as historical struggles against, negotations of, and challenges to, authority demonstrate (Furedi 2013, 3). For the concept of authority, a classical point of departure is Weber's "Typen der Herrschaft" (Weber 1980 [1921], 122–176; Weber 1922), which he sometimes uses interchangably with "Autorität" (e.g. Weber 1980, 122; Weber 1922; Breuer 2011). Weber's approach to authority has been widely used in the study of religions and the history of Christianity (e.g., Lincoln 1994; Lewis 2012), and recent studies show its continuing relevance (Rapp 2005).

Yet, Furedi, as Lincoln and Arendt before him, underlines first and foremost that authority is a relational concept, suggesting a compelling power to motivate and gain obedience, "without having to argue or threaten the use of force"; he suggests that authority is an influence which compels (Furedi 2013, 7–9; Lincoln 1994; Arendt 1961). So rather than discussing different authority types in the tradition from Weber, I here build on key ideas from Furedi and combine these with an attention to media and mediation. For my purposes, it is important to approach the authority which religious literature may be ascribed and compel, the obedience or influence it may command, as well as the importance of materiality, like objects and spaces, in the construction, maintenance and transformation of forms of authority (Law 2003). The approach to the discussion of authority here thus sees authority as intertwined with specific relational, narrative and discursive practices, as for instance Thomas Csordas (1997) and Olav Hammer (2016) have also indicated. A focus on media is arguably crucial for historical understandings of authority, for charismatic and other forms of authority are only available to research through the media by means of which authority is communicated and ascribed. Yet, first and foremost, as suggested by Furedi, it is crucial to provide a deeper historical context for transformations of authority (Furedi 2013, vii), as a key way of allowing new understandings to emerge, just as it is important to continually keep in focus how authority is a fragile and vulnerable accomplishment of social and mediated interaction. Here, my focus is on how a particular literary text attempts to enunciate and compel authority for the desert space, ascetic practice, as well as for itself, and I approach both space and literary texts as *media*, both of which have material aspects.

With regard to the desert and how the authority of a space such as the desert is mediated and practiced, I use insights from critical spatiality theory.[3]

3. The following exposition draws on and overlaps with previous ones, from when I have used the same theoretical perspectives on other empirical material, as in Feldt 2016b.

The understanding of space has been developed extensively and transformed in history and anthropology and also in the study of religion, with the recent spatial turn.[4] The field of critical spatiality theory *per se* developed in the social sciences. The basic presupposition is that space requires analysis as much as "history" or "sociality," because space is actively created through social and material practices.[5] Space should thus not be seen as "a substrate for the external imposition of arbitrary cultural form" (Ingold 2000, 214; Thrift and Whatmore 2004). Spatial analysis takes an interest in how space is produced, imagined, and lived, in addition to the conventional interest in space as a geophysical "reality." Space is thus not investigated only in terms of positions on a map or a passively existing materiality, but also in terms of spatial practices, spatial ideals, spatial experiences, modes of production and forms of materiality, and social relations. Both Edward Soja and previously Henri Lefebvre have introduced tripartite strategies for the analysis of social space (Soja 1996),[6] and while I recognize the complexities of both Lefebvre's and Soja's varying distinctions, for my purposes a reformulation for use in analyses of literary texts is necessary.[7] Thus, I will also use a tripartite distinction, but differentiate between *material space*, i.e., the concrete materiality of space, the geophysical, empirical realities, *designed space*, that is imagined space, ideas and models of space in culturally normative or authoritative forms, and finally *lived space*, which concerns the experience of social space, space as lived and practiced,[8] building on both *material space* and *designed space*, but marking the space from which a text is pro-

4. E.g., Kim Knott (2005) from the study of religions. Other academic disciplines such as philosophy, architecture, and cultural geography have played the key roles in the development of spatiality theory, as the work of scholars such as Henri Lefebvre, Edward Soja, David Harvey, Nigel Thrift, Susan Whatmore, and others demonstrates.

5. Especially the work of philosopher Henri Lefebvre and geographer Edward W. Soja demonstrates that space is not a mental construct alone, it is also always material, and representations of space in social thought and practice cannot be understood as projections of modes of thinking independent of socio-material conditions (Soja 1989,124–126; Lefebvre 1991).

6. Soja dubs the three kinds of spatial aspects *Firstspace*, *Secondspace* and *Thirdspace*, a distinction which is indebted—but not equivalent—to Lefebvre's distinctions between perceived space, conceived space and lived space.

7. Thus, I do not adhere strictly to Lefebvre's or Soja's theories, but only use their basic idea of a tripartite approach to space strategically, and I adapt it to Mieke Bal's tripartite approach to narrative (text, story and fabula , see Bal 1997). I view the different spatialities as different aspects that never appear separate in any text, but which may be distinguished for the purpose of analysis. I have previously presented this reformulation in Feldt 2016b.

8. As mentioned by C. Camp, Jim Flanagan has helpfully dubbed these aspects material space, designed space and lived space (Camp 2002); I have drawn the terminology from there.

duced and maintained.[9] I analyze material space by investigating mentions of the concrete geophysical/geographical materiality of space,[10] whereas I approach designed space aspects, which represent a discourse of power (Soja 1996, Camp 2002), by analysing normative, cultural models used to construct, explain and think space that are drawn upon in the texts (George 2009, 25–27; Bal 1997, 214–216).[11] Since designed space aspects must be seen as an authoritative appropriation of space, I combine this with attention to how the designed space models of the text are combined with other textual elements and utterances, because designed space aspects may be qualified, contested, questioned, or backed up in other discourse.[12] I focus on *lived space* aspects by looking at expressions of lived experience, combining this with data on the modes of production, and on the social space in which the texts were produced.[13] It is important to bear in mind that spatialities are invariably interwoven in intricate ways in texts, and that texts can be sites of negotiation and struggle between spatial aspects.

Since what is discussed here is also the text's authority, and how the text as a medium labours to construct not only the authority of the desert space but also its own authority, I supplement critical spatiality theory with insights from theories of literature and media. Ascetic letters may be approached in terms of theories of mediation and media technologies (McLuhan 1964; Meyrowitz 1994; 2001, 10). This means that the analysis approaches both content and form as devices which facilitate communication and enable relations. Media, including ancient ascetic letters, are—seen from this perspective—not neutral carriers of content or information,

9. It aim to move beyond the alternatives of describing spatiality only as material, physical, or as an imagined, mental construct (Soja 1996; Camp 2002; Lied 2005). Thirdspace is thus a term that aims to point to space as practiced in the lifeworlds of human beings; the field of social spatiality that uses and incorporates Firstspace and Secondspace aspects, but which cannot be reduced to the combination of the two (Lied 2005:108). In actual, human practice, these aspects cannot be separated. For purposes of analysis, however, they may be usefully distinguished.

10. This is far from simple with regard to ancient religions, as discussed by Lied (2005, 108 note 30), and we need also to draw on archaeological and other knowledge of the area with information supplied in the text.

11. Written texts, especially of the canonized sort, cannot be equated with designed space, on the assumption that "if it is written, it must be conceptualized," as Claudia Camp notes, using the distinctions of Soja. The boundaries between the three aspects of spatiality collapse in any actual text (Camp 2002).

12. Importantly, the secondspace aspects may be qualified, contested, questioned or backed up in other discourse, cf. in a narratological perspective (Bal 1997, 25, 34, 43–50, 52–61). To assess the ideological tenor of a text, its different voices must be analyzed (Bal 1997, 34).

13. Lived space in Soja's or Lefebvre's sense is of course beyond the texts, and therefore historians of ancient religions need to adapt the perspective for our usage.

and they are not approached here in the same way as traditional, historical sources. Rather, they are seen as content-in-form with physical, sensory, social, and other characteristics. They mediate not only information, but also social relations; they are material things which afford certain types of usage, relations, and interaction. They can be stored, copied, displayed, or burnt and destroyed. They are conditioned "internally" in their form and have particular characteristics, which constrain their reception and use (Heider 1959, 20), as well as "externally" in their materiality and in terms of their production and use (Meyrowitz 1994; Feldt 2016c). Here, I focus primarily on internal conditions and constraints. Here we need to keep in mind that the letter we are dealing with here is a highly literary letter, which is also clearly a religious letter, written, used, and circulated in a highly religious, monastic context.

It is relatively common, in the study of religion, to stress the authoritative force of religious texts (especially narratives), their capacity to orient identity and to found and maintain institutions and social order (Eliade 1960, 13–24; Assmann 1992, 75–79; McCutcheon 2000; Doniger 1998, 197; J. S. Jensen 2009, 8; Bremmer 2010).[14] Plausibly, we may assume some authoritative force for several kinds of ancient religious literature, as evidenced also for instance by their transmission histories. For letters, special characteristics apply. In a general literary-theoretical perspective, no literature is written entirely from scratch, and all texts participate in intertextual dialogues with previous works of literature. Similarly, religious literature continually re-negotiates and transforms earlier constellations of authority. The production of new literature always involves reception and transformation, or rewriting, of previous works of literature (Bloom 1997; Lachmann 2004), and so literature—including religious literature with its ascribed authority—is always in a process of change, re-negotiation, and potential subversion of older works, and their authority. So even as we can indeed often assume that religious literature is to some extent considered authoritative by a group of people, we should keep in mind how each piece of literature is involved in a process of maintenance, and/or re-negotiation of its own authority vis-à-vis other actors, including other textual conversation partners. This is exceptionally clear with regard to letters, which are often written with the specific purpose of persuading its recipient(s) of

14. One could perhaps also point to Bruce Lincoln's description of religion as "a human discourse that constructs itself as divine and unfailing" as well as "that discourse [along with associated practices and institutions] whose defining characteristic is its desire to speak of things eternal and transcendent with an authority equally transcendent and eternal" (Lincoln 2003, 16 and Lincoln 2005) as an example that points to similar general assumptions in the study of religion about the claim to authoritativeness of religious narratives.

something specific. It is well-known that the new Christian religion developed as a literate culture, highly dependent on books and the circulation of letters (Kloppenborg 2014; Horsfield 2015). With the crumbling of the Roman empire, the general decline of schools and literacy strengthened the networked power of the church due to its strategic use of literary media, through the constant circulation of news via letters and books (Horsfield 2015, 107–110; Brown 2003, 13–14), leaving the churches in key positions to assume the role of media authorities (previously more secular). From their earliest beginnings, ascetic milieus and monasteries were centres of literary culture, and considering the limited life span of a document, the copying and recopying of manuscripts necessary for their preservation can indeed be understood in terms of a media industry, as Peter Horsfield puts it (Horsfield 2015, 115). So while a specific monastic letter is of course always addressed to one or more specific persons, ancient literary letter writing was a social practice produced and used with a view to multiple, successive audiences (Morello and Morrison 2007, v–xii; Gibson and Morrison 2007).

Eucherius and his *Epistula de laude eremi*

Eucherius of Lyon came from the upper class, from a senatorial family in Gaul, and he joined the monastic milieu on the island of Lérins when he was ca. 30 years old, leaving behind his wife and children. He later became bishop of Lyon (between 433 and 439).[15] Eucherius' level of education is demonstrated in his works, in his reputation among his contemporaries as a man of letters, and finally also validated by his election as bishop (Pepino 2009, 34–35). The second part of John Cassian's *Conferences* is dedicated to Eucherius and Honoratus (Rapp 2005, 122–123; Kelly 2011, 130; Pepino 2009, 18). His *Epistula de laude eremi*[16] (from ca. 426–427) is a letter addressed to Hilary in order to congratulate him on his return to Lérins, probably after having escorted his kinsman and former abbot Honoratus to Arles for Honoratus' consecration as bishop.[17] The letter consists of 44 sections of varying length (between ca. 5–20 lines). After an introduction (1–3) follow some sections unfolding key references to authoritative desert mythology

15. See here Pepino's discussion of the evidence (Pepino 2009, 73–76).

16. Details of the extant manuscripts can be found in Pricoco 1965. I here use the edition of S. Pricoco (1965) throughout, and I have consulted the translations of Cummings (1976) and Vivian (1999). All translations are here quoted from Vivian 1999, unless otherwise noted. References to Vivian's translation are abbreviated EDLE—for *Epistula de laude eremi*, followed by reference to the numbered paragraphs of the text; references to the Latin text in Pricoco's edition are made by page number and then by reference to the individual lines in Pricoco (1965).

17. Hilary himself became bishop in Arles after the death of Honoratus (Pepino 2009, 203–204).

from the Old Testament, the gospels, and ascetic literature (7–27). Then, Eucherius praises the desert in general, outlines its advantages, and praises Lérins specifically (28–43). The conclusion touches upon Hilary (44). The letter is written in Latin and reflects a high level of education (Greschat 2007; Pepino 2009, 35–40).

Material space

Eucherius' text contains very few references to physical, material space. Almost all of the reflections on the desert focus on aspects of designed space—references to, and interpretations of, authoritative, normative religious narratives about the desert space. This is in itself an indication of the extent to which this text moves the idea of the desert wilderness into the realm of metaphor; how it transforms the desert or wilderness into an image of human existence. The first section of the letter references Hilary's previous stay at Lérins in oblique ways (1–3), and then only in section 42 we find direct some references to the material, physical world of Lérins. Even in section 42, the descriptions are overlaid with metaphorical and "existential" interpretation, as in this quote: "...but I honor my own Lérins above all. Faithful to her reputation, she takes in her faithful arms those who come to her from being shipwrecked in the stormy world" (EDLE 42, 4–5).[18] Here, the text is suggestive of the physical journey to the island of Lérins, but seen as a symbolic image placed in opposition to the world of shipwreck, storms, fire—over against the ascetic space of safety, calm, shade, the regaining of spirit and refreshment of the heart (EDLE 42).[19] While the entire text up until this section has focused on the solitude and sterile quality of the normative desert space, in the following section we get some of the only references to Lérinian material space, when the text refers to its bubbling fountains, beautiful flowers, and many visual and olfactory delights, which demonstrate to "those who possess this paradise" what they will possess in heaven (EDLE 42,8–10).[20] The stress on God's presence in the desert in the retellings of authoritative desert mythology from the Bible, in combination with the concrete materiality of space at Lérins, are probably factors which influence the metaphorical shift from desert to paradise references. It also shows that a considerable amount of textual and ideological work is necessary in order for Lérins to be viewed through the lens of a dry and barren desert (EDLE 5, 8–12; 8,1.5).[21] Lérins was a low-lying, off-shore island, which

18. Pricoco 1965, 75–76, lines 466–470.

19. Pricoco 1965, 75–76, lines 466–472.

20. Pricoco 1965, 75–76, lines 472–475.

21. Pricoco 1965, 49–50, lines 62–68.

was difficult to access, but it was quickly transformed by the monastic community into a cultivated estate, which was not threatened by violence as other similar villas on the mainland. Well-to-do ascetic recruits brought along their own slaves, and security and affluence characterized the place (Brown 2012, 419–421). The text passage also contains some resemblances to the ancient literary tradition of praise of the lush countryside as an ideal place for a retreat with educated friends (Rapp 2005, 108–109). Notably, this is a retreat limited in time.

The following section praises Lérins, not only for having been founded by Honoratus, for having been endowed with his wisdom, but Lérins is also presented as praiseworthy for having sent him forth into the world, just as it has sent out other monks and priests as missionaries (EDLE 42,15–16).[22] This sentence shows, I believe, in combination with other aspects, that Pepino's suggestion that Eucherius' aim in writing this letter is to persuade Hilary to come back to Lérins to stay there permanently (Pepino 2009) can be questioned, since it so clearly praises Lérins for its capacity to send monks out into the world.

Section 43 contains several references to the spatial practices of the ascetics at Lérins, which are surely idealized and normative, as the stress on virtues such as love, piety, hope, meekness and humility, constant prayer, praise of God, etc., suggests. Yet, the passage ends by suggesting that the desert life these monks desire can be lived *in the heart* (EDLE 43, 18–19).[23] This indicates, I argue, the metaphorical and symbolic nature of the desert space and desert practices analyzed here, and it entails that, seen from this text's perspective, the desert life can in principle be lived anywhere. Finally, when Eucherius asks Hilary to pray for him in the company of the Lérinian monks, this suggests that Eucherius himself is not at Lérins, but elsewhere.[24] This is another factor which implicitly sanctions a non-permanent stay at the monastic centre, in favour of a metaphorical understanding of desert life as a life which can be led "in the heart" in any context.

From designed space to lived space

Authoritative spatial models are referenced and interpreted in the letter and these indeed form the backbone of the letter, as mentioned above. Biblical wilderness mythology is used to outline a normative desert space with implications for ascetic spatial practice and piety. Notably, the Old Testament stories of Moses and Israel in the wilderness take up more tex-

22. Pricoco 1965, 75–76, lines 466–487.

23. Pricoco 1965, 77–78, lines 503–504.

24. Pepino discusses the context of the letter thoroughly (2009, 1–15.200–231).

tual space (EDLE 7–16) than the stories of Jesus (EDLE 21–26). The designed space or authoritative spatial models from the Old Testament and the gospels are sometimes difficult to distinguish from lived space aspects, because the Old Testament and gospel stories are extensively reinterpreted to fit the new context, as they are referenced and re-narrated.[25] I focus on how the designed space models from the Old Testament and gospel stories function as authoritative references, and on how they are re-interpreted as models and norms for the lived space practices of the monks at Lérins and the letter's recipients.

In the introductory passages of the letter, we find scattered characterizations of the desert in terms of its solitude, which is said to resemble that of heaven (EDLE 3, 14.21; 4, 4),[26] indications that it has God's favour and is his preferred place (EDLE 3, 15.21; 4, 6),[27] and finally it is characterized as dry, sterile, endless, pathless, and vast (EDLE 5, 8–9.12; 8, 1.5).[28] These introductory characterizations are verbalized in a clearly authoritative manner, and draw on normative ideas of the ideal desert, which use the Old Testament desert stories from Exodus through Numbers, but which also remould the desert space in their selectivity. The introductory sections take the desert space further in the direction of remote, dry, and pathless characteristics and to some extent away from the concrete.[29]

In the section re-narrating the stories of the Exodus and wilderness wanderings (EDLE 7–16),[30] Eucherius stresses first of all the desert's aptness for having conversations with God, and the authority of the desert in terms of nearness to God. The desert has merit and dignity (EDLE 7);[31] once there, there is no going back (EDLE 10).[32] The ability of a stay in the desert to transform identity is stressed (EDLE 7, 20–21),[33] and the Exodus and wilderness stories are interpreted in terms of which lessons can be learned, i.e., in terms of how the stories can function as authoritative guides for the inter-

25. Moreover, the references to the Old Testament and gospel stories are of course also filtered through earlier ascetic literature. The references to this literature are, however, much more oblique and will not be dealt with in the framework of this essay.

26. Pricoco 1965, 48–49, lines 32–50.

27. Pricoco 1965, 48–49, lines 32–50.

28. Pricoco 1965, 49–50, lines 57–68.

29. For a spatial analysis of the Torah wilderness stories, see Feldt 2012 and Feldt 2014. These analyses show the vast differences between the conceptualization of the desert space in The Hebrew Bible and in Eucherius' letter.

30. Pricoco 1965, 50–58, lines 78–182.

31. Pricoco 1965, 50–51, lines 78–95.

32. Pricoco 1965, 53–54, lines 117–122.

33. Pricoco 1965, 50–51, lines 94–95.

pretation of life and conduct. Eucherius deduces this lesson from the stories: People should only proceed to the desert (i.e., the ascetic life), when they are free of previous obligations and concerns (EDLE 7, 9–14);[34] the desert life represents taking a step towards a liberation from sin (EDLE 8,1–2).[35]

By referencing the authoritative and well-known Old Testament stories, and continuously re-interpreting them as ascetic literature, Eucherius positions the desert space as an uniquely authoritative space for ascetic practice: the desert is framed as a space for seeing God, hearing God's voice, speaking with God, receiving instructions and a new identity as God's instrument (EDLE 7),[36] and for being guided and guarded by God (EDLE 8–9).[37] In section 11, the merits and graces of a desert life are mentioned, and the Old Testament narrative desert space is fused metaphorically with the letter reader's heart to speak of conversion into the ascetic life, which is in this way framed as miraculous and as partaking in God's providence, i.e. divinely authorized and sanctioned (EDLE 11, 8–9.11–13).[38] The story of the manna (Ex 16) is used authoritatively to show that heaven will take care of those living the ascetic life, the desert life (EDLE 12),[39] and that those people are worthy of reading the letters of God. This can be read as a reference to ascetic literature and even as a mise-en-abyme reference to Eucherius' letter itself. The desert narratives, and the Old Testament wilderness mythology that it draws on, are here also used as stories to authorize the later visions and auditions of the desert dwellers, the ascetics (EDLE 13).[40] Their visions and auditions form part of their merits according to this text. This also explains the value of the ascetic men to society at large, which, I suggest, the text (also) attempts to argue.

Next, Eucherius stresses that Israel depended on God's miracles in the desert (EDLE 14),[41] and then he explains, in what is presumably a metacommentary on the text's ideal reception, how the Old Testament stories are to be read as signs, symbolically. The stories of outward appearances should be read as speaking of hidden mysteries, i.e., as having a spiritual meaning—in the manner of Paul's reading in 1 Cor 10: 2–4 (EDLE 15, 1–4).[42]

34. Pricoco 1965, 50–51, lines 78–95.
35. Pricoco 1965, 51–52, lines 96–99.
36. Pricoco 1965, 50–51, lines 78–95.
37. Pricoco 1965, 51–53, lines 96–116.
38. Pricoco 1965, 54, lines 129–135.
39. Pricoco 1965, 54–55, lines 136–144.
40. Pricoco 1965, 55–56, lines 145–157.
41. Pricoco 1965, 56–57, lines 158–168.
42. Pricoco 1965, 57, lines 169–174.

Nevertheless, the symbolic events should be understood as "true realities" (EDLE 15, 5–6),[43] even as they refer to mysteries and speak of ideals pertaining to the (future) eternal life (EDLE 15, 7–10).[44] In this way, the ascetic life is presented as divinely steered and ordained, and ascetic practice is ascribed a mysterious hidden power as sanctioned and authorized by God. Eucherius' re-interpretation of the Old Testament stories to authorize ascetic practice culminates in section 16, where the desert experience of Israel—and thus also by implication the desert life of the ascetics—is presented as a prerequisite for salvation:

> "In order for that people to take possession of the land 'flowing with milk and honey', they first had to possess this parched and sterile wilderness.... Let those who desire 'to see the good things of the Lord in the land of the living' take up their residence in an uninhabitable wasteland. Let those who strive to become citizens of Heaven be guests first of the desert."
>
> (EDLE 16, 2–5.7–9).[45]

Then follow a series of briefer expositions of stories from the Old Testament of leaders involved in politics, such as David, Elijah, Elisha, and their followers. While both Elijah and Elisha can be viewed as mediator-figures with clear ascetic traits in their Hebrew Bible context (Feldt 2014), it is noteworthy that these further Old Testament stories all involve leaders clearly taking part in contemporary power politics as leaders and political mediators (EDLE 17–20);[46] they were all religious leaders who were deeply involved in "the world." This could also suggest that Eucherius here communicates about the authority of the Lérinian monks, and their value as leaders for contemporary society. Eucherius stresses the strong and emotional devotion of David (his thirst for God is metaphorically merged with desert thirst (EDLE 17),[47] and the strong sacred power (ability to do miracles) of Elijah and Elisha, and their successors (EDLE 18–20).[48]

The gospel of Matthew's John the Baptist figure is referenced next as the institutor of baptism and a preacher of repentance in the desert. His preaching is framed as tied to the desert (EDLE 21),[49] and he himself as an angel (EDLE 21, 8).[50] In Matthew's version of this story, Jesus' desert experience, led by the Holy Spirit, is mentioned next, and so in Eucherius' letter

43. Pricoco 1965, 57, lines 173–174; Vivian's translation, as elsewhere in this paper.

44. Pricoco 1965, 57, lines 174–179.

45. Pricoco 1965, 58, lines 182–189.

46. Pricoco 1965, 58–60, lines 190–214.

47. Pricoco 1965, 58, lines 190–195.

48. Pricoco 1965, 58–60, lines 196–214.

49. Pricoco 1965, 60.

50. Pricoco 1965, 60, line 222.

the monks' departure into the desert becomes divinely authorized (EDLE 22).[51] Angels, alimentary marvels and other wonders, as well as the transfiguration (Matthew 17), are used as divine authorization of the desert's spectacular power in the past (EDLE 23–25).[52] Finally, Eucherius references Jesus as often praying in the desert, and uses this to authorize the desert as the appropriate place of prayer, indeed as a space in which prayers reach heaven more easily, and which gives more merit to the prayers (EDLE 26).[53]

In this way, I suggest, Eucherius offers solid authorization of "the desert" as key in ascetic life and backs up the popular understanding that the prayers of ascetics were more effective and meritorious than those of others (Brown 2012, 422–425) by means of his rewritings of previous desert mythology.[54] Re-interpreting Matthew's Jesus, Eucherius' Jesus is framed as full of strong and emotional devotion (he is "burning with ardour for the desert" EDLE 22, 11),[55] setting an example for enflamed desert ardour, intense devotion (EDLE 22, 12.16–17).[56] The text thus uses the authority of the Old Testament to persuade the readers of the necessity of ascetic practice (the desert) for salvation (EDLE 22, 14–15).[57] Indeed, the desert is presented as *the* way to salvation, and its authority is enhanced to surpass that of key protagonists in the Christian myth of salvation—their abilities are presented as stemming from and relating to their desert experiences.

One of the traits which is especially striking about this letter is the transformation of the desert into a broader and more metaphorical or symbolic image of ascetic life which the monks carried around with them, as also argued by Kelly (Kelly 2011). Eucherius' desert is a desert of the mind, body, and heart, not a physical desert, and only *partly* a physical place. This comes out clearly in for instance section 27, where the desert is clearly verbalized as a way of life, a transformation of the inner person (EDLE 27).[58] Here, it is also important to note that Eucherius frames the ascetics as a treasure of God, but interestingly not as a treasure meant to be locked up and stored, but meant to be brought out into the world when needed (EDLE 28, 8–10).[59]

51. Pricoco 1965, 60–61, lines 226–241.
52. Pricoco 1965, 62–63, lines 242–267.
53. Pricoco 1965, 63–64, lines 268–274.
54. This also offers pointers towards later understandings of the role of monasteries in society (Brown 2003, 219–231).
55. "Eremi tamen ardore flagrabat..." (Pricoco 1965, 61, lines 236–238).
56. Pricoco 1965, 61, lines 236–241.
57. The John (of Lycopolis, or Cassian) and Macarius mentioned next are monastic examples (Pepino 2009, 206).
58. Pricoco 1965, 64, lines 275–285.
59. Pricoco 1965, 64–65, lines 293–296.

Thus, Eucherius does not necessarily use this letter to argue that Hilary should stay on at Lérins permanently, but instead to authorize the monks as God's valuable goods which can be taken out into the world and used when necessary, as well as to transform the desert from being only or primarily a material, physical place into also being a way of life and a metaphor for the road to salvation.

According to the letter, divine providence is with the desert guests (EDLE 29),[60] their devotion is total, as are their virtues (EDLE 31).[61] They are presented as the illustrious men of former ages, who dedicated themselves to business affairs, and then took a break with philosophy. Nowadays, Eucherius suggests, such men can take a break in a solitary location, withdraw to the desert, practice virtues and nearness to God (EDLE 32–33).[62] Section 34 spells out directly that the desert life, and the ascetic practice, which Eucherius advocates here, is one pursued primarily "in the depths of their hearts" (EDLE 34, 11).[63] The desert life is described as a life of humility, of desire for heavenly things, of shunning wealth and the pleasures of this world; it is a life of manual labour, vigils, etc., in order to attain the "world without end" (EDLE 34, 11–22).[64] A material, physical stay in a concrete desert is seemingly not a requirement. Eucherius' desert life is not a life tied necessarily to a physical desert, or physical solitude.[65]

Finally, Eucherius stresses that the merit attained by the ascetics cannot be hidden forever, for the glory of God will pour out into exterior life (EDLE 36, 6–9).[66] This would suggest, again, that Eucherius sees the ascetics' contributions to public life as beneficial and necessary. This desert is a spiritual desert to be cultivated in the interior person (EDLE 41, 4–5);[67] such a person becomes in himself a temple of God (EDLE 41, 10–11).[68] Towards the end of the letter, Eucherius himself mentions the many illustrious ascetics and priests whom Lérins has nourished, and speaks matter-of-factly about how Lérins has raised missionaries and sent them out into the world (EDLE 42, 15–24).[69] He also stresses the power of the monks for doing blessed things

60. Pricoco 1965, 65, lines 297–311.

61. Pricoco 1965, 66, lines 319–326.

62. Pricoco 1965, 67–68, lines 327–350.

63. "... sed in cordibus..." (Pricoco 1965, 69, 359–366).

64. "...saecula sine fine...," Pricoco 1965, 69, lines 359–371.

65. Also in EDLE 42,1–2, it is clear that Eucherius believes that the desert life can be lived in many places (Pricoco 1965, 75–76, lines 466–472.

66. Pricoco 1965, 70, lines 386–391.

67. Pricoco 1965, 75, lines 457–460.

68. Pricoco 1965, 75, lines 462–465.

69. Pricoco 1965, 76, lines 474–487.

here on earth (EDLE 43, 11–12),[70] how the monks live a desert life *in their heart* (EDLE 43, 18–19; my emphasis),[71] and how they are able to do "heavenly" things in the present (EDLE 43, 20–21).[72] The final sections of the letter further indicate that Eucherius is not himself present at Lérins at the time of the letter's composition (EDLE 44); he assures Hilary that by spending time at Lérins he will be on the direct path to salvation (EDLE 44), without indicating that the stay will have to be permanent.[73] In so many ways, Eucherius has thus harnessed the authority of the Old Testament, gospel, and other religious literature's desert myths in order to demonstrate that the Lérinian ascetics are participants in a wider "desert" network; he has signalled their value to the world without spelling it out directly.

Many characteristics of the letter offer further indications towards the lived space of its author and readers. The literary character of the letter and the many references to the Old Testament and gospel literature suggest the elite and educated character of the producer and the users of the text (Pepino 2009, 5), and of the social milieu in which this text was produced and used. As Pepino points out, fifth century Provence possessed a keen literary and monastic milieu consisting of a group of men who shared the same aristocratic upbringing, including, we assume, rhetorical and grammatical education, and who shared their literary works with each other (Pepino 2009, 1–2). However, as Brown argues, it is important to remember that they were parts of the lesser nobility, not the key upper echelons of the empire (Brown 2012, 422).

Eucherius' application and transformation of the authoritative desert space into lived spatial practice is also reflected when he discusses how the Old Testament desert should be interpreted. He applies his interpretations to the everyday lives of the monks: While they should rely on the continued providence of God, they should not expect miracles like in the days of old or exotic lands, but rather that their needs will be taken care of in other, more subtle ways. This trait indicates an attention to, a preparedness to enter into, an ordinary, everyday life in the world, rather than an exoticization of the distant, secluded life in a fantastical desert, where marvellous things may happen. Rather, the desert is here transformed into a set of values for the ascetics to live by: Love, piety, hope, meekness, humility, modesty,

70. Pricoco 1965, 77, line 497. Most likely, the term "beata" (or the variant "beatam") does not refer to miracles.

71. Pricoco 1965, 78, lines 503–504.

72. Pricoco 1965, 78, lines 504–506.

73. Pricoco 1965, 78, lines 509–523.

silence, serenity (EDLE 43).[74] Rather than offering advice and ideals only for a life secluded from the world, Eucherius' text works to authorize an understanding of the desert which can *also* work as a metaphor for the ascetic way of life as an image of the path to salvation and offer ideals for the conduct and norms of the monks. Through the literary letter, he translates the authoritative mythology into practical advice on the performance of piety and how the ascetics can live the desert life in their hearts, anywhere. But Eucherius combines this with advocacy for the idea of a temporary stay in the desert, a monastic retreat, as a prerequisite legitimization of the authority of these men as worldly leaders, before they venture out into the world.

The desert Eucherius praises and advocates is accessed through reading practices, through literary media, which are to be interpreted symbolically, metaphorically, *mystice*, and performed out in everyday piety. Thus, we see here both how the authority of the desert is thoroughly relational, and how it is continually in a process of re-affirmation and concomitant transformation. Eucherius draws on authoritative texts from the Old Testament and the gospel of Matthew, which are here presented as uncontested and unquestioned in their authority for the readers, but which are nevertheless thorougly reinterpreted and transformed, in order to present his own perspective on the desert, which he also intends to be authoritative. He uses the medium of the letter to assert his influence, and the influence of the desert, through it. Clearly, both the letter medium and the desert space are key in the construction, maintenance and transformation of the authority of the ascetics.

The letter as a medium: Space as/in literature

Key to mediation and to what a medium is, is its capacity to travel, undergo circulation, and to pass, as a token, and to transform relations, beyond its communicative function. The media of the desert space, ascetic piety practices, and of the literary letter are here both at once material and literary. The desert space is a material island, Lérins, the letter is a concrete manuscript, and yet both space and literary text are metaphors for a Christian anthropological vision of life and Christian leadership. The letter's properties as a medium/thing constrain how it can be used. It encourages actions and practices in specific ways; it has particular affordances for social relations. The media affordances do not determine social relations or uses, as users naturally play a great role, but they do constrain it (Meyrowitz 1994; Bucher and Helmond 2016). Let us take a closer look at some of these aspects.

The text uses some aspects of the genre of the letter between friends. Considering what we know about Christian letters of this time, while the

74. Pricoco 1965, 77–78, lines 488–508.

letter was addressed to Hilary specifically, it is highly likely that it was circulated and used by a broader readership (Brown 2012, 419–428; Pepino 2009, 268–273; Horsfield 2015, 106–117). This means that the deictic pointers to the recipient ("you") will work in labile ways and extend to future recipients. The literary traits support a labile interpellation, as it were, for while the concrete addressee, Hilary, is noted at first, the repeated use of the pronoun (you) in the following sections ensures that all future ascetic readers can potentially feel directly addressed by the "you." These textual movements are supported by the imitatory structure of the culture of reception known generally from early Christian literature (Feldt 2016a). The intertextual references to other ascetic literature, which invite the readers to see the Lérinian monks as the heirs to previous, famous ascetics, as well as themselves, the readers, as participating in an extended network of friends and imitators of Christ, work towards the same goal.

Eucherius calls attention to his relationship to Hilary, and indicates that his authorship of the letter is an answer to Hilary's repeated requests to write a long and eloquent letter (EDLE 3).[75] The introductory sections thus use some of the epistolographic traits stressed by Rubenson (2015) in his discussion of the genre of ancient letters. Roberto Alciati, in his analysis of key persons in the Gallic monastic milieu, also emphasizes how Lérinian authors mix genres, and how key aspects of epistolographic form, especially that of the letter as a dialogue *in absentia*, are used in many works of other genres. Alciati suggests we might speak of "la lettre didactique," which was used for educational and parenetic purposes (Alciati 2009, 117–119), and this certainly seems appropriate for our letter. In Eucherius' letter, discourse on the desert and re-narration of biblical stories about the desert are framed by epistolographic traits. This influences the reception of the text and gives us an idea of which kinds of use, social relations, and practices the text stimulated and afforded. As Samuel Rubenson has suggested recently, the differences between letters and other kinds of monastic literature are not as strict as sometimes assumed (2015). In monastic literature collections, many kinds of text are combined, and generally the texts are preserved because they are deemed to have a pedagogic or instructive purpose or quality (Rubenson 2015, 77–78)—instructions, stories, legends, sayings, etc. appear all mixed up. As he suggests, letters of Christian ascetics from this era often express, in emotional terms, a close and special relationship to the addressees (Rubenson 2015, 75). We also get that aspect here; along with other traits named by Rubenson as particular to ascetic letters, namely references to the author's own experience and expressions of his knowledge

75. Pricoco 1965, 48, lines 32–50.

of what the recipients need and long for (Rubenson 2015, 76; EDLE 1–3).[76] Similarly to other ascetic letters, reference is here made to the importance of figurative readings (EDLE 15),[77] and to the close bond between the sender and the addressees.[78] In the very first section of the text, several different words are used to stress how the desert (and this text) is to be approached (EDLE 1–3).[79] Here we get the first clues that something interesting is going on in this text with regard to mediation, because the desert space is presented as something to be approached with affection and strong emotion, and as something not to be taken literally, and that the letter should be read as exemplary, instructive for practice.

As it has been pointed out with regard to Sulpicius Severus' letters, they do not demonstrate the classical epistolographic traits of salutation, valediction, and being addressed to a named recipient(s) in the second person, or the mentions of the recipients' physical distance from the sender (Yuzwa 2014). Yet, what Sulpicius Severus attains by using some aspects of the letter genre and form is an increased emphasis on the proper reception of the text and on the model recipients. Similarly to Sulpicius Severus mother-in-law, here Hilary is depicted as commissioning the letter, as occasioning its production. In this way, I argue that the text underscores the role of the reader, and of reading, in the production and reception of ascetic literature, similarly to what Yuzwa has argued about Sulpicius Severus (Yuzwa 2014, 337). The act of reading is put forward as an essential component of the literary program;[80] in other words, the letter's mediality emphasizes the act of reading and the presence of the reader. In EDLE, the audience's reading and presence is not external to the text; the reader is directly addressed, and the act of reading and reception gets a vital role within the text. The readers are meant to take Hilary as exemplum, in addition to the author. The recipient, Hilary, reads the text, just as the later readers will; the many deictic markers support this, so that the text can come across as direct speech from the author to the later readers.

The text's epistolographic traits thus underline how to read in an exemplary mode and demonstrate what the reader can expect to gain from doing so (Yuzwa 2014, 338). Placing the stories of miracles and other fantastic

76. Pricoco 1965, 45–49, lines 1–50.

77. Pricoco 1965, 57, lines 169–181.

78. Rubenson discusses the letters of Ammonas (2015).

79. Pricoco 1965, 45–49, lines 1–50.

80. Yuzwa: "Conceived most simply, what a letter does is introduce a second person—the addressee and primary reader—into the narrative space of the text." A letter is a media form for which its meaning and function is generated at least as much by the internal reader, the real or feigned recipient, as by the author (Yuzwa 2014, 337).

powers effectively in the past, interpreting such fantastic events as symbolic events and mysteries (EDLE 15),[81] and offering suggestions for how to reinterpret the special authority of the ascetics as exemplary conduct and values, seeing them as virtuous examples for the world, the text increases the merit of the ascetics, who have spent time in the desert, as leaders in the world, rather than as fantastic and extraordinary athletes in a remote and exotic desert:

> "But how can I acknowledge with appropriate words of praise the fruit of this desert spirituality? I cannot pass over in silence the virtues that are almost as well-known as they are well hidden in those desert dwellings. For when these monks give up human companionship and withdraw to remote places, they desire to be completely hidden, but merit cannot be concealed forever. The more they give themselves to the interior life, the more the glory of God pours out into their exterior life [...]" (EDLE 36[82])

Notably, Eucherius does not spend any attention on legitimizing and authorizing otherwise well-known media of religious power or charisma in ancient forms of Christianity, such as tombs, relics, persons, etc. Instead, this letter offers legitimization for the monks' presence in ordinary life—for monks without fantastic powers. Their specialness lies in their virtuousness, and in their literary skill in writing, reading, and interpreting "deeper mysteries." The letter is a very mobile, far-ranging, and in principle unlimited medium with which to intervene in social relations. The model readers are several times addressed explicitly, their life and conduct is described as lives of spiritual contemplation and progress. While Eucherius' letter certainly works to ascribe authority to a specific view of and perspective on the desert space, using authoritative texts from the Old Testament and the gospel of Matthew to back it up, it comes out clearly that the desert is already an authoritative space, with a long literary tradition connected to it, for the readers of the letter. This leads us to the letter itself as a medium through which the desert is experienced and seen, because the physical desert is so far removed. The letter also becomes a media-thing which labours to heighten its own authority, for the readers, to encourage them to spend time in the desert, to incorporate the desert as a state of mind into their lives, but also to use the letter as a medium of, and guide for, reading practices, interpretation practices, and for the (literary) formation of new ascetics and monastic piety and values.

81. Pricoco 1965, 57, lines 169–181.

82. Pricoco 1965, 70, lines 382–390. The text segment continues with some reflections which underline how the desert dwellers are exemplary in relation to the world (even if hidden). It is also their light will penetrate the world, and those who are metaphorically in the dark, and in danger, will be healed/saved by drawing near to their light.

Discussion: Materiality, media, and authority in late antique Gaul

The emperor, the holy man, and the bishop are key figures in most discussions of authority in late antiquity. Men in these positions functioned as practical leaders, they offered moral guidance, and they dispensed favours, just as they were also among the key subjects of ancient literary production (Rapp 2005), in which they often appear with ascribed fantastic or miraculous abilities and qualities. Ascetics feature in considerable numbers among the "holy men."[83] At the centre of literary production about ascetics and the role of the desert was the Life of Antony by Athanasius of Alexandria, which quickly became the authoritative text on the subject (Bremmer forthcoming). Aspiring Western ascetics sought out the desert wilderness in their own home regions, and among these we find the ascetics who created the monastic community on the island of Lérins. Many ascetics from Lérins did not stay on for their entire lives, but went on to become bishops, priests, and missionaries in Gaul—what Markus has termed "the ascetic invasion" in Gaul (Markus 1990, 199–213). As we have seen in the above analysis, rather than portraying the monks as exceptional holy men with fantastic abilities and qualities, the desert space—rather than the monks themselves—is here presented as the key to religious authority, as the focal point in a literary network. As witnessed by this text, the desert played a tremendous role in constructing the authority of the Lérinian ascetics, but Eucherius found it important to reframe the desert's authority literarily and turn it into a metaphor, an image of a way of life and a sanctioned path to salvation, rather than (only) as a literal location. Not everyone agreed with Eucherius' perspective on the desert, as this comment by the Roman aristocrat Rutilius Namatianus of Capraia shows: "A filthy island filled by those who flee the light."[84] Certainly, Eucherius' strong view of the desert as a straight path to salvation alarmed other Latin Christians, who found it elitist (Leyser 2006, 120).

As Pepino points out, at the time in which Eucherius wrote his letter, the role of monks in the secular world was a matter of discussion and contention in southern Gaul (Pepino 2009, 215). Markus has shown how one significant aspect of Cassian's contribution to the discussions was an evolution from an ideal of the monk in complete withdrawal from the world,[85] to one of the monk, with his special merits and graces, influencing the world, interacting

83. The classical discussion here is of course Brown's (1971).

84. Rutilius Namatianus, *De reditu suo* l.440–448; quoted from Leyser (2006, 120).

85. This was, of course, an ideal view. The monks and ascetics who adhered to this view naturally interacted in many ways with the world, from tourism to their role as benefactors and societal hinge persons (cf. Peter Brown's many contributions to the study of holy men, and others).

with it (Markus 1990; Brown 2012, 419–415).[86] While both Leyser and Pepino have argued that the point of Eucherius' letter is to persuade Hilary to stay at Lérins and not assume a position of authority on the mainland (Leyser 2006; Pepino 2009), my argument is instead that the text betrays much more tension than that interpretation suggests.[87] As I have indicated above, several passages of the letter imply the utility and merits of the monks for society in general and suggest that the stay in the desert can both be temporary and metaphorical. Most plausibly, I think, we should view the letter as an attempt to participate in a relational construction of the authority of the desert, which would function as a legitimizing prerequisite for the assumption of authority positions in society and in the church. On the one hand the letter does praise Lérins and the value of a physical stay in the desert, in a state of withdrawal from the world, but on the other hand it certainly also renders the idea of the desert metaphorical and thus more versatile, in as much as a desert life can be practiced anywhere, in the heart. The text suggests that a spiritual understanding of the desert is preferable to a physical, and a symbolic-mystical to a miraculous-fantastic understanding. It also suggests the value and merits of those who have been guests of the desert to society at large, also when speaking of the special effectiveness of their prayers.[88] As Moreschini and Norelli point out, we do not find a strong discourse of opposition to, or contempt of, the world in this text (Moreschini and Norelli 2005, s.v.); rather, we find an unperturbed optimism that this learned and comparatively unspectacular asceticism can be combined with authority positions in the secular world. Indeed, Eucherius positions his metaphoricized desert space as a prerequisite for the religious authority of an ascetic or a monk. Many of the Lérinian monks went on to assume positions of power on the mainland and they used the desert to bolster episcopal authority (Leyser 2006, 117). As Brown points out, questions can be raised with regard to the social status of key Lérinian monks, and it is more likely that people such as Honoratus and Hilary were small-time nobles and not part of the empire-wide class of the superrich (Brown 2012, 422). These men of the lesser nobility—and not the key power brokers of the empire—had experienced the violence of migrations and civil wars, and they needed the

86. This ideal points onwards to what Brown has dubbed the powerhouse of prayer function for later Benedictine monasticism (Brown 2003).

87. See here also Kelly 2011 for a different analysis, which also argues in favour of a broader interpretation and impact.

88. Indeed, Eucherius' version of the desert seems to suit Cassian's practical approach to monasticism well; recognizing the value of the physical desert and physical withdrawal, but nevertheless placing prime emphasis on the transformation of the interior man, the cultivation of virtues, and a metaphorical understanding of the desert, as Kelly brings out (Kelly 2011).

desert as a medium to transform their identity, their authority as nobility, into one with a different quality from the normal, lesser aristocrat (Brown 2012, 422). In this text, we thus get a valuable glimpse of the many tensions that came to characterize the performance of authority in the Latin West, where in centuries to come the authority of church leaders, as parts of an institutional network which had survived the fall of the empire, was manifestly insecure and vulnerable and in need of various forms of material media support. The desert and literary letters featured prominently among the media used to negotiate positions of authority.[89]

Conclusion

As pointed out by Conrad Leyser and others, Athanasius' *Life of Antony* functioned as an authoritative foundation myth of the Christian, ascetic pioneer, breaking open the wilderness for monasticism (Leyser 2006). It also became pivotal in spreading not only ascetic ideals, but also key ideas of the attainment of sacred power in the desert space and through the ascetic's body. Through letters and narratives, the desert quickly became an important, and fetishized, part of the new Christian landscape, along with the idea of the powerful ascetic body. By the end of the fourth century, aspiring Western Christians sought out the wilderness experience by venturing out into the local forests, mountains, and islands. Among these were, from the 420s, a group of Christians who travelled to the island of Lérins, off the coast of modern Cannes, to live the ascetic, desert life. One of them, the later bishop of Lyon, Eucherius (ca. 380–450), wrote the letter *In Praise of the Desert* (*De laude eremi*; Pricoco 1965; Vivian 1999), to a fellow monk, Hilary. In my analysis of the letter, I used spatiality and media perspectives to investigate how this text connects the concrete, material space of the island of Lérins with its bubbling springs, green grass and flowers to key aspects of the designed space of Christian desert mythology from Moses to Elijah, Jesus, and beyond, in order to frame the entire Christian existence as a desert life, a life of travelling towards the prize in the other world. The move towards assigning a metaphorical value to the desert or wilderness life is seen in a statement such as "From the dwelling places in the desert, the road lies always open to our true homeland" (*De laude eremi*, 16), or "The prayer of a humble petitioner will more easily penetrate the clouds if it rises from the desert" (*De laude eremi*, 26; the translation of Vivian 1999). In conclusion I suggest that the lived space of this particular letter can be understood as firmly entrenched in elite, urban power struggles on the mainland. It is well

89. Leyser makes a similar point with regard to the use of the living and dead holy men (Leyser 2006, 122–123).

documented that many former monks from Lérins went on to play lead roles in contemporary public life on the mainland. Contrary to arguments that Eucherius wrote this particular letter in order to persuade Hilary to stay on permanently at Lérins, rather than assume a position of power in Arles (Leyser 2006; Pepino 2009), the analysis here has suggested instead that the letter functioned as a medium for raising the authority of the desert, but also transforming it into a more metaphorical, and thus more versatile form, as a necessary prerequisite for the assumption of authority positions on the mainland. The authority of the Lérinian desert was the result of literary media, of a literary circle of cultivated and politically active men (cf. Brown 2012, 412–414). This particular text is thus a testimony of how dependent key developments not only in Christian understandings of the legitimate exercise of authority, but also in Christian anthropology and soteriology, have been on literary culture and literary media forms, and how bound up the metaphorical understanding of Christian life as a pilgrimage towards the treasure in heaven is with contemporary issues in ancient, social life.

References

Alciati, Roberto. 2009. "Eucher, Salvien, et Vincent: Les Gallicani doctores de Lérins." In *Lérins—une île sainte de l'antiquité au Moyen Age*, edited by Y. Coudou and M. Lauwers, 105–119, Turnhout: Brépols.

Arendt, Hannah. 1961. "What is Authority." In *Between Past and Future*, by H. Arendt. London: Penguin.

Assmann, Jan. 1992. *Das kulturelle Gedächtnis. Schrift, Erinnerung und politische Identität in frühen Hochkulturen*. München: C. H. Beck.

Bal, Mieke. 1997. *Narratology*. Toronto: University of Toronto Press.

Bloom, Harold. 1997 [1973]. *The Anxiety of Influence: A Theory of Poetry*. Oxford: Oxford University Press.

Bremmer, Jan N. 2010. "From Holy books to Holy Bible: An itinerary from ancient Greece to modern Islam via Second Temple Judaism and Early Christianity." In *Authoritative Scriptures in Ancient Judaism*, edited by Mladen Popovic, 327–360. Leiden: Brill.

———. forthcoming. "Athanasius' *Life of Antony*: Composition, readership and impact." In *Marginality, Media, and Mutations of Religious Authority in the History of Christianity*, edited by Laura Feldt. Leuven: Peeters.

Breuer, Stefan. 2011. *"Herrschaft" in der Soziologie Max Webers*. Wiesbaden: Harrasowitz.

Brown, Peter 1971. "The Rise and Function of the Holy Man in Late Antiquity." *The Journal of Roman Studies* 61: 80–101.

———. 2003. *The Rise of Western Christendom: Triumph and Diversity A.D. 200–1000.* Second edition. London: Blackwell.

———. 2012. *Through the Eye of a Needle: Wealth, the Fall of Rome, and the Making of Christianity in the West 350–550*. Princeton, NJ: Princeton University Press.

Bucher, Taina and Anne Helmond. 2016. "The affordances of social media platforms." In *The SAGE Handbook of Social Media*, edited by Jean Burgess, Thomas Poell and Alice Marwick, 233–253. London and New York: SAGE.

Camp, C. 2002. "Storied space or Ben Sira tells a temple." In *"Imagining" Biblical Worlds: Studies in Spatial, Social and Historical Constructs in Honor of James W. Flanagan*, edited by D. M. Gunn, P. McNutt and J. W. Flanagan, 64–80. JSOT Supplement 353. Sheffield Academic Press: Sheffield.

Csordas, Thomas. 1997. *Language, Charisma and Creativity: The Ritual Life of a Religious Movement*. Berkeley: University of California Press.

Cummings, Charles. 1976. "In praise of the desert: A letter to Hilary of Lérins from Eucher of Lyon." *Cistercian Studies* 11: 60–72.

Dijkstra, Jitse H. F. and Mathilde van Dijk, eds. 2006. *The Encroaching Desert: Egyptian Hagiography and the Medieval West*. Leiden: Brill.

Doniger, Wendy. 1998. *The Implied Spider: Politics and Theology in Myth*. New York: Columbia University Press.

Eliade, Mircea. 1960. *Myths, Dreams and Mysteries: The Encounter between Contemporary Faiths and Archaic Realities*. New York: Harper Colophon Books.

Feldt, Laura. 2012. *The Fantastic in Religious Narrative*. London: Routledge.

———. 2014. "Wild and wondrous men: Elijah and Elisha in the Hebrew Bible." In *Credible-Incredible: The Miraculous in the Ancient Mediterranean*, edited by Janet Spittler and Tobias Nicklas, 323–352. Tübigen: Mohr Siebeck.

———. 2016a. "Ancient wilderness mythologies: The case of space and religious identity formation in the gospel of Matthew." *Archiv für Religionsgeschichte* 16: 163–192.

———. 2016b. "Religion, nature, and ambiguous space in ancient Mesopotamia: The mountain wilderness in Old Babylonian religious narratives." *Numen* 63: 347–382.

———. 2016c. "Contemporary fantasy fiction and representations of religion: Playing with reality, myth, and magic in *His Dark Materials* and *Harry Potter*." *Religion* 46: 550–574.

Furedi, Frank. 2013. *Authority: A Sociological Approach*. Cambridge: Cambridge University Press.

George, M. 2009. *Israel's Tabernacle as Social Space*. Atlanta, GA: Society of Biblical Literature.

Hammer, Olav. 2016. "Towards a secular theory of religious experience." In *Contemporary Views on Comparative Religion*, edited by P. Antes, A. W. Geertz and M. Rothstein, 115–126. Sheffield: Equinox.

Gibson, Roy K. and A. D. Morrison. 2007. "Introduction: What is a letter?" In *Ancient Letters: Classical and Late Antique Epistolography*, edited by Ruth Morello and A. D. Morrison, 1–16. Oxford: Oxford University Press.

Greschat, K. 2007. "Spätantike Bildungstraditionen im Umkreis des Klosters von Lerinum. Die Kompendienwerke des Eucherius von Lyon." *Zeitschrift für Antike Christentum* 10: 320–335.

Heider, F. 1959. "Thing and Medium." *Psychological Issues* 1: 1–34.

Horsfield, Peter. 2015. *From Jesus to the Internet: A History of Christianity and Media.* London: Blackwell.

Ingold, Tim. 2000. *The Perception of the Environment: Essays in Livelihood, Dwelling and Skill.* London: Routledge.

Jensen, Jeppe S. 2009. *Myths and Mythologies: A Reader.* Critical Categories in the Study of Religion. London: Equinox.

Kelly, Christopher. 2011. "The myth of the desert in western monasticism: Eucherius of Lyon's *In Praise of the Desert.*" *Cistercian Studies Quarterly* 46: 129–141.

Kloppenborg, John. 2014. "Literate media in early Christian groups: The creation of a Christian book culture." *Journal of Early Christian Studies* 22: 21–59.

Knott, Kim. 2005. *The Location of Religion: A Spatial Analysis.* London: Equinox.

Lachmann, Renate. 2004. "Cultural memory and the role of literature." *European Review* 12: 165–178.

Larsson, Göran. 2015. "Power." In *Vocabulary for the Study of Religion*, edited by R. A. Segal and K. von Stuckrad, 103–109. Leiden: Brill.

Law, John. 2003. "The Manager and His Powers." Lancaster: Centre for Science Studies, Lancaster University. http://www.comp.lancs.ac.uk/sociology/papers/Law-Manager-and his-Powers.pdf

Lefebvre, Henri. 1991. *The Production of Space.* Oxford: Basil Blackwell. [Translated from *La production de l'espace*, 1974].

Lewis, James R. 2012. *Cults.* London: Equinox.

Leyser, Conrad. 1999. "'This Sainted Isle': Panegyric, nostalgia, and the invention of 'Lérinian Monasticism'." In *The Limits of Ancient Christianity: Essays in Honor of Robert Markus*, edited by W. Klingshirn and M. Vessey, 188–206. Ann Arbor: University of Michigan Press.

Leyser, Conrad. 2006. "The uses of the desert in the sixth-century west." In *The Encroaching Desert: Egyptian Hagiography and the Medieval West*, edited by J.H.F. Dijkstra and M. van Dijk, 113–134. Leiden: Brill.

Lied, L. I. 2005. "Another look at the Land of Damascus: The spaces of the Damascus document in the light of Edward W. Soja's Thirdspace Approach." In *New Directions in Qumran Studies: Proceedings of the Bristol Colloquium on the Dead Sea Scrolls, 8-10 September 2003*, edited by J. G. Campbell, W. J. Lyons and L. K. Pietersen, 101–125. London: T&T Clark.

Lincoln, B. 1994. *Authority. Construction and Corrosion.* Chicago, IL: University of Chicago Press.

———. 2003. *Holy Terrors: Thinking about Religion after September 11.* Chicago, IL: University of Chicago Press.

———. 2005. "Theses on Method." *Method and Theory in the Study of Religion* 17(1): 8–10.

McCutcheon, R. T. 2000. "Myth." In *Guide to the Study of Religion*, edited by W. Braun and R. T. McCutcheon, 190–208. London: Cassell.

McLuhan, Marshall. 1964. *Understanding Media: The Extensions of Man.* New York: Signet.

Markus, Robert. 1990. *The End of Ancient Christianity*. Cambridge: Cambridge University Press.

Meyrowitz, Joshua. 1994. "Medium Theory." In *Communication Theory Today*, edited by D. Crowley and D. Mitchell, 50–77, Cambridge: Polity Press.

———. 2001. "Morphing McLuhan: Medium theory for new millennium." *Proceedings of the Media Ecology Association* 2: 8–22.

Morello, Ruth and A. D. Morrison. 2007. *Ancient Letters: Classical and Late Antique Epistolography*. Oxford: Oxford University Press.

Moreschini, C. and E. Norelli. 2005. *Early Greek and Latin Literature: A Literary History*. Peabody: Hendrickson Publishers.

Pepino, John. 2009. *St. Eucherius of Lyons: Rhetorical Adaptation of Message to Intended Audience in Fifth Century Provence*. Washington, DC: Catholic University of America Dissertation.

Pricoco, Salvatore 1965. *Eucherii De laude eremi*. Recensuit, apparatu critic et indicibus instruxit. Università de Catania: Centro di studi sull'Antico Cristianesimo.

Rapp, Claudia. 2005. *Holy Bishops in Late Antiquity: The Nature of Christian Leadership in an Age of Transition*. Berkeley: University of California Press.

Rubenson, Samuel. 2015. "The letter-collections of Antony and Ammonas: Shaping a community." In *Collecting Early Christian Letters from the Apostle Paul to Late Antiquity*, edited by B. Neil and P. Allen, 68–79. Cambridge: Cambridge University Press.

Soja, Edward W. 1989. *Postmodern Geographies*. New York: Verso.

———. 1996. *Thirdspace: Journeys to Los Angeles and Other Real-and-Imagined Places*. Cambridge, MA: Blackwell.

Thrift, Nigel and Susan Whatmore, eds. 2004. *Cultural Geography: Critical Concepts in the Social Sciences*. London: Routledge.

Vivian, Tim, Kim Vivian and Jeffrey B. Russell, trans. and eds. 1999. *The Life of the Jura Fathers: The Life and Rule of the Holy Fathers Romanus, Lupicinus, and Eugendus, Abbots of the Monasteries in the Jura Mountains*. With Appendices: *Avitus of Vienne Letter XVIII to Viventiolus, Eucherius of Lyon: The Passion of the Martyrs of Agaune, Saint Maurice and His Companions, In Praise of the Desert*. Cistercian Studies Series178. Kalamazoo, MI: Cistercian Publications.

Weber, Max. 1922. "Die drei reinen Typen der legitimen Herrschaft: Eine soziologische Studie." *Preussischen Jahrbüchern* 187: 1–12.

———. 1980. *Wirtschaft und Gesellschaft: Grundriss der Verstehenden Soziologie*. 5th revised edition by J. Winckelmann. Tübingen: J.C.B. Mohr (Siebeck) [1921].

Yuzwa, Zachary. 2014. "Reading genre in Sulpicius Severus' letters." *Journal of Late Antiquity* 7: 329–350.

About the author

Laura Feldt is Associate Professor of the Study of Religions at the University of Southern Denmark, head of the research programme *Authority, Materiality and Media*, and managing editor of *NVMEN—International Review of the History of Religions* with G. D. Alles. Her research has mainly focused on myth, the fantastic, and monsters in ancient Mesopotamia, The Hebrew Bible and ancient Christianity, as well as on religion and contemporary popular culture. Her current research project is about wilderness mythology, space, and religious identity formation in ancient religions.

— 3 —

The Authority of Translators: Vendors, Manufacturers, and Materiality in the Transfer of *Barlaam and Josaphat* along the Silk Road

Christian Høgel

Texts—and the stories and teachings they contained—travelled far along the Silk Road in the hands of merchants, missionaries, monastic communities and many more. The intricate itineraries and the many languages and scripts used on the way have received much attention, and we can therefore follow some of the stages and versions that stories like the *Barlaam and Josaphat* (as it was known in the West) went through in its long journey from Sanskrit India to e.g. Norse-writing Norway. But in studies of such transfer of texts, translation has mainly been seen as a linguistic enterprise, requiring language skills and linguistic strategies of translators. The present paper aims at involving also material aspects of this process, focusing on the material conditions into which texts were inscribed on the way. The transformation from stringed palm leaves, to single parchment leaves or rolls, and then to bound codices also had an impact on the structure, presentation and symbolic value of these texts. Layout, the place and possibility of illuminations, as well as the portability and physical resilience of the written text all depended on the traditional manners of book production, and these varied immensely over the expanse of the Silk Road. Being authoritative to various degrees in themselves, texts entered, when translated and re-circulated, into a universe of multiple authority holders where translators (in a broad sense) would have to reinvent authoritative presentations of the new text, acting in many ways as vendors of it. This would in itself imply a—brief—authoritative position, comparable to the "authority of the seller" *auctoritas venditoris*, as expressed in Roman law.

Introduction

It has long been known that texts—and the stories and teachings they contained—travelled far along the Silk Road, in the hands of merchants, missionaries, monastic communities and many more. The intricate itineraries, the many languages and scripts used on the way, and the many interventions into the texts and stories have received quite some scholarly attention.[1] To some extent, we can thus follow some of the stages and versions that a story like *Barlaam and Josaphat* (as it was known in the West) went through in its long journey from Sanskrit India to Norse-writing Norway in the European Middle ages (Cordoni 2014).[2] Most of the far-travelling texts that crossed linguistic and political borders were sacred texts, fable stories, tales of kings and heroes (or, primarily, of Alexander the Great), and philosophical treaties, forming what could be called the earliest global or world literature.[3] Within this pattern, the Barlaam-story attracts special attention as a sacred narrative which changed its religious affiliation along the way. Unlike the Bible, the Qur'an, or the works of Mani, which were primarily disseminated by believers of the respective religious formations, the Barlaam-story—originally a version of the story of the Buddha—changed from its original Buddhist outlook, first to a Manichaean, then to a Muslim, and finally—in its most Western versions—to a Christian perspective. Along with this transmogrification in religion we find other parallel changes: in names, in narrative structure and details, and—not least—in language.

But yet another and equally parallel transformation is less often taken into account when talking of the geographical translocation of texts and stories along the Silk Road, namely that of the physical embodiment or the materiality of the text.[4] In the case of the Barlaam-story, the text went from being written on—presumably—stringed palm leaves, perhaps on to birch bark, before passing on to single parchment or paper leaves or rolls, then to book-like parchment codices, and finally to being integrated into large codices in which the text appeared only as one among many parallel tales. As this paper will show, the transformations in materiality were often interlinked with changes in language, narrative structure, and names. New places had their established literary habits, with a primary literary language normally going along with certain manners of speaking, of telling a story, and of manufacturing a text. So the success of this kind of travelling literature relied heavily on the performance of a number of skilled people that we normally refer to as the translators. To make the text retain or regain its authority in new contexts, a multi-fac-

1. After decades of intense study of specific languages and texts, studies into a more complete picture of the process are at the present picking up at an enormous speed. To refer only to some recent works, see Foehr-Janssens and Uhlig 2014; Gaullier-Bougassas 2011.
2. The brilliant overview and study of Cordoni 2014 has made this immensely easier.
3. On world literature, see Damrosch 2003; Thomsen 2008; and Beecroft 2015.
4. This is only partly covered by Pym (1998, 150–151).

eted craftsmanship would be needed. Script, language, layout and the material aspect of a book as well as its narrative or religious contents often went hand in hand when persuading an audience or a buyer. Advanced knowledge on the side of translators would be required to take a story successfully from one cultural/linguistic/material sphere into the next. In this paper, I will look at some of the common features relevant to far-reaching translations in the Middle Ages. I propose to see translations as very specific stations in the dissemination of texts/stories, as verbal-material or verbal-pictorial-material compounds, which bring particular issues of authority to the fore, not least in transformations and adaptations of materiality. I suggest that such analyses can improve our understanding of trans-cultural exchange and of the double vision needed by the translators in order to make this travelling literature so successful. This double vision worked towards a complex transfer of authority, which placed translators in a situation comparable to that of a seller of goods, as expressed by Roman law in the *auctoritas venditoris*. The vendor established a position of authority for him- or herself when investing an object with a certain price, and this position was legally binding but at the same time precarious (not requiring any prior transfer of authority). Yet, as shown by its very mention among defined positions of authority in Roman law, as those of rulers and magistrates, this position was of central importance in the sphere of holders of authority.

Shifting authority in translations

In the process of translating texts and transferring them to new contexts, various holders of authority were involved, just as the status or authority of the text or story in itself was crucial. The texts that went successfully through the process of translation were not chosen haphazardly in the first place, but were often those that carried a specific authority in their original sphere, having obtained a solid place for themselves in social life whether as holy, entertaining and/or informative. Some texts would have gained institutional support or become basic reading in schools, as with religious and philosophical texts and, to some extent, the tales of Alexander, which were used as a mirror of princes at many courts (Agapitos 1998). Holy texts would have carried an ascribed authority as such, for the believers but also for others in the community.[5] The authority of philosophical/scientific texts had increased, as the influence of Greek but also of Indian/Tibetan scientific traditions spread along the Silk Road, probably starting already in the

5. The status and authority of "authoritative texts" in religions is discussed extensively in the field of Second Temple Judaism and emerging Christianities, as well as with regard to new religious movements using fiction as core texts in various ways. See here most recently the 2016/4 issue of the journal *Religion*.

age of Alexander and peaking with the translation movement under the Abbasids (Gutas 1998).[6] Philosophical treatises promised a kind of knowledge that, even if hardly connected to production, administration or any direct accumulation of wealth, would still be desired and valued wherever there was a need for a well-educated class to run an empire or manage larger religious institutions (De Weerdt 2007). But some far-travelling texts or stories do not display a secure, authoritative status and seem to have carried their claim to importance and authority in their media form and their very verbal structure, pertaining to no fixed societal or institutional structure. The high occurrence of fable stories may be seen as reflecting a wish for tales on human wisdom and folly. Fable compounds, on the other hand, such as the classical Arabic *Kalila wa-Dimna* (originating from the Sanskrit *Panchatantra*) were often structured as to become images of court life, which may to some degree explain their popularity and their canonical status as exempla within Arabic prose (Versteegh 1997). The success of the *Barlaam and Josaphat* story, changing religious affiliation at several stations, cannot be explained through its attachment to any fixed institutions. So if religion has anything to do with its success, we would have to posit some common religiosity uniting all the religions involved. If not, the story was simply too good not to be copied, translated, and inserted into new contexts.

But despite the measure of authority that a text could carry in the first place, in its context of origin, nothing guaranteed that this authority would be in place at the receiving end, in the target sphere of a translation. Status could be secured by various (e.g. institutional) means, but of central importance was the highly specialized intervention performed by translators. 'Translator' is here taken in its traditional sense, but with broader implications. In the process of "carrying over" (the original meaning of Latin *translatio*), translators were brokers between two cultures not only in performing the linguistic transformation, with the ensuing narrative alterations,[7] but also in transferring the new text to a suitable—often traditionally acceptable and context-sensitive—physical form. To some degree, this feature differentiates far-travelling translations from those that did not travel far. The latter would, when successful, often have their authority secured by the same structures that formed the context of the original texts. And many translations did not have to travel far. The Syriac and possibly also the first Arabic translations of Greek philosophy were produced at centres in which intellectual exchange shifted repeatedly from being based on one language into another, creating a demand for translated versions (Gutas

6. See also the controversial Beckwith 2012.

7. On translation in general, see Pym 1998.

1998). Vernaculars, rising in many places to challenge the status of a well-established and privileged written language, created a need for translations that in most instances did not imply a change in geographical setting.[8] In many other cases, however, translation involved the prospect of a future displacement of the text or a present displacement. Translation centres, such as Antioch, Jerusalem, Sinai, the Tarim basin (or the outskirts of the Taklamakan desert), and many others, formed multi-lingual milieus with multi-directional motions in the displacement of persons and texts. Many readers would be found among travelling passers-by, speaking and reading a variety of languages, and local intellectual readerships must have been thriving. Still, translators in these places must in many cases have envisaged larger cities and states placed further along the trade routes as primary receivers of their new versions. Gratitude for their luck is often expressed by translators that found a brilliant story in places far away from home: the Latin translator of the *Barlaam*-story in Constantinople in 1048–1049 thanked a certain Leo for directing his attention to the text; the Greek patriarch Methodios when in Rome in early ninth century; an early Chinese translator in India around 800 CE (Cordoni 2014, 59; Volk 2006, 88; Krausmuller 2007; Houben and Rath 2011). Translators would often be travellers, as travelling was one of their means of acquiring proficiency in more than one language. The famous translator of Greek philosophy into Arabic, Hunayn ibn-Ishaq, seems to have acquired knowledge of Greek in Mesopotamia, which must still have been partly Greek-speaking in his day, and had travelled far to find manuscripts, but in order to get an even fuller grasp of Greek, he probably also went to Constantinople (Griffith 2009, 138–139).

In this way, translation depended in many cases on the displacement of texts and translators to and from translation hubs like Sinai and Tarim/Taklamakan, which were not strong political centres. Translators often performed in borderlands, with all that this implies in terms of cultural mix and physical insecurity. Embassies and missions, the origin of so much translation activity implied work offers for translators but also placed them in vulnerable positions.[9] But, even if displaced, much of the success of translating depended on the authority that texts held somewhere. When Chosrau I, according to the Greek historian Agathias (*Histories* 2.31), invited the philosophers of the newly closed-down Platonic academy to Persia, the former status of the institution in the Greek-Roman world must have played

8. On the rise of vernaculars and comparison between Sanskrit-Indian and Latin-European situations, see Pollock 2009, part 2.

9. It would have been an asset to know the circumstances of Mani's visit to the court of Shapur I in third century CE, leading to his composition in middle Persian of a summary of his teaching, see Lieu 1992, 6–7 and 58–59.

an important part in the invitation. The well-informed commentaries that tenth-century Baghdadi intellectual al-Nadim was able to give to the many texts mentioned in his impressive *al-Fihrist*, show that the origin of a text was by no means neglected. Al-Nadim was careful to note when a text had travelled far, notably from Greece or India, and he also listed e.g. the translators of Greek philosophy into Arabic (Dodge 1970, 156–589). The authority of a text could also work the other way. Translation could be undertaken in order to counter a text and the beliefs that others venerated, to work with the aim of contesting the authority of the text in its source environment. The Latin translation of the Qur'an, produced by Robert of Ketton at the initiative of Peter the Venerable in mid-eleventh century, was meant to serve polemical aims, which wholly depended on the authority that the text held elsewhere (Burman 1998). But then Peter Venerable had no aim—as had al-Nadim—of increasing the sale of the translated text, and in this sense his project was an exception. By far the most translations were meant to become respected, to become authority holders in their target environment, probably even to become an object of exchange and trade.

The authority of the vendor

When taking a look at the Silk Road as an example of an early book market, we see much trade of books taking place as mere transportation from producer to buyer and further on to subsequent buyers and possessors. However, for the texts/stories that travelled far, like our Barlaam-story, from India to Norway, transportation was obviously not enough. Indian palm-leaves in Norway would have served no other purpose than wonder, and no use could have been made of their textual contents. In fact, several stations and linguistic/physical transformations would be needed on the way to make such exchange possible (no medieval Sanskrit-Norse translator is ever mentioned). And at every station somebody—and in many cases the translators of the linguistic aspect of the book—would have to carefully plan and execute the physical transformation of the book as well. Detailed decisions on writing material, layout, placing of illuminations and commentaries would demand much more than linguistic skills of the translator, and in some cases collaboration with illuminators and other professionals. Many translators (in the broad sense of the word) would have been familiar with the conventions of both source and target text production and formats, but commissioners and buyers much less so. All choices made to bridge this gap would have an impact on the structure, presentation and the symbolic value of the text or story. And changes were unavoidable. Layout, the place and possibility of illuminations, as well as the portability and physical resilience of the written text, all depended on the traditional manners of book production, and these varied immensely over the expanse of the Silk Road. So if any transfer was to succeed, the texts would have to transform accordingly.

Even if often invisible later, translators therefore stood in a crucial, even if less permanent, position of authority, having to negotiate with the first recipient(s) of the translated text in its new sphere. In this part of their activities, we may see translators as comparable to that of the vendors of goods, who were actually one of the four envisaged holders of authority in Roman law. As discussed by Lincoln, Roman law listed three persons or bodies officially and more permanently vested with power (the senate, the emperor, the trustee); but a fourth one was the performer of a sales transaction, vested in action with *auctoritas venditoris*, the "authority of the seller" (Lincoln 1994, 1–3). Al-Nadim, mentioned above, was as son of a book-seller bent upon giving texts the best possible recommendations, and this would often be based on evoking original status and authority as well as the high qualifications of the translators. In his *al-Fihrist,* al-Nadim offers a (partly mis-informed) variety of origins or background stories to the transmission of Greek learning into Arabic, giving accounts of shifting imperial borders, enormous libraries in far-away locations, and of rulers' dreams, like that of al-Ma'mun whose account of how he meet Aristotle is given in al-Nadim's book (Dodge 1970, 572–586).

The catalogue of al-Nadim offers us a glimpse of the books that a son of a bookseller in Baghdad could come across in the late tenth century. And many of his praises of authors, stories and conceptions can be seen, I suggest, as mirroring those that were performed in front of buyers on the market. Al-Nadim, and his father, would thus ensure (or increase, as in the etymological root aug- from *augeo* "to increase" in Latin *auctoritas*), the value and authority in their own interest, but running at the same time the risk of angry costumers, who could complain if the text somehow did not live up to the description. In this way, book transactions invested a wide range of people, also in much less urban areas, with the authority of the seller. The many caves on the slopes of the Tarim basin (or Taklamakan desert) would not only be the shrines of various deities and their religious communities, lavishly decorated with statues, mural paintings and holy texts; they were also the forum of linguistic negotiation and of book trade.[10] And at specific times, the translators, in the broad sense of the term, would perform the role of authority holder in the eyes of people who would depend on the skills of the translators for understanding what interest a book, sometimes written thousands of kilometres away, had to offer. Descriptions may at times have run beyond

10. On the texts coming out of the Turfan expeditions and the Dunhuang caves, see van Schaik and Imre Galambos 2012, 13–34; Encyclopaedia Iranica (http://www.iranicaonline.org) 'Turfan expeditions'.

reality and expectations may have gone beyond what the text could actually fulfil. But this misuse of authority would only mirror the common problem of trade, especially if transacted through travelling sellers or itinerant buyers.

Phases of transfer and the interplay between specific languages

Writing the history of translation along the Silk Road offers some difficulties. In most cases, we do not know the individual translators or even possess copies of their texts, and so we have no way of ascertaining their specific aims or the wishes of individual commissioners or buyers etc. Yet, we do know that the process took place, so somebody must have had the necessary transcultural ability to see the potentials of new texts and to mediate between cultural contexts. And these translators would not be working in a void, since both linguistic and material procedures would have been affected, or even guided, by preceding translations between the specific languages and/or cultural spheres. In fact, the entire process depended in many ways on whether a translation industry had already developed between the two languages/cultural spheres, and on how much common cultural ground had been established between them in general. The following exposition will, supported by a few examples, claim that translations between two languages and their cultural spheres would often go through two phases, of which the second would only be reached in case translations between the specific languages became widespread and the sphere of origin had attained some authority *per se* in the target sphere.

If we think of the first translators between two specific languages, these would be pioneers or perhaps people who had performed such duties in less extensive ways, like the translators at court, bilingual educators, or people engaged in other strands of society. When first venturing into translating longer texts, the need for the translation and the possibility of it being accepted at the receiving end would have been less than clear. For many reasons, such initial translations would often depend on serious reworking and large-scale intervention. The target audience would be people who had heard only extracts or short presentations of the story etc., if anything at all. To make the text work in the new setting, where such texts would have little resonance, the translator would have to insist on the utility, truth and/or exoticism of the restated text, while at the same time offering explanations and other means of verbal support to the new readers and listeners. Much has been written on the distinction between translations that are mainly oriented towards the target language, as opposed to translations which retain features of the source language to a higher degree (Pym 2010, chapter 2). But only very few studies attempt to trace the gradual development between two specific languages, as presented here, from an early phase of pioneering work to a later stage of more settled and steady production. In such a second phase, a target audience would to some extent have become accustomed to the new cultural context, and new texts would thus join an existing body of translated texts and perhaps even an existing commentary discourse, thereby reducing the need for support on the part of the translator.[11] To put this in literary terms, little or no intertextuality would support the reading or listening of a translated text in phase one. Since readers and listeners would have nowhere else to go to find information, translators would have to take this into account. At a later stage, the translated literature had much better chances of performing authoritatively on its own, on the basis of acquired knowledge in the audience.

Translators working on the conditions described in phase one are known from many places. When Cicero translated Greek philosophy and rhetoric into Latin, substantial remodelling went into the process. And whether offering his texts as mere support for the reading of the Greek originals, as suggested by some scholars, or actually trying to make the Latin translations perform on their own in the eyes and ears of newcomers, the result is the same: a too close verbal correspondence with the Greek original would not do the job (Powell 1995). A similarly concerned attitude, leading to a looser correspondence between the original and the translation, was also perceived by later readers of the early Arabic translations of Greek philosophy (Gutas 2012). Re-translation of the Greek philosophical tradition was therefore widespread.[12] Very little was ever translated into Greek in the Byzantine period, and the Septuagint was in a sense the only wholesale (Greek, but pre-Byzantine) translation of a text corpus that became integrated into Byzantine literature, though some translations from Latin (Ovid, Thomas Aquinas, etc.) from the thirteenth and fourteenth centuries point in the direction of a broader interest on the rise. Other translation initiatives in Byzantium—hymns and hagiography and from Syriac and Latin (the latter only hagiography), technical treatises from Arabic, and originally Indian texts from Arabic, Syriac and Georgian—depended primarily on the initiatives of individuals and never made it beyond our first phase.[13]

But this happened in other places. In Tibet an earlier phase of translating Buddhist texts was, by the late eighth century CE, supplanted by a

11. On the issue of writing into an existing body of texts or "library," see Mortensen 2018, 71–90.

12. On re-translation see e.g. Brentjes 2006, with an example of consecutive and—at least according to the translators—improved translations is that of Arabic translations of Euclid; om re-translation in general see also, Pym 1999, 82–84.

13. See "translation" in Kazhdan 1991.

much more intensive and centrally controlled translation activity, which would also adhere much closer to the source language. Emperor Khri-srong lDe-btsan (755–794? CE) invited the learned Śāntarakṣita to Tibet. In collaboration with Tibetan peers, he produced an extensive Buddhist literature in Tibetan (Scherrer-Schaub 2009, 161–162). On the basis of a translation manual, an Indo-Tibetan dictionary, and a list of primary Buddhist works, all produced for the same purpose, Śāntarakṣita and his group, in accordance with an imperial decree, produced Tibetan translations that followed the Sanskrit word order and manners of expression as closely as possible. The same development is seen in the case of Georgian translations from Greek. After centuries of looser, and more inventive, adaptations of Byzantine literary genres and modes, Georgian translators shifted course in the eleventh century and began producing translations that followed their Greek models as closely as possible, putting serious demands on Georgian readers and listeners (Tarchnisvili 1955, 7–79).

All in all, the shifting authority positions of texts and translators, in interplay with the perceived standard norms and languages, shifting from region to region, would make the successful transfer of texts and stories hinge on specific performances of authority. The original status of authority of a text would in these cases be transferred, transformed, or contested. We now turn to a short case study to see these forces at work more closely.

The story of Barlaam and Josaphat

The story of Barlaam and Josaphat is that of a king, who at the birth of his long-expected child, is told that the son will convert to an unwanted religion or belief, if he discovers the sorrows of the world. The young prince Josaphat (his name occurs in various versions) is therefore kept inside the castle, and everyone around him is instructed to be joyful. When reaching puberty or such, the young prince becomes distressed. Faced with his son's pleas, the king allows him to take some trips out into the world beyond the castle, which he has not yet seen. Again, instructions are given to ensure that the young man will only encounter happy people on his way, until the prince, on an excursion, meets first a blind person and a cripple, and then on a following trip a very old man whose lifetime is almost up. Faced with the frank answers from court attendees to his questions—that the sorrows of humankind are many, and that death is unavoidable—the young prince falls into a depression. His father soon recognizes that some cure is needed and hires a teacher for his son. The choice falls on Barlaam, a virtuous man who claims to have a most valuable treasure. The reader quickly realizes that this treasure is the teaching of the religion or belief that the king was warned against, and Josaphat gradually adopts this belief. At first, the king is unaware of this, but as soon as he finds out, he launches a sequence of threats and allurements in order to draw back the prince to his paternal beliefs. He does not succeed, and at the end the father is also converted. This short summary not only leaves out all the lovely details in the story, such as the normally lively dialogues full of wonders, questions and frank answers, but also the many fables or embedded tales that support or further develop the many deliberations on humankind's place in the world, with some Buddhist colouring that stays on through all the versions (Lang 1957).

As already mentioned, the ability of this story to transgress linguistic/cultural borders did not rest on institutional or confessional support. Originally Buddhist, it became Manichaean, Islamic, and Christian on its way westward. So no continuous institutional support guided the transfer of this religious text. It is hard to avoid the suggestion that in the many phases of its translation, literary beauty itself was a factor in its acceptance. One very striking trait of the story is that it tells of a slow conversion, of a young person who is first lost in distress and depression, and only gradually finds relief in a new way of viewing the world and his place in it. These striking features, which are closely knitted to the story's original Buddhist teaching, stand out also when the story appears as a Christian saint's life, where the young protagonist experiences a much more gradual conversion than is normal for Christian saints.

The many embedded tales in the story of Barlaam and Josaphat almost certainly go back to early versions, and many of the inserted stories are known from other Indian contexts (see Lang 1967). But otherwise it is difficult to ascertain exactly what was there from the start. Probably based on three different versions of the life of Buddha (two written in Sanskrit, one in Pali), our earliest extant "versions" of the Barlaam-story are found in Old Turkic fragments (Cordoni 2014). In one of these, found among the many Manichaean texts from the Turfan expedition (1902–1914), the scene of the young prince's meeting with the old man appears. The name of the prince makes this Turkic text a likely link (or a copy/reworking of the link) between the Indian and later versions. "Boddhisatva"—Buddha's name—has here become "Bodisav," which resembles the later Arabic "Būḍāsaf" (or "Būḍāsf"). This form slid, probably because of the easy confusion of "b" and "y" in Arabic, into "Yodasaph" in Georgian, "Ioasaph" in Greek, and finally "Iosaphat" in Latin and Western vernacular languages. This corruption in the name was part of the clues that led to the modern recovery of the origins of the story of Barlaam and Josaphat, known in the West for centuries as a Christian tale, as originally a narrative about the Buddha (Lang 1957). The gradual transformation of the name also shows that nobody, in this long process, intentionally kept the origins a secret. Translators simply stuck to the name, though adjusting it—to add e.g. Old Testament associations, as in the Latin form—or in some cases, they simply misread it. Still, the religion to which the text was ascribed changed on the way. The Turkic, and most probably Manichaean, translation was probably close to the Middle Persian (or Pehlevi) version, which gave rise to several Arabic versions according to al-Nadim.[14] Two of these are direct forerunners to the transmitted Arabic version, which has a slightly Islamicized hue, with references to Allah only in short expressions and the like (Lang 1957, 36). This light Islamic touch makes the story stand out more as a parable of a virtuous life than as a text of fundamental importance for any religion. Still, the text's dissemination in Arabic predominantly happened via Shia-Muslim milieu; this is evident especially in the reworkings which we see in encyclopaedic summaries etc. (Cordoni 2014, 11–18).

As we see in the Arabic (and Ismaili Shia) *Kitab Bilawhar wa-Būḏāsaf*, the story clearly resembles the later Georgian and Christian versions. Yet, one of its features, that large sections of the main story are narrated by the protagonists of the story, does not surface in the later versions. Here we see a common transformation which recurs in much of the originally Indian literature that travels West: originally complex layers of narration are simplified, with more parts being told simply by one, general narrator, and a reduced number of tales being told within other tales.[15] Another originally Indian tale, the *Kalila wa-Dimna,* uses embedded tales extensively, peaking with small narrations that are subordinated into the fourth degree of tales within tales (thus, an N4 in the annotation system of Genette). This narrative strategy is substantially reduced in the Greek version produced by Symeon Seth, at the end of the eleventh century in Constantinople (Niehoff-Panagiotidis 2003). In accordance with more Eastern habits, Symeon Seth called these tales *paradeigmata,* 'paradigmatic tales' (hereby translating the Arabic *maṯal/amṯāl*), but the argumentative capacity that they were now made to serve (and which also became part of Latin *exempla*) was foreign to the Eastern models (Niehoff-Panagiotidis 2003, 117–135). We can hardly avoid deeming the reduction in embedded tales/subordinate narrators a common distinguishing feature between Eastern and Western narrative tra-

14. Al-Nadim (Dodge 1970, 717) lists these among the Persian texts that ibn al-Muqaffa translated into Arabic. Though very productive, ibn al-Muqaffa is nowhere else credited with a translation of the Barlaam-story, and it seems more likely that al-Nadim simply listed them there, because he knew ibn al-Muqaffa had done translations from Middle Persian (and at least one—*Kalila wa-Dimna*—which was also an originally Indian text). We have fragments of a versified version of the story from a tenth century manuscript, see Cordoni 2014, 18–19.

15. On embedded tales and narrative subordination in an East-West perspective, see Taylor 2014.

ditions, though this is a hotly debated issue in scholarly circles.[16]

As is clear from the many versions that these multi-layered narratives take, embedded tales are likely to change position in the narrative flow, and they also have the tendency to become the words spoken by differing characters in the narrative. This play with narrative voices, though almost certainly a key part of oral traditions, seems somehow connected also to the writing material. Indian stringed palm-leaves, the most important writing material for early Sanskrit and Pali writing, would structure a text into smaller bits than would paper or parchment pages, and a clear layering and possible easier restructuring would be part of the way a text presented itself. Such modern observations are impossible to substantiate with medieval examples; nobody seems to have made a note of it. Likewise unsupported by direct evidence is the following observation: the lavishly illuminated Byzantine manuscripts that offer us the Barlaam text supported by pictures all have very horizontal images (wide and low dimensions).[17] Is it possible that this feature, which is found only rarely elsewhere in Byzantine manuscripts, was a remnant from a more Eastern pictorial programme originally designed for palm-leaves? Again, we have no means of corroborating this, but we know that pictorial features travelled far and often on the same light material as portable texts. An example of this is found in Manichaean book production. Mani, the founder of Manichaeism, was both a writer and a renowned illuminator, and Manichaean books are often luxuriously embellished with images in strong colours (Lieu 1992, 139–140). One feature, which is found in several Manichaean books and nowhere else, to the knowledge of the present author, is the placing of images on the manuscript page not so that they correspond with the view of the reader, but turned ninety degrees, so that these become easily accessible to anybody sitting next to the reader. A whole performative and social/communal usage of Manichaean books may be envisaged from this, and the habit of turned images is found in Manichaean books originating thousands of kilometres apart.[18]

What we may state with a high degree of certainty is, however, that when the Barlaam story left India and travelled west, it was also transferred to other materials. In Arabic, this material would soon be paper. Paper was an extraordinary commodity that soon became so important to the Silk Road as portable writing material that it made modern historians suggest that the route be called the Paper Road (Bloom 2005). We do not know when and

16. See the references in Taylor 2014.

17. The most comprehensive overview is still in der Nersessian 1936.

18. Distinct Chinese pictorial features (eyes of characters, how horses, trees and perspective are rendered, etc.) spread westward, not least through Timurid manuscript art. by the thirteenth century reaching Mediterranean ports, see Titley 1983, 11–25.

by whom the text was translated into Georgian,[19] but due to the close connections between Greek and Georgian book production, it is probable that the text now was transferred to parchment, which remained, in the Greek world, and most probably also in the Georgian sphere, the primary writing material until the eleventh century, with paper only slowly picking up after this. The transferral of the text to parchment is not only a sign of it joining a different textual culture. From this point on, the Barlaam story entered a new distinct religious context, with its specific textual habits, modes of sanctity and constellations of authority. In the Georgian version—and then again in the Greek—the story is now a saint's life, with Ioasaph as the primary saint and Barlaam as his holy assistant. In the Orthodox (and other) churches, saints were venerated on their feast days. Most saints had a proper "life" written which supported their status, and various liturgical books would include a mention of the saint or give a short or full version of his or her life.

The inclusion of the Barlaam-story into this textual scheme presented some difficulties that seem, however, to surface most clearly in its Greek version. First, the text had to explain the rise of a new saint so far away from the original Christian world. Since Late Antiquity, apostles had been known to roam the world, and the common notion was that the apostle Thomas christianized (parts of) India. The Georgian version seems not to be particularly preoccupied with making any link; it simply refers from the start to 'Christians multiplying' in India (Lang 1966, 53–54). The Orthodoxy of the Christianity taught by the Barlaam story could easily be questioned, since the story had no clear source or original teacher of his faith. In all the versions Barlaam gains access to Josaphat by claiming to possess a treasure or precious stone with distinctly magical powers (Lang 1966, 71–73; Volk 2006, 50–51). The Georgian version is content with this—in the first place enigmatic—marker of Barlaam's holiness. It is hard to indicate in what way a Greek audience would be different from a Georgian in the late tenth century, but the translator from Georgian into Greek, Euthymios the Iberian or the Athonite, felt the need to add further support for the saint's claim and explain how his new saint fitted into ecclesiastical history. In presenting the story in Greek, Euthymios carefully pointed out India as the same as the land of the Ethiopians, an obvious mistake that was nevertheless common in Byzantium (perhaps envisaging a land connection encircling the Indian Ocean). He also made reference to the apostolic mission of Thomas, and to avoid any suspicion to the contrary, a complete treatise (the so-called Apology of Aristeides) was put into the mouth of Barlaam when presenting

19. A short presentation of various modern hypotheses is given by Cordoni 2014, 25–26.

the Christian faith (Volk 2006, 269–283). The story may have fascinated with all its foreign details and narrative inventiveness, but to become accepted into Byzantine hagiography, which offered promising aspects of dissemination, the translator saw the need for an adjustment to connect it to various existing narratives. Euthymios did not envisage a Byzantine audience ready for too many features from the source (or intermediary source) setting.

Euthymios, the translator, was a person who knew how to mediate between Georgian and Greek. Born around 955 and having spent his first years in Georgian Tao-Klardžeti under Byzantine sovereignty, in 964 Euthymios was, at the age of about nine, included among the royal hostages who were taken to Constantinople, in accordance with an agreement between the Byzantine emperor Nikephoros Phokas and the Georgian regent David.[20] Presumably, Euthymios received his thorough training in Greek literature in Constantinople, where he was probably attached to the court. Not many years later he was involved in the construction of the first Georgian settlement in the monastic area of Mount Athos (in northern mainland Greece). After a successful campaign for the emperor Basil II, the general Tornik, the cousin of Euthymios' father, founded the Georgian monastery Ton Iviron in Athos where Euthymios was later to become abbot. In this context Euthymios translated not only the Georgian version of the Barlaam story into Greek, but also more than hundred translations of Greek Biblical and patristic writings into Georgian. As these activities show, Euthymios is a fine example of a translator involved in the displacement of texts, who thinks in terms of translating for a larger centre at a distance from his original geographical position. Though placed in Athos, the primary readers of his Greek translation would have been found in cities as Constantinople and in monastic milieus all over the Byzantine world. His translations into Georgian soon found readers in Georgia, a prospect he must have counted on.

Further details about Euthymios place him as a clear example of a broker between cultures. Not only was he well versed in Georgian and Greek, but the names of his father, Abulherit, and his maternal grand-father, Abuharb, reveal an Arab background or at least an Arabic cultural influence. It is impossible to determine the direct importance of this (was the Arabic-Georgian translation also a product of Euthymios' family?), but Euthymios was clearly a man of many cultures, and his expert ability to adjust the Georgian original to a Byzantine readership finds a clear confirmation in the many extant manuscripts of his Greek Barlaam-text, even from the eleventh century.[21]

20. For his biography, see Volk 2006, 1–96.

21. See the list of manuscripts in Volk 2006, 240–495.

As far as we can see, the strategy of Euthymios was to make the new text appear in the Greek world as a specific type of hagiography that was becoming widespread, perhaps even popular, in Byzantium at the end of the tenth century, namely the saint's life of a type that included whole treatises and extensive documentation, in some cases approaching historiographical dimensions. These texts, such as the *Life of Gregentios*, the *Life of Basil the Younger*, and to some extent also the *Life of Andrew the Fool*, were lengthy texts (more than one hundred pages in modern editions), which despite their clear mirroring of ordinary saints' lives took the genre beyond its liturgical limits, and instead focused on convincing its reader through narrative inventiveness (as in the *Life of Andrew the Fool*) and massive documentation (as in the *Life of Gregentios*) (Berger 2006; Sullivan 2014; Rydén 1995).

The transformation of the text into something closer to a treatise mirrors other aspects of Byzantine book production. It was common in Byzantium to exchange (probably mostly shorter) texts in lose leaves or rolls (Bernard 2014, 90–96), but once texts were meant to serve more institutionalized purposes, such as the liturgy, they seem always to have been transferred onto parchment and to have been incorporated into manuscripts that were 'complete' texts, in the sense that they filled out the needs of the whole or a specific part of the liturgy.[22] This orderliness mirrors the general manner of using hagiographical manuscripts in Byzantium, which based on the lack of any indications to the contrary must be deemed rather utilitarian. As repeatedly indicated in *typika* (the Byzantine liturgical manuals), books were taken down from the shelf in order to be read out. If we compare with e.g. Buddhist material from Gilgit, where liturgical books were wrapped in multi-coloured cloths and set up in pure places (Schopen 2009, 197–203), the more practical handling of liturgical or holy books in Byzantium becomes clear. Images, icons, were shown respect, but not books, only the words they contained. This dematerialized view of books and manuscripts in the West (here including Byzantium) was an important part of what the inclusion of the Barlaam-story onto parchment implied. Further west, especially in the Latin hagiographical collection, the *Legenda aurea,* produced by Jacob de Voragine towards the end of the thirteenth century, the complete circle of converting Josaphat (and to some extent Barlaam) into ordinary Christian saints was completed. Authority now resided less, or not at all, in the materiality of the writing, but primarily in systematized textual structure. This, however, did not prevent the text from having many readers all over Europe and the Middle East, as the number of extant manuscript copies and rich illumination programmes show.

22. It is hard to establish a statistics on this, but compare the sections on ordered and non-ordered Byzantine hagiographical manuscripts in Ehrhard 1936–1952, vol. 1, p. 52.

In moving, both the concrete materiality of texts and their perceived materiality were of importance. When arriving in the West, the Barlaam and Ioasaph story would become incorporated into larger contexts and at the same time lose some of its perceived corporeality. Assimilating the text to many of the local factors and conditions, e.g. supplying it with dogmatic treatises upon entering the Byzantine sphere, translators enabled it to retain or obtain a status of authority. Yet, much Buddhist wisdom can still be found, even in the most Western versions, and on some of the shining white parchment folios of the Byzantine manuscripts horizontal images probably mirrored the shape of much earlier versions. Euthymios, bridging in his personal story the gap between two spheres, languages and book cultures, is a prime example of a translator performing as a broker or mediator, in a situation comparable to that of the vendor, vested also according to Roman law with a short but crucial authority position.

Conclusion

The transfer of the story of Barlaam and Ioasaph passed through a sequence of translations, also requiring shifts in the material. Scholarship related to the many philologies covering the languages and literatures of the world has accumulated an immense knowledge on textual production in all its phases, but translation has mainly been seen as a linguistic enterprise, requiring primarily or only the language skills and the linguistic strategies of the translators. The present paper has suggested that we change perspectives to also include the material and networked aspects of text production and dissemination into the discussion of this process, thereby hopefully supporting a gradual build-up of a truly comparative philology. When wanting to compare textual procedures in various parts of the world, translators and the full requirements of their job becomes an obvious point of focus. Since all languages and areas each had their own ideas, conventions, and norms with regard to how texts should be produced and presented, translators would have to know the procedures of the source language (or source area) in order to read and understand the source text, while at the same time taking the target format of books into consideration for the final product; he—or she—would have to translate the text but also transform one type of material book shape into another. This demanded knowledge about differing front matter, layout, illuminations etc. and serious planning, in order to avoid incompatible solutions. It also put into focus the various aspects of authority involved. Texts, often adopted for translation due to their status of authority, could easily loose their status in new and untried contexts, particularly in what has here been described as phase one in the translation between two languages. In phase two, more settled conditions would support the acceptance of a new text. Yet in both cases translators would often have to undertake the brief but important stance of authority, comparable to that of a vendor of goods (and therefore compatible with the fourth position of authority according to Roman law, that of *auctoritas venditoris*). Translators would have to communicate what was of value from one culture to a new one. And the variation found in what aspects of a text would survive and be of importance at each new station of translation—its institutional or school status, its narrative richness, its performative potentials—is crucial to understanding how sacred texts and translations travelled along the Silk Road and in some cases retained their status all the way.

References

Agapitos, P. A. 1998. "Teachers, pupils and imperial power in eleventh-century Byzantium." In *Pedagogy and Power: Rhetorics of classical learning*, edited by Y. L. Too and N. Livingstone, 170–191. Cambridge: Cambridge University Press.

Beckwith, Cristopher. 2011. *Empires of the Silk Road: A History of Central Eurasia from the Bronze Age to the Present.* Princeton, NJ: Princeton University Press.

———. 2012. *Warriors of the Cloisters: The Central Asian Origins of Science in the Medieval World.* Princeton, NJ: Princeton University Press.

Beecroft, Alexander. 2015. *An Ecology of World Literature. From Antiquity to the Present Day.* London: Verso.

Berger, Albrecht. 2006. *Life And Works of Saint Gregentios, Archbishop of Taphar.* Berlin: de Gruyter.

Bernard, Floris. 2014. *Writing and Reading Byzantine Secular Poetry, 1025-1081.* Oxford: Oxford University Press.

Bloom, Jonathan M. 2005. "Silk road or paper road?" *The Silkroad Foundation Newsletter* 3(2). http://www.silk-road.com/newsletter/vol3num2/5_bloom.php.

Brentjes, Sonja. 2006. "An exciting new Arabic version of Euclid's Elements: MS Mumbai, Mullā Fīrūz R I.6." *Revue d'histoire des mathématiques* 12: 169–197.

Burman, Thomas E. 1998. "Tafsir and translation: Traditional Arabic Quran exegesis and the Latin Qurans of Robert of Ketton and Mark of Toledo." *Speculum* 73: 703–732.

Cordoni, Constanza. 2014. *Barlaam und Josaphat in der europäischen Literatur des Mittelalters. Darstellung der Stofftraditionen—Bibliographie—Studien.* Berlin: de Gruyter.

Damrosch, David. 2003. *What Is World Literature?* Princeton, NJ: Princeton University Press.

De Weerdt, H.G.D. 2007. *Competition over Content: Negotiating Standards for the Civil Service Examinations in Imperial China (1127-1276).* Harvard East Asian Monographs 289. Cambridge, MA: Harvard University Asia Center.

Der Nersessian, S. 1936. *L'illustration du Roman de Barlaam et Joasaph.* Paris: de Boccard.

Dodge, B. 1970. *The Fihrist of al-Nadīm: A Tenth-Century Survey of Muslim Culture*. New York: Columbia Univeristy Press.

Ehrhard, A. 1936–1952. *Überlieferung und Bestand der hagiographischen und homiletischen Literatur der griechischen Kirche. Texte und Untersuchungen zur Geshichte der altchristlichen Literatur*. Vols. 50–52.2. Leipzig: Hinrichs.

Foehr-Janssens, Yasmina, and Marion Uhlig, eds. 2014. *D'Orient en Occident: Les recueils de fables enchassees avant les mille et une nuits de Galland (Barlaam et Josaphat, Calila et Dimna, Disciplina Clericalis, Roman de Sept Sages)*. Turnhout: Brepol.

Gaullier-Bougassas, Catherine, ed. 2011. *L'Historiographie médiévale d'Alexandre le Grand*. Turnhout: Brepols.

Griffith, Sidney. 2009. *Hunayn Ibn Ishaq and the Kitab Adab Al-Falasifah: The Pursuit of Wisdom and a Humane Polity in Early Abbasid Baghdad*. Piscataway: Gorgias.

Gutas, D. 1998. *Greek Thought, Arabic Culture: The Graeco-Arabic Translation Movement in Baghdad and Early ʿAbbāsid Society*. London: Routledge.

Gutas, Dimitri. 2012. "Arabic into Byzantine Greek: Introducing a survey of the translations." In *Knotenpunkt Byzans*, edited by A. Speer and P. Steinkrüger, 246-262. Berlin: De Gruyter.

Houben, Jan E. M. and Saraju Rath. 2011. "Introduction, Manuscript culture and its impact in 'India': Contours and parameters." In *Aspects of Manuscript Culture in India*, edited by Saraju Rath, 1-53. Leiden: Brill.

Kazhdan, A. P., ed. 1991. *The Oxford Dictionary of Byzantium*. 3 vols. New York: Oxford University Press.

Krausmuller, Dirk. 2007. "Patriarch Methodius, the first hagiographer of Theodore of Stoudios." *Symbolae Osloenses* 81: 144–150.

Lang, David Marshall. 1957. *The Wisdom of Balahvar: A Christian Legend of the Buddha*. London: George Allen and Unwin.

———. 1966. *The Balavariani: A Tale from the Christian East*. Los Angeles: California University Press.

———. 1967. "Introduction." In *John Damascene. Barlaam and Ioasaph*. Translated by G. R. Woodward and Harold Mattingly. Cambridge, MA: Loeb Classical Library.

Lieu, Samuel N. C. 1992. *Manichaeism in the Later Roman Empire and in China*. 2nd ed. Tübingen: J.C.B. Mohr.

Lincoln, Bruce. 1994. *Authority. Construction and Corrosion*. Chicago, IL: University of Chicago Press.

Mortensen, Lars Boje. forthcoming. "Latin as vernacular: Critical mass and the 'librarization' of new book languages." In *Origin Stories: The Rise of Vernacular Literacy in a Comparative Perspective*, edited by Norbert Kössinger, Elke Krotz, Stephan Müller, Pavlina Rychterova and Pavlína Rychterová, 71-90. Munich: Brill.

Niehoff-Panagiotidis, Johannes. 2003. *Übersetzung und Rezeption: Die byzantinisch-neugriechischen und spanischen Adaptionen von Kalila wa-Dimna. Serta Graeca*. Wiesbaden: Reichert.

Pollock, Sheldon. 2009. *The Language of the Gods in the World of Men. Sanskrit, Culture, and Power in Premodern India*. Berkeley: University of California Press.

Powell, J.G.F. 1995. "Cicero's translation from Greek." In *Cicero the Philosopher*, edited by J.G.F. Powell, 273–300. Oxford: Oxford University Press.

Pym, A. 1998. *Method in Translation History*. London: Routledge.

———. 2010. *Exploring Translation Theories*, London: Routledge.

Rydén, Lennart. 1995. *The Life of St Andrew the Fool*. Studia Byzantina Upsaliensia. 2 vols. Uppsala: Uppsla University.

Schaik, Sam van and Imre Galambos. 2012. *Manuscripts and Travellers: The Sino-Tibetan Documents of a Tenth-Century Pilgrim*. Berlin: de Gruyter.

Scherrer-Schaub, Christina. 2009. "Copier, interpreter, transformer, représenter ou Des modes de la diffusion des Écritures et de lécrit dans le bouddhisme indien." In *Écrire et transmettre en Inde classique*, edited by Gérard Colas and Gerdi Gerschheimer, 151–172. Paris: École francaişe d'Extrême-Orient.

Schopen, Gregory. 2009. "On the absence of Urtexts and otiose Ācāryas: Buildings, books, and lay Buddhist ritual at Gilgit." In *Écrire et transmettre en Inde classique*, edited by Gérard Colas and Gerdi Gerschheimer, 189–219. Paris: École francaişe d'Extrême-Orient.

Sullivan, Denis F., Alice-Mary Talbot and Stamatina McGrath. 2014. *The Life of Saint Basil the Younger: Critical Edition and Annotated Translation of the Moscow Version*. Dumbarton Oaks Studies. Washington: Dumbarton Oaks,.

Tarchnisvili, Michael. 1955. *Geschichte der kirchlichen georgischen Literatur: Auf Grund der ersten Bandes der georgischen Literaturgeschichte von K. Kekelije*. Vatican City: Biblioteca Apostolica Vaticana.

Taylor, Barry. 2014. "Frames Eastern and Western." In *D'Orient en Occident. Les recueils de fables enchâssées avant les Mille et une Nuits de Galland (Barlaam et Josaphat, Calila et Dimna, Disciplina clericalis, Roman des Sept Sages)*, edited by M. Uhlig and Y. Foehr-Janssens. Turnhout: Brepols.

Thomsen, Mads Rosendahl. 2008. *Mapping World Literature: International Canonization and Transnational Literatures*. New York: Continuum Publishing.

Titley, Norah M. 1983. *Persian Miniature Painting*. London: British Library.

Versteegh, Kees. 1997. *The Arabic Language*. Edinburgh: Edinburgh University Press.

Volk, Robert. 2006. *Die Schriften des Johannes von Damaskos. Historia animae utilis de Barlaam et Ioasaph*, edited by H. C. Brenncke and E. Mühlenberg. Patristische Texte und Studien, vol. 6/2. Berlin: Walter de Gruyter.

About the author

Christian Høgel is Professor (wsr) of Byzantine Literature and co-director of the Centre for Medieval Literature at the Department of History, University of Southern Denmark, Odense (www.sdu.dk/cml). He has published on Byzantine hagiography (*Symeon Metaphrastes. Rewriting and Canonization* 2002), Arabic-Greek translation (especially the early Greek translation of the Qur'an), and on the Ciceronian concept of *humanitas* (*The Human and the Humane*, 2015).

— 4 —

The Material and the Implied Library: Book Collections, Media History, and Authority in Twelfth Century Papal Europe

Lars Boje Mortensen

In this contribution, I discuss authority, materiality, and media in relation to medieval libraries and textual culture in Western Europe in the twelfth and thirteenth centuries. More specifically, I focus on some aspects of textual retrievability, storage and authority that I find both important and relevant for a literary media history, but which have tended to fall out of focus both before and after a material turn in literary studies—possibly because they are located in between a concrete material and a more abstract space of intentionality and ideals. I draw on examples from twelfth and thirteenth century historical writings in order to analyse the specific conditions under which a new avenue to authority opened up in literary culture, and the roles played by forms of materiality and media for understandings of or transformations of authority, in medieval text culture in Western Europe. My key prism for this investigation is the medieval library, in terms of its material and physical form, but also of its accumulated and imagined form.

Introduction

The authority of the book is an obvious feature of most forms of Christianity historically, and the ways in which this authority is sustained and transformed are not only determined by social and religious factors, but also deeply connected to media history. Among the key contributions in this field we find, naturally, studies of the materiality and mediality of the copies of the sacred texts themselves. This interest should, however, be supplemented by a book- and library-historical approach, in which questions are posed about the place of the sacred texts within the wider range of books and texts available in specific historical contexts. For the medieval period, which is in focus here, it does not suffice to understand that the Christian Scriptures are found at the top of the hierarchy of texts. Rather, the historically changing character of the entire population of books/texts and their internal hierarchy affected and changed the attitude to books in general as well as to The Book. A great number of other books/texts thus supported and extended the authority of the Scriptures, first of all liturgical and exegetical texts, but also historical, philosophical, and fictional books.

The same holds true if we flip the perspective to that of medieval literary history or the study of medieval textual culture in broad terms. If our vantage point is not the study of medieval religious communities but rather—as in this chapter—intellectual and literary history, and we want to grasp some of the main features of textual production and reproduction in the medieval period, we need to analyze the relations that hold between the whole and the parts: in the European Middle Ages, all textual compositions had some link to Biblical (or Quranic) exegesis, some a close relationship, others a more distant one. Liturgical, exegetical, historical, philosophical, and fictional books all borrowed whatever authority they might obtain from a dialogue with the Scriptures—both in terms of textual relations and in terms of material similarity, in terms of the text as a material object.

The more specific aim of this chapter, however, is to point to the role of an overlooked material aspect of medieval books that goes beyond the materiality of the individual item and the authority generated by one-to-one intertextual relations. In this paper, I want to call attention to the authority that was bestowed on texts through the libraries or the book collections of which they, almost invariably, were produced to form a part, and whose precarious retrieval and storage mechanisms formed an important part of the horizon of textual copying and creation. This kind of authority is not easy to demonstrate as institutional book collections were taken for granted and not commented much upon, and the modest physical structures of medieval libraries have largely disappeared as well. The hundreds of thousands of individual medieval books that survive today are like archaeological finds and they often come without a material context. This does not mean, however, that the physical and institutional frameworks of medieval libraries did not play a role in the mediation of the authority of the book. I suggest that literary and intellectual history can be of considerable help in establishing and imagining this otherwise "invisible" authoritative space.[1]

1. An excellent if rare example of the combination of literary history and manuscript studies aiming to map a specific geography and chronology of a medieval book horizon is Lapidge 2006. A recent special issue of the journal *French Studies* 2016 also approaches library history from a literary angle, but it is concerned with a later period of the Middle Ages than the present chapter and focuses on Francophone literature. Especially relevant for the present analysis of real and imagined libraries of the twelfth century is the article by Campbell (2016). For the dynamic interplay between reading, book col-

I wish to illustrate the importance of this library aspect of textual authority via a discussion some examples from the textual culture of the High Middle Ages in Papal (or Latin) Europe, a highly dynamic and expansive period in the history of the book, which resulted in unintended consequences for both intellectual and religious authority: while a larger body of authoritative texts was created, and a larger group of expert authors and interpreters emerged, this expansion also transformed the locus of textual authority into more complex and abstract forms, gradually opening up new possibilities of contesting the authority of experts and interpreters.[2] This trajectory is accompanied—as I will exemplify—by a dialectic between the growth of (fragile) material libraries, and the emergence of notions of knowledge understood as an eternal "virtual" library.

These aspects have partly been neglected because Papal Europe possessed no large, central and iconic library, but instead consisted of a system of smaller collections, even in this expansive period. While I cannot outline a proper medieval library history here, it should be kept in mind that during the twelfth century well-equipped libraries in Latin Europe held some 400–500 books. The majority of these books would contain not one, but a number of texts, so in terms of modern bibliographical units, the figures should be multiplied by several factors. These large collections were all housed by ecclesiastical institutions, either monastic or episcopal ones. Usually, the books were organized into three groups: Liturgical books (often kept separately in, or close to the church), school books (if there was a monastic or cathedral school), and books for study and reference. This last part of the library is the most interesting for our purposes, as this was where an author would hope to place a collection of sermons, a chronicle, an exegetical, philosophical, theological, scientific, or legal treatise or commentary—next to the commented copies of the Scriptures.[3]

lections, and the composition of new texts, discussing both antiquity and the period around 1200, see Mortensen 2017.

2. Cf. the emphasis Furedi puts on the medieval legacy of the contestation of authority from the Investiture Contest through the conciliar movements and finally the Reformation (Furedi 2013, chapters 5–7). A detailed study of the Investiture Contest as the first instance of a Western medieval public sphere is Melve (2007).

3. The understudied, difficult, and non-iconic library history of medieval Papal Europe has led to the neglect of this period in general overviews: Battles (2003) is just one example of a popular historical narrative that leaps straight from Antiquity to the Renaissance. In the highly interesting and ambitious collection edited by Eliot, Nash and Willison (2007), which takes a global view of book culture, again the Western medieval period is covered by one chapter about the Carolingians and one about Petrarch as a book collector, thus skipping the entire period from c. 800 to c. 1350. In the overview edited by Cavallo on ancient and medieval libraries (1989), we find one (important) article about the eleventh and twelfth centuries in the West. A long and very substantial series of

From the modern to the medieval book: The contribution of media studies

Before entering the more specific historical context, it may be useful to review some key features of medieval book culture as they have been recognized through sustained media- and book-historical research during the last half century, coinciding with the new media awareness kindled by the modern media revolutions from the radio to the internet (Havelock 1963, 1986; Eisenstein 1980; Clanchy 1979; Green 1994; Johns 1998; Neddermeyer 1998; Rouse and Rouse 2000; Gillespie 2007; Hobbins 2012; de Hamel 2013a).

As we have now, rather suddenly, come to live in a world in which texts from all times and places can be accessed regardless of time and place, it can be argued that humanist scholars of our generation are the last to possess a uniquely medieval experience, as it were—an experience of the age before the internet when place and material access completely determined the scope of one's reading and studies. The best humanist scholarship was in some way or other related to a good research library, and the enjoyment of literature was equally dependent on private or public physical book resources. We may not feel very medieval, but the present radical accessibility of almost everything we can think of, including, probably sometime soon, translating machines that could give some insight at least into the contents of writings in most languages, has made my generation of scholars' experience from the 1980s and early 1990s belong to an almost ancient or medieval world.

There are of course many fundamental differences between our own pre-internet experiences of literature and humanist scholarship and medieval ones—in terms of basic technologies, taxonomies and forms of conceptualisation, as well as in terms of institutional frameworks. In order to work our way back to the extraordinary dynamics of textual culture in Western Europe of the twelfth and thirteenth centuries that is my concern here, we need to leave two major upheavals behind us.

First, we must discuss how fundamental the changes of the nineteenth century were: the Romantic turn shaped basic taxonomies that are still with us. When the field of "literature" and its academic study emerged in the nineteenth century, it was constituted by the nexus of the reading public, the critics, the publishing houses, and the authors—all of which were necessary for its subsequent autonomy, which lasts until this day, where it is, of course, challenged by new media, genres, and academic fields. A key feature of

meticulous scholarship exists with regard to different national text cultures (e.g. for Britain, Gameson ed. 2011 and Morgan and Thomson eds. 2008), and of specific medieval libraries, but still the only attempt to provide a narrative of all of medieval European library history is the impressive, but obviously outdated volume edited by Thompson (1939).

nineteenth-century literary and academic culture was the idea of intellectual property, which had gradually emerged together with national and international copyright laws (which protected printers and publishing houses).

The idea of intellectual property was accompanied by a *l'art pour l'art* aesthetic and an adoration of the genius writer that enabled each national literature to line up a privileged series of authors and works—the canon—and put a clear emphasis on the works as abstract objects of art. As analysed by Bourdieu (1992), the resulting ideology of the field is underpinned by theoretical and philosophical assumptions which confirm both the canons and the status of individual texts as literary masterpieces, as "works." The texts thus acquired an immaterial life of their own, and literary interpretation (of the pure work) and reception studies (dealing with the social, cognitive and material conditions of storing, retrieving, and reading, etc.) were sharply separated. The distinction between interpretation of the work and reception studies became professionalized and institutionalized only with the rise of the discipline of comparative literature after World War II, but its basis is clearly the idea of the pure work of literary art that emerged in the nineteenth century. The delimitation of literature as strictly fictional accompanied the establishment of a number of humanistic disciplines, most importantly for our purposes the discipline of history. Gradually, other humanistic fields of inquiry emerged, like the history of religions, the history of law, the history of literature, the history of philosophy, and more (each with their founding father representatives of "genius" in scholarship). This clear division thus severed, on an epistemological level at least, the links between artful and scholarly writing: the former was regarded as fiction, the latter was concerned with scientific truth (Leerssen 2006; Rigney 2001; Berger, Eriksonas and Mycock 2008; Berger and Lorenz 2010).

In the present context of literary storage and retrieval, it is also important to add one more feature to the system of literature and learning as it emerged in most of post-Napoleonic Europe: the national library. Functioning as each nation's ultimate place of textual memory, the national library (often with extensions into one or more "state" or subsidiary national libraries) became a symbolic treasure in the building of nations (and their mutual contests), as well as a physical guarantee and a spatial framework for the establishment of national literature and learning, with top level security. Aiming to hold all national publications, these institutions guaranteed a material, eternal life for the nation's textual heritage (fictional and scholarly), and the libraries, through their priorities of collecting, displaying, ordering, and guarding, also provided the arena for an ideal hierarchy of texts and a canon to which future writers could relate.

In a fast-track rewind back to the Middle Ages, the second important juncture is the early modern (sixteenth–eighteenth centuries) "Republic of Letters" made possible by the late medieval invention of print (c. 1450). The importance of the moveable type print media technology for the development of European letters and science remains unquestioned, but the debate on the where to place the emphasis continues unabatedly: should we ascribe the new dynamics mainly to technological, institutional, linguistic, ideological, or other factors? Elizabeth Eisenstein's *The Printing Press as an Agent of Change* (1979) has had a defining impact on the discussion, but her views have been both nuanced and challenged in recent decades, for instance by Adrian Johns in his *The Nature of the Book* (1998) (focused on England) and more recently in his *Piracy—The Intellectual Property Wars from Gutenberg to Gates* (2009). While print technology is of course only one minor aspect of the Scientific Revolution, of Rationalism, Antiquarianism, and ultimately the Enlightenment, and while much of early print culture *was* as messy and uncontrolled as Johns emphasizes, I still think that one of Eisenstein's basic insights holds to this day: without this particular media change, entailing the ability of a number of scholars to consult *identical* copies of books, with identical tables, diagrams, images, maps, texts, indices, etc., the accumulative effect of knowledge in a large number of scientific and humanist fields would simply not have started to build in a qualitatively new way. This was a necessary pre-condition for the "Republic of Letters" and the Scientific Revolution, and it illustrates well how different conditions were before the moveable type print (c. 1450) and copper engravings (sixteenth century). Much recent research has also emphasized the necessary conditions for the invention of print by pointing to the much cheaper handwritten books on paper, overtaking parchment significantly around 1400, and the sharp increase in the book trade, and in the size and number of private libraries, etc.—which makes it possible in many respects to describe a common book culture for the entire fifteenth century, but one which does not invalidate the radical novelty of the sudden appearance of hundreds of identical copies of the same texts and illustrations (Hobbins 2012; Neddermeyer 1998; Gillespie 2007).

In contrast to the Romantic turn and its insistence on national languages, the print revolution ushered in a new era of the common learned language, Latin. The much increased availability and production of texts and the common idiom has made comparisons with our age of English and the Internet quite obvious, as in McGann's manifesto for philology and textual history as the main methodology in the humanities, *A New Republic of Letters. Memory and Scholarship in the Age of Digital Reproduction* (2014). Important factors in the horizons of media, writing, and scholarship in the early modern period, however, were not only the enabling elements such as the accumulation of knowledge, the "openness" provided by undefined intellectual property rights and the international learned exchange, but also restrictive factors in the form of pervasive censorship by (Catholic and Reformed) ecclesiastical authorities and by kingdoms and empires (Vega, Weiss and Esteve 2010). We need to keep in mind that the grand libraries of the period were princely or imperial and mostly aristocratic and private. Even when they were in principle public, like the Vatican library, access to university libraries and, gradually, some royal libraries, was in practice limited: these were the defining book repositories of the age, into whose beautifully bound folio volumes—predominantly written in Latin, but increasingly in French, German, etc.—aspiring writers, scholars, and scientists envisaged and hoped that their own contributions would survive in the long term.

Key features of the medieval book and its expansion c. 1100–1300

When we turn to high medieval book culture and the rapid expansion it went through in the twelfth and thirteenth centuries in Papal Europe (as also elsewhere), we are looking at a world in which many features contrast sharply with modern conditions: a quick listing of the most important differences—with the changes of the early modern and the Romantic period sketched above in mind—is perhaps the best way to enable a modern reader to imagine the medieval media situation and what it meant for the authority of books and book collections. One of the few constants is, perhaps to the surprise of those who automatically take the book to be the printed book,[4] the basic codex form laid between two covers, where you leaf through pages with writing on both sides, and which could be made in as many sizes as modern books. In many languages we still find a strong tradition to use the term "manuscripts" for medieval books, but the more unambiguous term today would be "handwritten books" or "books copied by hand." Apart from the codex form and the Latin alphabet in the West—almost every aspect of textual culture was different from today:

Every book was unique. Even when texts were copied as accurately as possible, there would still be errors, omissions, corrections and alterations in the resulting copy. Sometimes these might be small, sometimes substantial, and there was no good way of ascertaining the fidelity of a copy. If a text passage was poorly copied or physically damaged, it would be difficult to trace another copy and to find the passage again. The most faithful textual copies

4. As in Johns' (1998) confusing title: *The Nature of the Book*—dealing only with print.

would still look different from their exemplar in script, layout, paratexts, illustrations, etc., and they would often be combined with other texts within the same binding and thus contextualized differently. The most canonical texts, not least the Scriptures, were copied very carefully and with an idea of perfection, but medieval readers were always alert to the possibility of textual corruption.

Books were very expensive. Before paper, which become widespread in Western Europe from c. 1400, books were made of animal skins (parchment) and therefore even modest books were time-consuming and labour-intensive to produce, but usually very durable.

There was no copyright. Due to the technology of reproduction (copying by hand), the grey zone of textual production between "original" composition, rephrasing (and translating) and copying proper was very large. It was the order of the day that extensive portions of texts were compiled from somewhere else, either with or without a reference. In effect, this meant that in most cases it is difficult today to draw a line between a concrete medieval text and a "work." A number of texts *were* clearly written based on an idea of a self-contained, authored work, but considering how it was usually copied in part, reused, made part of a compilation, etc., always makes it relevant to study the exact textual version appearing in specific, individual copies. This point is well made by scholars in the "New Philology"/the material turn research trend from the 1990s onwards (*Speculum* 1990; Driscoll 2010).

A very large proportion of texts were anonymous. Even when authors had done what they could to attach their name to a text, it could easily be anonymized or re-appropriated in subsequent copies or compilations. Apart from the core canonical texts, there was usually no way of establishing to whom a quotation belonged as there were no standard reference editions (a problem of which contemporaries were acutely aware) (Munk Olsen 2014; Delle Donne 2016). Even a substantial portion of para-biblical texts—bestowing authority to the Scriptures as well as deriving their authority from them—were unattributed commentaries, biblical glosses, liturgical or para-liturgical texts with no other authoritative power than the ritual and material context and their appearance.

There were no professional authors. Teachers, bishops, canons, abbots, monks, preachers, scribes, notaries, bureaucrats, lawyers, noblemen (warriors), merchants, magistrates, entertainers, story-tellers, musicians, singers, and more wrote (or dictated) texts, but before the fourteenth century in the West (Dante, Petrarch), and perhaps not even then, no-one would self-identify as an "author" or "writer" (Ascoli 2008). Peter Abelard was a nobleman, teacher, and later a monk; Thomas Aquinas was a nobleman, a

Dominican theologian and a university teacher, Saxo Grammaticus was a nobleman and a canon in Lund, Snorri Sturluson was a nobleman, counsellor, warrior, and a poet, Gottfried of Strassbourg (possibly) an influential town magistrate, William of Rubruk a Franciscan missionary, a traveller, and probably a spy for the French king. When we speak of scholars, scientists, intellectuals and authors in this period, they are all sensible modern categorisations, but it must be kept in mind that these were not seen as positions then; their writing was often a natural extension of their social position, not the other way around (and this is again connected to the lack of intellectual and copy-rights).

No overview of existing books or texts was possible. Although individual libraries occasionally had lists produced, there was, due to the uniqueness of each book, no golden standard for bibliographical identification; this meant that no interlibrary overview was possible; nor was it practically imaginable. Libraries of hand-copied books would always (and still do) contain surprises, unidentified texts, previously unknown versions, etc. The best one could do in bibliographical research was to ask the most learned people and study in the largest or most authoritative libraries. I will return to the libraries and the effects of this situation below, but the thrill of entering a great library of handwritten books, admittedly a much bigger collection than anything similar in Europe at the time, can best be conveyed in the famous description by Ibn-Sina (Avicenna), the Arab scientist and philosopher (980–1037), who as a young man was summoned to Sultan Nuh ibn-Mansur's court in Bukhara:

> I found there many rooms filled with books which were arranged in cases row upon row. One room was allotted to works on Arabic philology and poetry; another to jurisprudence, and so forth, the books on each particular science having a room to themselves. I inspected the catalogue of ancient Greek authors and looked for the books which I required; I saw in this collection books of which few people have heard even the names and which I myself have never seen either before or since. (Nicholson 1907, 265–266)

The overwhelming majority of books were in a non-native, schooled language, Latin. Although exactly the twelfth and the thirteenth centuries are characterized in most of "Latin" Europe by a vernacular revolution in book production (Middle High German, French, Old Norse, Dutch, Castilian, and more), from a statistical point of view, in most contexts a book would still be expected to be in Latin, and the production of Latin books expanded significantly with the rise of universities, bureaucracies, etc. (Boureau 2007; Neddermeyer 1998). The thirteenth century did see a distinct rise in the number of books in the vernacular which was, in many ways, a turning point in literary and media history (Gaunt 2015; Doubleday 2015; Mortensen 2017). This crucial development, however, did not make vernacular books overtake Latin books in quantitative terms, although one is often left with this impression in handbooks and standard narratives which privilege literature in what was later was perceived as "national languages" (*Interfaces* 2015). The book collections were also characterized by a conservative feature in as much as they—to a large degree—took care of older precious books and readers kept on using them.

Books were authoritative. As already stated, the Christian Scripture as a material object compelled great authority, and worked together with a number of para-biblical books in doing so (de Hamel 2001; van Liere 2014). Although the expansion of book culture in this period *did* open up new possibilities, attitudes, and changes in authority—such as the rise of a self-consciously fictional literature (Green 2002, Agapitos and Mortensen eds. 2012)[5], philosophical and theological disagreements and troubles in writing (Wei 2012; Godman 2000)—books were overwhelmingly a serious and expensive matter, deriving from an exclusive social layer of high-standing, well-connected and educated people. Books were endowed with authority via the networks of noblemen they formed part of, and via their ecclesiastical or lay institutional leaders, who paid for them and kept them in their libraries. The period saw the first signs of more widespread private, non-institutional, non-ritual writing and reading (Mortensen 2017), of small lay book-collections, books designed for travel, a growth in the number of female readers, etc. (Green 2007)—but all of these were emergent features which really came to fruition in the fourteenth and fifteenth centuries. Therefore, in the twelfth and thirteenth centuries, again statistically speaking, a reasonably well-made handwritten book would first of all impart impressions of religious authority: the main public appearance of books was in the domain of the divine service, and books that were not liturgical were routinely associated with monastic, episcopal, or princely authority. An important aspect of the authority of books was their aspiration to eternity—to be extensions of the sacred biblical and liturgical books written for the honour of the saints and God, in the same eternal language as that of the sacred writings. Book production was broadly perceived as a human gift to the divine powers (through the local saint or patron), in the same way as was the building of churches (Rider 2001; de Hamel 2013a, 2013b). The book as an artefact among others for divine offering—whether of a piece of new writing, of a copy of an existing text or of something in between (compilations)—is an

5. While fictional literature became widespread in books already in the High Middle Ages, it did not constitute a separate field of "literature" as in the nineteenth century (cf. above and *Interfaces* 2015).

important aspect of the library perspective I am concerned with here. I shall now discuss some concrete examples from twelfth-century literature which illustrate the ways in which book collections were considered a sacred and authoritative space.

Finding, composing, and placing historical literature in the twelfth century

In 1139, the archdeacon of Lincoln, Henry of Huntingdon, one of many great chroniclers of the twelfth century, made a remarkable discovery in one of Europe's richest libraries, at the abbey of Le Bec in Normandy (close to Rouen). Henry had finished his first version of his *Historia Anglorum* (History of the English People) in 1129, but continued updating and rewriting it until his death in 1154 (Greenway 1996). In Le Bec, he was shown a book completely unknown to him, called *Historia regum Britanniae* (The History of the Kings of Britain). Startlingly, it gave a full narrative of the British kings reigning from before Roman times all the way up to the Anglo-Saxons—an unexpected narrative of what was otherwise a serious gap in the history of the island, which put the native Britains (and Welsh and Bretons) at centre stage (and famously introduced King Arthur of later literary fame). Henry immediately copied down an abbreviated version and included it in some subsequent copies of his own history.

The new text was in fact entirely fresh, having been completed by a Welsh cleric (and a canon of Oxford), Geoffrey of Monmouth in 1137 or 1138 (edited and translated by Reeve and Wright 2007). To give his elaborate fabrication some credibility, the author himself had taken advantage of the lack of cross-library bibliographical standards or guidelines and of the haphazard access to books by claiming that he had come across an old book written in Welsh, and that his history was simply a Latin translation of this. He even ended the work by pointing out that other historians would not be able to tell this story as they did not have access to that book. In spite of these bold indications, Geoffrey's book was taken to be authoritative throughout the Middle Ages.[6]

Let me quote a further example of the nice surprises a major library might provide for a twelfth century historian. Around 1180, a certain Tore (also known as Theodoricus) from Norway, a high-standing cleric and probably identical to the future archbishop of Trondheim (1206–1214), finished his small, but pioneering Latin work, *Historia de antiquitate regum Norwagiensium*

6. Only one or two skeptical voices emerged in the twelfth century, cf. Green 2002. The ploy of the privileged access to a secret book was used several times in the twelfth century, in fabricated history as here, and in outright fiction; this motif itself reflects the proliferation of books in the twelfth century; cf. Agapitos and Mortensen 2012.

(History of the Norwegian Kings) (ed. Storm 1880; tr. McDougall and McDougall 1998) The work is dedicated to Eystein Erlendsson, the influential archbishop who held office from 1161 to 1188. Trondheim had been separated from the great Nordic see of Lund and had become its own ecclesiastical province in 1152/1153; the cult of the royal saint, Olav Haraldsson, who had been killed more than a century earlier (in 1030), took on a new urgency and it was promoted in writing, liturgy, and building activities, successfully attracting pilgrims on his feast day. Stories about Olav had so far only been transmitted orally, but now the official hagiography was taking form (Jirouskova 2014). A crucial point in the story was the circumstances of the martyr king's conversion and baptism.[7] Several versions, placing it in Norway or Iceland, seem to have circulated. In his *History*, Tore reports:

> But I, for my part, have read in the "History of the Normans" that he was baptized in Normandy by Robert, Archbishop of Rouen. For it is certain that duke William of Normandy took him with him to help him in his fight against king Robert of France, whose by-name was Capet (he was the son of the most noble duke Hugh Capet), when together with the count of Flanders Robert was preparing to wage war against duke William.
>
> (transl. McDougall and McDougall 1998, 17)

This was a finding of some impact as Rouen figures as the place of Olav's baptism in the beginning of the saint's life (of Trondheim origin from the same decades, cf. Mortensen 2000; Jirouskova 2014). But how and where did Tore find this? The Norman History is the one by William of Jumièges who composed his work in several different versions between 1050 and 1070, thus being quite close to the lifetime of Olav, including a mention of his role as an ally of the Normans against the French. It has been established that Tore (like Eystein and many other Nordic noblemen) had studied in Northern France, and that he had a connection to the important Royal foundation of St Victor in Paris, a school of great renown in the twelfth century. Whether it was here or in another French or Norman library that Tore had the good luck of stumbling upon the passage in the Norman Chronicle of William of Jumièges, we do not know—but what is certain and quite interesting for our discussion here is that the authority and status ascribed to a book coming from one of those rich libraries settled the matter (and, incidentally, modern historians agree regarding the value of William's testimony).

So we should picture a cleric from the farthest periphery of papal Europe who had been doing research for his work at the very centre of European Latin learning and who must have envisaged his own little book being placed at the cathedral library in Trondheim as a lasting point of reference

7. The following draws on Mortensen 2000 with further references.

for the local cultural memory—as we would phrase it today. Tore's text does its best to inscribe Norway and its saintly king into a greater scheme of Christian learning and understanding of the world—in fact one can read the chronicle as a small encyclopaedia of "universal" historical knowledge. This is achieved by including references to old and more recent canonical authors such as Jerome and Hugh of St Victor, historical comparisons between Norwegian kings and Roman Emperors (including Charlemagne), proverbial quotations from popular classical poets, and by means of a series of digressions which link the local to the divine order as it emerges from the Bible, its acclaimed exegetes and later historical writers (Bagge 1989, Mortensen 1993). The highlight of Tore's narrative is the martyrdom of Olav, and this place in the text he endows with the heaviest excursus on chronology and time. In effect, what Tore has done, on a small scale, is to bring the whole Latin historical exegetical library into one book—whose role it was to represent this section of a big library in a small and peripheral one. In this manner, not only are Norway and Olav firmly inscribed into the greater unfolding of a divine scheme at the level of textual meaning, but the physical presence of organized excerpts copied from authorities found in the greater research libraries also establishes an access point from the local small repository of knowledge into the greater "virtual library" of knowledge to be found in books all over Latin Christendom. The "eternity"-dynamics involved in the medium of the beautifully handwritten and solidly bound parchment book, the Latin language, and the storage in an archiepiscopal library ensured this mutual partaking—the local in the universal and vice versa.

On a much bigger scale, a similar dynamics is attested in a masterpiece of twelfth-century historical writing from another distant corner of papal Europe, the Kingdom of Jerusalem.

The voluminous learned Latin chronicle of the Crusades and the Christian Kingdom established after the conquest in 1099 was written by William of Tyre between c. 1170 and 1184, when the Chronicle stops abruptly (Huygens ed. 1986; trans. Babcock and Krey 1943). William had enjoyed the full education of the leading French and Italian schools in the mid-twelfth century, including in the arts (rhetoric, philosophy, classics, and more), theology, and law. When he returned to the East around 1165, he started to climb the ladder of ecclesiastical offices as well as the royal administration, and he became directly involved with king Amaury (1163–1174) and was a teacher of his unfortunate successor, the leper king, Baldwin 4 (1174–1185). During these years he became the archbishop of Tyre (1175), and travelled officially on behalf of the Kingdom both to Constantinople and Rome, attending the

Third Lateran Council in 1179. In the final power struggle around the weak and dying king, however, William was side-lined, not being elected as the Patriarch of Jerusalem in 1180 and he might even have been excommunicated by the dominant party around the king's mother, Agnes of Courtenay. He must have died in 1185 or 1186 just in time to avoid seeing the conquest of Jerusalem by Saladin in 1187 (Edbury and Rowe 1988).

William's intellectual background is much better attested than for most contemporary authors, including Tore, as he wrote an autobiographical chapter in his Chronicle:

> In the same year [1165] I, William, by God's patience unworthy minister of the holy church of Tyre, author of this history, which I have compiled to leave something of the past to those who come after, after nearly twenty years in which I had most avidly followed in France and Italy the schools of the philosophers and the study of liberal disciplines, as well as the improving dogmatics of the celestial philosophy and the prudence of canon and civil law, returned home to the memory of my father and to my mother—may her soul now receive eternal rest—and was received with embraces.
>
> I was born in the holy city of Jerusalem, beloved by God, and was brought up there by my parents. During this middle period, in which I spent my adolescence across the sea in the [various] disciplines and dedicated my days to the study of letters in voluntary poverty, I was taught by the following distinguished doctors in the liberal arts."
>
> (transl. by Loud and Cox in Murray 2006, 1305–1308)

William goes on to mention a long series of prominent teachers at the great schools of France and Italy. During these studies and his later travels and work as a top-level cleric and royal diplomat, William lived a life among books and documents, as is very apparent from his work. He probably even had experience with Arab learning and libraries as he also wrote a history, now lost, of the Middle East, to some extent probably based on Arab learning (Murray 2001). Unfortunately, he only offers one direct mention of what must have been the numerous libraries and archives he had seen and used in both the West and the East. The libraries in the centres of the Christian East—like Jerusalem, Tyre, Tripoli, Antioch, Ascalon and others—are also very poorly attested in the form of surviving books or library lists in the twelfth century (cf. Munk Olsen 1987), but no doubt several of the (arch-) episcopal collections were of substantial volume and quality (Minervini 2002). What he does say is this—prompted by his own role as secretary in the Third Lateran Council in 1179:

> If anyone desires to know the statutes enacted and the names of the bishops, their numbers and titles, he may read the writing which, at the earnest request of the holy fathers who took part in this synod, we have carefully

> compiled. We have directed that this be placed in the archives of the holy church at Tyre among the other books which we have collected for that same church, over which now for six years we have presided.
>
> (21.26, tr. by Babcock and Krey 1943, 438).

Here we get a good impression of the kind of difference one (arch-)bishop could make in building a local collection as a reflection of larger collections (e.g., in Italy and France where William had studied). Furthermore, it becomes clear how place-bound references to books and documents were, as they really only resided within the authority of the institution housing the collection, and subject to its current material organization and status. At the same time, they all pointed to the universality and virtual existence of the eternally valid documents—a tension we also find in William's own writing.

William's chronicle exhibits the same encyclopaedic ambitions we saw on a small scale in Tore's work. Although the codification of historical and geographical knowledge in William's chronicle is of a much higher order, it can be analysed in the same terms of bringing relevant parts of the virtual "Library" and its authority into one book, and then aspiring to bring that book into one or more authoritative, material libraries as a lasting piece of writing, and codifying in depth the history and overall significance of the conquest and Christian rule of the Holy Land. In contrast to Tore, however, William's subject matter made sure that not only could he plunder the libraries "across the sea" for knowledge, authority, and the general level of learning, he could also hope to give something back to those Western libraries: a first-hand knowledge of all the important biblical sites and their long history. Before the Crusades, commentaries on biblical geography and topography had usually just repeated undigested patristic material, but William made a point of offering thorough descriptions of buildings, towns, scenes of war, holy places, landscapes and so on, and of delving into discussions about the meanings and etymologies of relevant biblical names. He thus combined his own first-hand knowledge with learned discussions and was quite aware, it seems, of the superiority and authority of his text. The descriptions artfully follow the chronology of the scenes of war (especially of the First Crusade)—thus making the reader focalize through the crusaders' experience, most strikingly by placing the elaborate description of Jerusalem just before the crusaders took the town in 1099 (William, Book 8).

Given the scope of William's chronicle and of his own broad experience and travels, it seems quite clear that he planned and executed the work not only with real and implied readers in mind, but also with a horizon of authoritative libraries in mind, in which his book might serve as the best reference available far into the future—just as he himself had built on and excerpted texts that were centuries old, and—including the Bible and the classics—even more than a thousand years old. It is also not too daring to suggest that he had both Eastern and Western libraries in mind: in the Kingdom of Jerusalem itself, the text would be a strong statement rendering authoritative a local cultural memory (with specific political and cultural preferences). It was also an official text of historical self-understanding meant to be available at (arch-)episcopal libraries along with local archives, perhaps also as part of a few private princely book collections. In the West, William must have had some of the great episcopal and monastic libraries in Italy and France in mind, and here his text would serve as a repository of information on the Holy Land as well as a triumphant and complete narrative of the crusades and the Kingdom of Jerusalem.

What actually happened to the text of *Chronicle* is another matter which has not been thoroughly examined. Today, it survives in 13 copies, mostly from the thirteenth century, and all of them, it seems, were produced in the West (Huygens 1986). Most of the great narrative compiled and composed by William, however, survived in a way that would have surprised him, namely in a French translation (or rather paraphrase) made in Paris around 1220, which was then disseminated in much greater numbers than the Latin original (Handyside 2015). As mentioned, this move into the vernacular was typical of the thirteenth century, and partly related to new attitudes towards books among the nobility (Aurell 2011, 106–114, and Mortensen 2017), partly to other developments. William's target audience was thus partly missed, although his original Latin book *did* survive to this day and *did* make it into some book collections in the France and Italy that he had become acquainted with during his own studies in the mid-twelfth century.

Conclusion

In this chapter, I have tried to make the argument that in order to appreciate the elevated status of books and book collections and the material authority they projected in the High Middle Ages, it is necessary first, from a modern perspective, to divest ourselves, with the help of media studies, of ideas generated in nineteenth-century Romanticism and in the early modern Republic of Letters, both based on print, about authorship, texts, and the prestigious book collections of nations and aristocrats. In this way, going back to an age of precarious small collections of hand-copied books—more obviously sharing a space with the Scriptures—we can better assess a dynamic period of book culture in the Middle Ages themselves, namely that of the twelfth and thirteenth centuries. While books were here already multiplying beyond control and bibliography, they were still, in this watershed period, largely kept, consulted, and studied in ecclesiastical institutional collections. As the examples have illustrated, we must take this horizon of writing and usage into account: it was not only the material hand-copied book itself, but also the library—in concrete, material form, as well as in a virtual, implied form—which served as a locus of textual authority ranging from the Scriptures to new writing and back, all supporting each other on the shelves of eternity.

References

Agapitos, Panagiotis and Lars Boje Mortensen, eds. 2012. *Medieval Narratives between History and Fiction. From the Centre to the Periphery of Europe, c. 1100–1400.* Copenhagen: Museum Tusculanum Press.

Ascoli, Albert Russell. 2008. *Dante and the Making of a Modern Author.* Cambridge: Cambridge University Press.

Aurell, Martin. 2011. *Le chévalier lettré—Savoir et conduite de l'aristocratie aux XIIe et XIIIe siècles.* Paris: Fayard.

Babcock, E. A. and A. C. Krey, trans. 1943. *William, Archbishop of Tyre, A History of Deeds done beyond the Sea*, 2 vols. New York: Columbia University Press.

Bagge, Sverre. 1989. "Theodericus Monachus—clerical historiography in twelfth-century Norway." *Scandinavian Journal of History* 14: 113–133.

Battles, Matthew. 2003. *Library: An Unquiet History.* New York: Norton.

Berger, Stefan, Linas Eriksonas and Andrew Mycock, eds. 2008. *Narrating the Nation: Representations in History, Media and the Arts.* New York–Oxford: Berghahn Books.

Berger, Stefan and Chris Lorenz, eds. 2010. *Nationalizing the Past: Historians as Nation Builders in Modern Europe.* Basingstoke: Palgrave Macmillan.

Bourdieu, Pierre. 1992. *Les régles de l'art—Genèse et structure du champ littéraire.* Paris: Seuil.

Boureau, Alain. 2007. *L'empire du livre. Pour une histoire de savoir scolastique (1200–1380). La Raison scolastique II.* Paris: Les belles lettres.

Campbell, Emma. 2016. "The library in twelfth- and thirteenth-century French literature: Benoît de Sainte-Maure's *Roman de Troie* , Chrétien de Troyes's *Cligès*, and Adenet le Roi's *Berte as grans piés*." *French Studies* 70: 187–200.

Cavallo, Guglielmo, ed. 1989. *Le biblioteche nel mondo antico e medievale.* Rome: Editori Laterza.

Clanchy, Michael. 1979. *From Memory to Written Record, England 1066–1307.* London: Edward Arnold [rev. 3rd ed. 2013 Malden, MA: Wiley-Blackwell].

de Hamel, Christopher. 2001. *The Book: A History of the Bible.* London: Phaidon Press.

———. 2013a. "The European Medieval Book." In *The Book: A Global History*, edited by M. F. Suarez and H. R. Woodhuysen, 58–79. Oxford: Oxford University Press.

———. 2013b [repr.]. *Scribes and Illuminators* (Medieval Craftsmen). Toronto: University of Toronto Press.

Delle Donne, Fulvio. 2016. "Perché tanti anonimi nel medioevo? Note e provocazioni sul concetto di autore e opera nella storiografia mediolatina." *Rivista di cultura classica e medioevale* 58: 145–166.

Driscoll, Matthew. 2010. "The words on the page: Thoughts on philology, old and new." In *Creating the Medieval Saga: Versions, Variability, and Editorial Interpretations of Old Norse Saga Literature*, edited by Judy Quinn and Emily Lethbridge, 85–102. Odense: University Press of Southern Denmark.

Doubleday, Simon R. 2015. *The Wise King: A Christian Prince, Muslim Spain, and the Birth of the Renaissance*. New York: Basic Books.

Edbury, Peter W. and John Gordon Rowe. 1988. *William of Tyre: Historian of The Latin East*. Cambridge: Cambridge University Press.

Eisenstein, Elizabeth. 1979. *The Printing Press as an Agent of Change*, 2 vols. Cambridge: Cambridge University Press.

Eliot, Simon, Andrew Nash and Ian Willison, eds. 2007. *Literary Cultures and the Material Book*. London: The British Library.

Furedi, Frank. 2013. *Authority: A Sociological History*. Cambridge: Cambridge University Press.

Gameson, Richard, ed. 2011. *The Cambridge History of the Book in Britain, vol. 1.: c. 400–1100*. Cambridge: Cambridge University Press.

Gaunt, Simon. 2015. "French literature abroad: Towards an alternative history of French literature." *Interfaces* 1: 25–61.

Gillespie, Alexandra. 2007. "The history of the book." *New Medieval Literatures* 9: 245–286.

Godman, Peter. 2000. *The Silent Masters: Latin Literature and Its Censors in the High Middle Ages*. Princeton, NJ: Princeton University Press.

Green, Dennis H. 1994. *Medieval Listening and Reading: The Primary Reception of German Literature 800–1300*. Cambridge: Cambridge University Press.

———. 2002. *The Beginnings of Medieval Romance: Fact and Fiction, 1150–1220*. Cambridge: Cambridge University Press.

———. 2007. *Women Readers in the Middle Ages*. Cambridge: Cambridge University Press.

Greenway, Diana, ed. 1996. *Henry, Archdeacon of Huntingdon: Historia Anglorum (History of the English People)*. Oxford: Oxford University Press.

Handyside, Philip. 2015. *The Old French William of Tyre*. Leiden: Brill.

Havelock, Eric. 1963. *Preface to Plato*. Oxford: Oxford University Press.

———. 1986. *The Muse Learns to Write: Reflections on Orality and Literacy from Antiquity to the Present*. New Haven, CT: Yale University Press.

Hobbins, Daniel. 2012. *Authorship and Publicity Before Print: Jean Gerson and the Transformation of Late Medieval Learning*. Philadelphia: University of Pennsylvania Press.

Huygens, R.B.C., ed. 1986. *Guillaume de Tyre* [William of Tyre], *Chronicon* (CCSL 63–63A). Turnhout: Brepols.

Interfaces. 2015. *Interfaces 1: Histories of Medieval European Literatures: New Patterns of Representation and Explanation*. https://doi.org/10.13130/interfaces-4960.

Jirouskova, Lenka. 2014. *Der heilige Wikingerkönig Olav Haraldsson und sein hagiographisches Dossier: Text und Kontext der Passio Olavi (mit kritischer edition)*, 2 vols. Leiden: Brill.

Johns, Adrian. 1998. *The Nature of the Book*. Chicago, IL: The University of Chicago Press.

———. 2009. *Piracy—The Intellectual Property Wars from Gutenberg to Gates*. Chicago, IL: The University of Chicago Press.

Lapidge, Michael. 2006. *The Anglo-Saxon Library*. Oxford: Oxford University Press.

Leerssen, Joep 2006. *National Thought in Europe: A Cultural History*. Amsterdam: Amsterdam University Press.

Liere, Frans van. 2014. *An Introduction to the Medieval Bible*. Cambridge: Cambridge University Press.

McDougall, David and Ian McDougall, trans. 1998. *Theodoricus Monachus: Historia de antiquitate regum norwagiensium: An Account of the Ancient History of the Norwegian Kings*. Translated and Annotated by David and Ian McDougall, with an Introduction by Peter Foote. Viking Society for Northern Research Text Series, vol. XI. London: Viking Society for Northern Research.

McGann, Jerome. 2014. *A New Republic of Letters. Memory and Scholarship in the Age of Digital Reproduction*. Cambridge, MA: Harvard University Press.

Melve, Leidulf. 2007. *Inventing the Public Sphere: The Public Debate during the Investiture Contest (c. 1030–1122)*, 2 vols. Leiden: Brill.

Minervini. Laura. 2002. "Modelli culturali ed attività letteraria nell'Oriente latino." *Studi Medievali* 43: 337–348.

Morgan, Nigel J. and Rodney M. Thomson, eds. 2008. *The Cambridge History of the Book in Britain, vol. 2: 1100–1400*. Cambridge: Cambridge University Press.

Mortensen, Lars Boje. 1993. "Det 12. århundredes renæssance i Norge: Teoderik Munk og Romerriget." In *Antikken i norsk litteratur*, edited by Øivind Andersen and Asbjørn Aarseth, 17–35. Bergen: Det Norske Institutt i Athen.

———. 2000. "The Anchin Manuscript of Passio Olaui (Douai 295), William of Jumièges, and Theodoricus Monachus: New evidence for intellectual relations between Norway and France in the 12th century." *Symbolae Osloenses* 75: 165–189.

———. 2017. "The sudden success of prose. A comparative view of Greek, Latin, Old French and Old Norse." *Medieval Worlds* 5: 3–45. https://doi.org.10.1553/medievalworlds_no5_2017s3

Munk Olsen, Birger. 1987. *L'étude des auteurs classiques latins aux XIe et XIIe siècles*, vol III.1 *Les Classiques dans les bibliothèques médiévales*. Paris: CNRS Éditions.

———. 2014. *L'étude des auteurs classiques latins aux XIe et XIIe siècles*, vol. IV, 2, *La réception de la littérature classique: Manuscrits et textes*. Paris: CNRS Éditions.

Murray, Alan. 2001. "William of Tyre and the origin of the Turks: On the sources of the Gesta Orientalium Principipum." In *Dei gesta per Francos: Etudes sur les croisades dédiés à Jean Richard / Crusade Studies in Honour of Jean Richard*, edited by M. Balard, B. Z. Kedar and J. Riley-Smith, 217–229. Farnham: Ashgate.

Murray, Alan, ed. 2006. *The Crusades—An Encyclopedia*, vol IV. Santa Barbara: ABC-CLIO.
Neddermeyer, Uwe. 1998. *Von der Handschrift zum gedruckten Buch: Schriftlichkeit und Leseinteresse im Mittelalter und in der frühen Neuzeit, quantitative und qualitative Aspekte*, 2 vols. Wiesbaden: Harrasowitz.
Nicholson, Reynold A. 1907. *A Literary History of the Arabs*. New York: Charles Scribner's Sons.
Reeve, Michael D., ed. and Neil Wright, trans. 2007. Geoffrey of Monmouth: *The History of the Kings of Britain: An Edition and Translation of De gestis Britonum (Historia Regum Britanniae)*. Woodbridge, Suffolk: Boydell Press.
Rider, Jeff. 2001. *God's Scribe: The Historiographical Art of Galbert of Bruges*. Washington, DC: Catholic University of America Press.
Rigney, Ann. 2001. *Imperfect Histories: The Elusive Past and the Legacy of Romantic Historicism*. Ithaca, NY: Cornell University Press.
Rouse, Richard H. and Mary A. Rouse. 2000. *Manuscripts and their Makers: Commercial Book Production in Medieval Paris, 1200-1500*, 2 vols. Turnhout: Brepols.
Speculum 1990. *Speculum* 65: *New Philology*.
Storm, Gustav, ed. 1880. "Theodrici monachi Historia de antiquitate regum Norwagiensium." In *Monumenta Historiae Norvegiae. Latinske Kildeskrifter til Norges Historie i Middelalderen*, 1–68. Kristiania: A. W. Brøgger.
Thompson, James Westfall, ed. 1939. *The Medieval Library*. Chicago, IL: The University of Chicago Press.
Vega, María José, Julian Weiss, Cesc Esteve, eds. 2010. *Reading and Censorship in Early Modern Europe: Barcelona, 11-13 de Diciembre de 2007*. Bellaterra: Universitat Autònoma de Barcelona.
Wei, Ian. 2012. *Intellectual Culture in Medieval Paris: Theologians and the University, c.1100-1330*. Cambridge: Cambridge University Press.

About the author

Lars Boje Mortensen is Professor of Ancient and Medieval Cultural History and Director of the Centre for Medieval Literature at the Department of History, University of Southern Denmark, Odense (www.sdu.dk/cml). He has published on Latin literature and historiography from Antiquity to the Renaissance and on the practice and theory of pre-modern literary history.

II

Claiming Authority through Forms of Materiality—Ancient and Modern

— 5 —

Claiming Authority in the Sphere of Roman "Deathscapes": Tomb 100 in the Isola Sacra Necropolis

Jane Hjarl Petersen

This paper explores burial culture and tombs as material media through which ancient Roman non-elite citizens could lay claim to authority and thus obtain social recognition and standing in the local community, as well as exercise power over members of their familia. The focus of the paper is a case study of a second century tomb complex, Tomb 100, in the Isola Sacra necropolis near Rome's main harbour city of Portus. It argues that the design, in particular the decoration and dedicatory inscription on the façade of the tomb, constitutes a condensed communication of identity manifestations which served to bring the patron and her family into the limelight in terms of social status and standing within the local community. The tomb in question thus serves as an example of how the "deathscapes" of Roman cities offered an obvious opportunity for both the living and the dead to stage authoritative positions and social status via self-representations aimed at the local contemporary community, as well as posterity.

Introducing the Roman Necropolis

In contrast to many cemeteries of modern-day Western societies, where strictly defined grave plots are often lined with uniform, well-trimmed hedges and the voices of visitors are kept respectfully low and dignified, ancient Roman[1] necropoleis were bustling, disorderly places filled with activities and people at most hours of the day. Mainly arranged alongside

1. This paper is based primarily on evidence from the cities of Rome and Ostia/Portus as well as nearby urban centres from the period of the late Republic to the late Empire, ca first century BC to AD 300. The very broad term "Roman" is of course much more complex than the picture offered here by this snapshot and encompasses vastly diverse geographical, cultural, social and chronological meanings, encompassing the vast Roman Empire with its many different cultures and people of diverse economic means and social standings; a detailed consideration is beyond the scope of the present study.

the primary roads leading into cities and towns, necropoleis were part of the lived urban space, and anyone travelling into or out of the city would pass by them. Grave plots varied greatly in size and design, and, although strict instructions on the size of individual grave plots are often cited in the epitaphs of the grave markers, the reality was that larger tombs and smaller burials of all types were scattered amongst each other. Many Romans were intensely preoccupied with proper burial in an actual tomb, notably members of the poorer segment of society, who faced the frightening prospect of ending up as a cadaver preyed on by dogs and birds rather than as a corpse treated with respect and dignity by caring relatives (Bodel 2000, 129).[2] In general, the regulations for the design of tombs were quite loose, in some periods more so than others, and often the personal taste and economic means of the family of the deceased set the order of the day (Toynbee 1971, 74). The lack of overall control or authority over the spatial layout and design of necropolis areas permitted the development of a rather diverse and individualized range of options for the final resting places of the Romans (Hope 2009, 154–163). In terms of activities centred in and around the necropoleis, the Roman customs of visiting the tomb and engaging in commemorative activities such as banquets, the scattering of flowers and gifts, and the making of offerings of food and drink to the dead, as well as maintenance or rebuilding of the grave plot, frequently brought family and friends of the deceased to the necropoleis (Hope 2009, 99–102; also Graham 2005).[3] The necropolis areas were also used for practical purposes related to their siting along the main roads. Thus, along the road between Ostia and Rome the tired traveller could find food and a bed in one of the small inns which were situated amongst the tombs of the Porta Romana necropolis.[4] But the necropoleis were also notorious as hideouts for tomb robbers, pickpockets and low-class prostitutes.[5] Moreover, fear of the rest-

2. Bodel (2000, 129) estimates that an average of ca 30,000 individuals died in the capital city every year; at times of epidemic this number would increase. With such high numbers, the pressure on the necropolis areas was constant, and often the less fortunate would die in the streets and lay unclaimed and unwanted. These corpses would be disposed of by dumping them in large, open mass graves, so-called *puticuli*, where they would be left to scavengers and general decay (Bodel 2000, 131; Graham 2006, 63–84).

3. There is also evidence for the establishment of market gardens around tombs (so-called *cepotaphii*), from which produce could be sold to help maintain the tomb monument and added to the offerings of foodstuffs used in tomb rituals. This implies that gardeners and their assistants were a part of the living population of a necropolis (Campbell 2008, 31–33; Hope 2009, 173–174).

4. Heinzelmann 2000, 28–30, identifies clusters A5b–A6–B2–B3 and A15–A17–B15–B16b–B17 as utilitarian structures.

5. Hope 2009, note 31 gives full list of references to ancient sources pertaining to this phenomenon.

less dead—those persons whose relatives failed to fulfil the ritual duties of regular tomb visits and offerings—along with criminals and the like, added a sense of marginality to the necropolis spaces (Hope 2009, 176–177; also Alfayé 2009).[6] Thus, Roman necropoleis were busy spaces buzzing with the activities of the various people from very different social backgrounds who frequented them.

Contextualizing Roman burial culture

The close relationship between the living community and the "city of dead" meant that necropolis areas constituted an excellent arena in which to communicate social status and identity manifestations. The visibility of a tomb, its architectural features, decoration and epitaph(s) were potentially major instruments in the competition for attention from passers-by. The wish for attention could be fuelled by various motivations; often fear of oblivion was one. This was a central theme in the Roman preoccupation with what happened after life had ended. The fear of being forgotten with no one to perform the appropriate rites of commemoration was grounded in the belief that the soul would be doomed to wander restlessly about, haunting and seeking the attention of the living (Hope 2009, 37–38, 116–117; 2011, 176–177). We see a reflection of this phenomenon in the epitaphs which call out directly to passers-by to stop and say aloud the name of the deceased, to ponder on his/her life story and to think about life and death in general (Hope 2009, 37–38). The fate of humans after death was a major preoccupation for many Romans. What happened after death, however, was only vaguely described or dealt with in Roman eschatology, and a wide range of beliefs and presumptions prevailed. Again, epitaphs provide examples of the diverse range of ideas and thoughts on death and a potential afterlife. Statements on epitaphs encouraged passers-by to enjoy life today, because tomorrow we may be gone (a *memento mori*), or simply noted that after death there is nothing but dust and darkness (Hope 2009, 22–27). Other epitaphs, as well as iconographic symbolism in, for example, wall paintings, mosaics and sarcophagi, explicitly expressed hopes for a happy afterlife of harmony and prosperity, as well as for the prospect of reunion with loved-ones (Hope 2009, 97–120; Ewald and Zanker 2012, 96–103, 170–173).

Another reason for the explicit wish for attention which could motivate the construction of a conspicuous tomb complex was the opportunity to promote one's social status. A tomb could thus serve as a medium through which a family or an individual could communicate their identity and social standing (real or perceived) in contemporary society, and for posterity.

6. On the relations between tombs and ghosts, evil spirits and witchcraft, see Ogden 2001, 2002.

Epitaphs, again, are helpful testimonies to this habit. While some chose only a very brief text for their epitaph, stating just the name of the deceased and perhaps the number of years, months and days—and even hours—which the person had lived, more lengthy epitaphs would also specify the occupation, the social status (for example freedman/woman or slave) and the country or city of origin of the deceased, as well as the exact size of the tomb plot and the name of the patron and others who were permitted burial within the monument.[7] Later on, from around the second century CE onwards, very personal and emotional epitaphs commemorated and praised the deceased in verse or prose, thus giving the bereaved an opportunity to come to terms with their grief and ensure long-lasting commemoration of their loved-ones (Hope 2011, 177–179). Further, it seems evident that such epitaphs could serve to reassure the wider community that the family was acting according to the correct precepts and also secure or even enhance their respectability in the eyes of the local community. All in all, it follows that the composition of tomb epitaphs was quite free. There were some stock phrases and standardized expressions at hand—such as *D(is) M(anibus)*, "to the spirits," or *H(oc) m(onumentum) h(eredem) n(on) s(equetur)*, "this monument shall not pass to the heirs"—but, generally speaking, the wording of the epitaph could be composed specifically and individually to the liking of the patron who commissioned it (Bodel 2001, 30–31; also Feraudi-Gruénais 2003, 155–156).

While we may expect a certain degree of reflection of the will and wishes of the deceased in a burial complex, the ultimate decisions and execution of the burial and monument were in most cases left to the relatives or friends who buried the deceased. A monument might have been commissioned and built by the patron before death had occurred, but the living had the final say in the chain of events surrounding the burial of an individual. A response to this can be seen in the example of several heirs who mounted inscriptions on burial monuments reassuring the general public that the will of the patron had been honoured (Hope 2009, 31–32). Similarly, the standard phrase *H(oc) m(onumentum) h(eredem) n(on) s(equetur)*, "this monument shall not pass to the heirs," touches upon the anxiety of patrons regarding what will happen once control of events is out of their hands (Toynbee 1971, 74–75).[8]

7. The phenomenon was so common that a standard phrase existed for this: *et sibi et suis, / libertis libertabusque / posterisque eorum.*

8. Apart from epitaphs, other means of attracting attention were the architectural designs and decorations of the tombs. For Rome and surrounding areas the late Republican period seems to have been the most liberal in terms of fanciful architectural tomb designs and decoration schemes; examples from later periods under the emperors tend to feature more conformist attitudes towards these aspects of burial culture (Petersen 2014, 27–28).

However, it is important to keep in mind that attitudes towards tomb designs and burial culture in general varied greatly within the vast Roman Empire, where cultural, economic and social contexts were all determining factors for the manner in which burial was conducted. Nevertheless, their suitability as arenas for displays of identity and social status was a common feature of the Roman necropoleis, and through their firm integration within the urban spaces of the living, these "deathscapes" provided an obvious opportunity for communications and manifestations on various aspects of human life, as an "edited impression of the dead" (Hope 2011, 177).

Roman burial material and authority

As reflections of the thoughts and beliefs of those who commissioned them and used them, burial monuments and material remains related to the funerary sphere were, and still are, ideal media for representing who and what we are or wish we had been. Furthermore, on an emotional level, necropoleis and burial monuments facilitated the continuation of bonds between the bereaved and the deceased. Through preparations for the burial, handling of the actual interment, and continued interaction with the plot and the burial monument, the bereaved created a memorial for the deceased while simultaneously dealing with and articulating their own personal grief. This could ensure an emotional continuity between the living and the dead, and serves to underline the strong liminal character of the necropolis space as a realm in which the living could interact with the dead and come to terms with their emotional experiences and life-situation, both at the time of the burial and also in the future, as a continuing dialogue with loved-ones.[9] Thus, the study of tombs, burial spaces and their related material remains can grant us access to a wide range of aspects pertaining to a society and its members, be they political, social, religious, economic, personal, emotional or other.[10] In this respect the notion of the necropolis as a lived space enables us to ask specific questions about the concept of authority in this particular ancient context and to approach the concept of authority through material remains and objects; a line of approach which is rarely given much in-depth treatment in the literature on authority as already touched upon in the Introduction to this volume. The use of imagery as a medium through which claims of authority can be made was lightly touched upon by Lincoln in his renowned 1994 study of authority. Here he

9. This theme is studied in detail, from various perspectives of Roman literary and material culture, in Hope and Huskinson 2011. For a study of these mechanisms in contemporary Danish society, see Sørensen 2010.

10. See also Petersen 2010, 32–33, for a discussion on the interpretative limitations and pitfalls of burial data.

emphasized the ability of iconic emblems and items to announce the authority of their bearer for a given audience (1994, 7–8). Lincoln identified a variety of attributes and items—from objects, costumes and physical postures to facial expressions—through which an individual can lay claim to authority. Through the handling and possession of legitimate items, emblems and body language, individuals can thus strive to win the attention, respect and trust of the audience whose recognition of their authority is desired. The emblems and items are instrumental in signalling that their bearer is acting in an official capacity and thereby serve to announce and verify the authority of an individual before an audience. However, Lincoln argued, the success with which these elements are set in play and articulated depends on the willingness of the audience to recognize, accept and respect the claimed authoritative position of the individual (1994, 7–8). Relationality is at the core of Lincoln's definition of authority: authority exists when the person claiming authority plays his/her part correctly and convincingly and when the audience acknowledges and respects this (Lincoln 1994, 4–6, 10–11).[11] For the present study both the definition of objects as potential bearers of authority and the emphasis on the social relations as the structural fabric of authoritative positions are crucial. In an archaeological study the starting point will obviously be the material record through which we seek to explore and shed light on social relations and patterns of human interaction. It therefore seems like an obvious path to explore the ways in which analyses of archaeological material can contribute to our understanding of how authority claims could be made, how authority could be sought established and communicated. Further, there seems to be much to gain from considering ancient Roman burial material in the light of concepts of authority since this avenue has been poorly investigated up until now. In the following, I shall examine how aspects of social identity pertaining to professional occupation could be communicated through visual representations in the funerary sphere through a case study of Tomb 100 from the Isola Sacra necropolis and consider how we may understand concepts of authority in relation to the professional identities of the non-elite members of Roman society.

The Isola Sacra necropolis

The Isola Sacra necropolis, situated some 30 km southwest of Rome between the main port cities of Ostia and Portus, is one of the best preserved Roman necropoleis of the second century CE (Figure 5.1). Here it is possible to walk

11. For a discussion of authority as a relational concept and its definitions by scholars such as Weber, Foucault, Arendt and others, see Furedi 2013, 7–10.

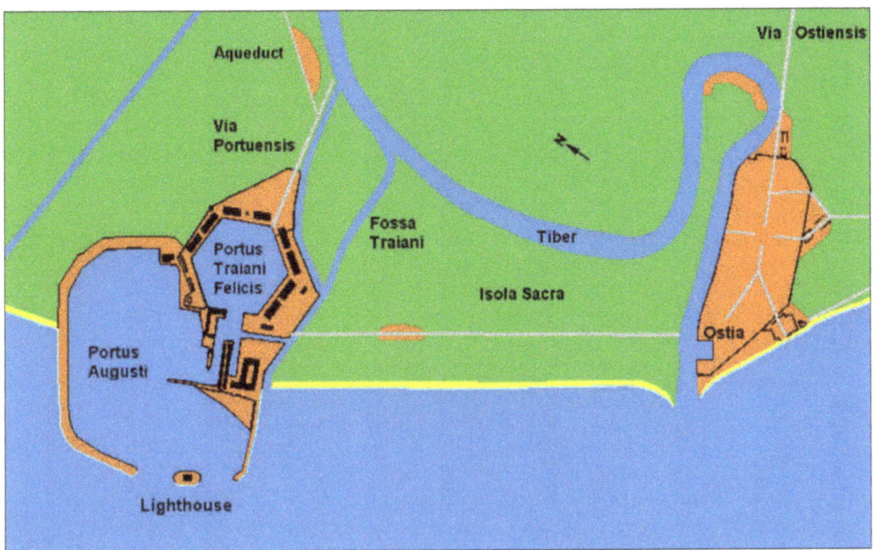

Figure 5.1 Map of Portus and Ostia. Reproduced with kind permission from Jan Theo Bakker: http://www.ostia-antica.org/portus/claudius.htm

amongst the well-preserved house tombs and *columbaria* complexes[12] which line the main road between Ostia and Portus, the Via Severiana-Flavia, in neat rows (Figure 5.2). A smaller area of the necropolis has been investigated systematically since the 1920s, and well over 100 tombs and smaller burials have been unearthed. These constitute, however, only a small percentage of the total number of tombs originally erected here. Scattered amongst the larger tomb complexes of the wealthy is an array of smaller tombs and simple burials, indicating that the necropolis also accommodated the less well-to-do strata of society (Baldassare *et al.* 1996, 19–24). The necropolis has been the focus of intense study due to its well-preserved tombs, but also because of the vast array of epigraphic evidence which the excavations have revealed.[13] From this evidence, it is clear that the majority of people who built tombs and were buried at the Isola Sacra belonged

12. *Columbaria* are tomb complexes with dovecote-like niches in which urns containing ashes could be placed together with various offerings to the dead. Above or under each niche, an inscription plaque commemorating the deceased could be inserted. *Columbaria* became popular in Rome and its surrounding areas from the end of the first century BC onwards. Some of the larger *columbaria* in Rome could accommodate hundreds of burials. For a recent comprehensive study, see Borbonus 2014.

13. Helttula 2007 is the most recent comprehensive publication of the epigraphic material from Isola Sacra. Calza 1940 and Baldassare 1996 constitute the main excavation reports. An extensive bibliography (up to 2009) can be found at http://www.ostia-antica.org/biblio/keywords/key1073.htm.

Figure 5.2 The Isola Sacra necropolis. Private photo by Tom Birch Hansen.

to the non-elite social strata of nearby Portus; free working-class citizens, freedmen/women and slaves are the main patrons and recipients of the epitaphs, while magistrates and members of the local aristocracy are virtually absent (Baldassare 1996, 24; Petersen 2006, 185–188; see also Helttula 2007, 389–390). This particular social set-up lends itself to a wide range of approaches to the study of the social history of an ancient harbour area; among others, it offers the opportunity to assess how tombs could be used as media for staging authoritative positions and social status. This is exemplified in the following analysis of burial complex Tomb 100.

Tomb 100

Tomb 100 is located in the second row of tombs beyond the Via Severiana, with no other tomb structures in its immediate vicinity, and is dated to the early 140s CE. The complex consists of a relatively small structure which was probably covered with a barrel-vaulted roof (now missing). The structure in its original design consisted of a single room fitted with small wall niches for cremation urns as well as larger *arcosolia* (niches) for inhumations; later, *formae* (rectangular recesses) covered with marble slabs were sunk into the floor to provide room for more inhumations (Baldassare *et al.* 1996, 42–44). In front of the entrance, two large *klinai* (concrete benches) were initially found, but these are no longer visible. *Klinai* are common features in the necropolis and were part of the more elaborately equipped tomb complexes, allowing visitors to the tombs to engage in dining and banqueting activities in the closest possible proximity to their dead relatives. The tomb's marble epitaph, the so-called titulus inscription, is placed centrally on the façade above the entrance. It reads as follows:

> May this monument be protected against all evil
>
> To the spirits
>
> Scribonia Attice made this for herself and for her husband Marcus Ulpius Amerimnus and for her mother Scribonia Callityche and for Diocles and for his and for her freedmen and freedwomen and their descendants except Panarato and Prosdocia
>
> This monument will not pass to the heirs[14]

The epitaph serves to name, and thus attract attention to, the prominent "inhabitants" and patrons of the complex, but it also gives testimony to the many elements which made up the Roman *familia*, as discussed further below.[15] Flanking the epitaph are two terracotta reliefs (Ostia Museum). The relief to the left (Figure 5.3) is a shallow, free-modelled relief with traces of red and blue paint (Calza 1940, 248–249; D'Ambra 2006, 78; also Kampen 1981). It depicts three women: one standing, one sitting on a chair and one kneeling. The central, seated figure is partially undressed and wears a veil over her head. She grips the armrests of the chair firmly and, from her considerably sized stomach, we may assume that either she is pregnant and going through a gynaecological examination or, more likely, she is in labour. The latter assumption seems to be backed up by the presence of the woman standing behind the chair who supports the pregnant woman with her arms and by the fact that the woman is seated on a special birthing chair, also known from ancient literary sources on gynaecology.[16] The third woman on the relief kneels in front of the pregnant woman with her right arm between her companion's legs; but she looks away from the pregnant

14. Helttula 2007, 154–156.
 H(uic) m(onumento) d(olus) m(alus) a(besto)|
 D(is) M(anibus)|Scribonia Attice|fecit sibi et M(arco) Ulpio Amerimno|
 Coniugi et Scriboniae Calli|tyche matri et Diocli et suis|et libertis libertabusque poste|risque eorum praeter Panara|tum et Prosdocia(m)|
 H(oc) m(onumentum) h(eredem) n(on) s(equetur)

15. The extended Roman *familia* encompassed blood relatives, relatives by marriage, slaves and freedmen/women (Rawson 2010 offers a comprehensive overview of the overwhelming output of research into ancient families and provides ample bibliography on the many and varied aspects of this field of research).

16. E.g. Soranus *Gyn.* 2.5. On Roman midwives, see French 1987; D'Ambra 2006; Laes 2010; 2011; Porter 2016.

Figure 5.3 Terracotta relief of a midwife from Tomb 100 (Ostia Museum, inv.no 5203. Archivio Fotografico del Parco Archeologico di Ostia Antica).

woman, facing directly outwards towards the viewer in a very striking, glaring *en face* representation. She is most certainly a midwife (*obstetrix*) and the woman behind the patient is her assistant.[17] The averted gaze of the midwife has been interpreted as a professional gesture of the experienced midwife, who, in consideration of the modesty of her patient, avoided eye contact during examinations in order to lessen the patient's possibly shameful feelings about the situation (D'Ambra 2006, 78; Porter 2016, 291). As noted by D'Ambra and Porter, the physician Soranus, in his *Gynaecology*, offers an invaluable and detailed account of gynaecology and obstetrics in the Roman world, describing the work and role of the midwife, the female anatomy, conception, childbirth and the care of the new-borns. Incidentally, he was writing at the time of the construction of Tomb 100, and his description of the professional ethics, assurance and compassion of the midwife during

17. Olson (2008, 46) notes that the short, calf-length tunic was perceived as a marker of lower social class, and this implies that the assistant in the relief was most likely either a slave or a freedwoman working for the midwife. A study by Laes (2011, 156) demonstrates that the vast majority of inscriptions from the Roman world pertaining to midwives classify them as freedwomen and "possibly slaves" (42% and 29%). We may speculate that Scribonia Attice was a freedwoman who had established herself as a midwife in her "new life" post manumission, but we cannot be sure that she was not a freeborn Roman woman. The inscription gives no information about her legal status and the term *Liberta* (freedwoman) was not a compulsory part of the epitaphs of ex-slaves (Petersen 2006, 11).

labour (*Gyn.* 2.4.3–2.6.2) very closely mirrors, in literary form, the visual depiction on this relief. He recommends that the face of the patient should be visible to the midwife: hence a veil is positioned over the head of our parturient woman but her face is visible. He advises that the midwife should avert her gaze so as to avoid the patient feeling shame during her contractions (*Gyn.* 2.4.3–2.6.2; also D'Ambra 2006, 78, note 37). The careful composition of the scene on the relief (assistant, patient, midwife), the birthing chair, the position of the veil and the professionally averted gaze underline not only the professional identity of the patron of the tomb, Scribonia Attice —who must have been a midwife—but also convey a strong visual message of occupational authority. The assistant and the birthing chair are motifs which serve to symbolize the controlled professional environment offered by Scribonia Attice in her capacity as a trained midwife.[18] They are probably depicted here as *pars pro toto,* at least if we draw on the advice offered by Soranus, who recommends at least three assistants and an array of equipment (*Gyn.* 2.4.3–2.6.2).[19] The body language with its conveyed compassion and reassurance, symbolized by the unveiled face of the parturient woman and the adverted gaze of the midwife, serves to create an impression for the viewer of the unquestionable professionalism and authority of Scribonia Attice. In this potentially life-threatening situation, a woman would feel safe in these hands—the hands of an undisputed authority.[20] Here we can

18. Depictions of Roman midwifes at work are rare. Apart from the Isola Sacra relief, French (1987) offers just two other depictions: an ivory relief from Pompeii and a marble relief from a private collection. The Science Museum of London holds a very interesting marble relief with a parturition scene (no. A129245). Further illustrations can be found in Dierichs 2002. Common features of these depictions are midwife, woman in labour and assistant(s). It seems that the Scribonia Attice relief is set apart from the other depictions by focusing on an undetermined moment during an examination or child birth rather than the crucial moment of delivery. By choosing this approach Scribonia Attice perhaps sought to widen the depiction of her professional services and abilities to encompass various examinations and assistance during both pregnancy and birth.

19. On the various aspects of the midwife's profession as discussed by Soranus, including giving legal advice and acting against superstition and accusations of witchcraft, see D'Ambra 2006, 79–80.

20. The fatal dangers of pregnancy, childbirth and post-natal complications are attested and described in numerous ancient epigraphic and literary sources (see Laes 2010 for a through presentation; also Todman 2007). Roman girls tended to marry young, commonly in their mid-teens or even earlier (Rawson 2003, 95–97; Laes 2010, 262–263), and pregnancy at such an early age, before the body is fully developed, is significantly more dangerous than pregnancies later in life (Rawson 2003, 96; see also Nutton 2004, 198–199 on the advice of Soranus that girls should remain virgins until the unset of menstruation because of the dangers of early pregnancy and childbirth). Women repeatedly found themselves in life-threatening situations throughout their child-bearing years, as infant and child mortality rates were terrifyingly high and the production of offspring was the main duty of a Roman wife. Furthermore, female slaves were the physical prop-

bring in Lincoln's considerations on the relational character of authority; namely that authority exists when the person claiming authority plays his/her part correctly and convincingly and when the audience acknowledges and respects this (Lincoln 1994, 4–6, 10–11). The relief of Scribonia Attice gives us *one* side only of this relation, namely her own claim to professional authority through the carefully selected elements of the visual composition.[21] Whether her ambition to be recognized as an authority was successful and acknowledged amongst her contemporaries and, more specifically, her potential patients/clients we can only guess: manipulations and idealizations lie at the very heart of identity expressions in the funerary sphere (Tarlow 1999, 22–23; Fowler 2013). What we may deduce from the representation is that Scribonia Attice herself was well aware of the relational significance between the individual in authority and the person(s) she is interacting with—her patient is carefully placed at the very centre of the composition. She could have commissioned a relief with a self-portrait accompanied only by representations of objects and symbols pertaining to her occupation—as we shall see in another example discussed below—but she chose instead to stress the respectful and professional nature of her engagement with a patient, who has in return placed confidence in her professional abilities and thereby acknowledged her as an authority.

The evidence at hand here offers the opportunity to study the strategies used in the claim for authority, which Scribonia Attice herself pursued. The fact that she was the patron of the tomb complex confirms to us that she, in contrast to her husband, was alive when the reliefs were commissioned and installed on the façade, and she may very well have still been practising as a midwife at this point in her life. It is thus possible to credit her with the direct agency of the design of the reliefs, in an act of conscious self-representation. In the midwife relief we thus encounter the end product of her expression of identity, as well as her claim to occupational authority, communicated through carefully staged motifs of professional capability. The self-same strategy was employed by her on behalf of her deceased husband in the relief on the other side of the epitaph (Figure 5.4).

erty of the master, in every respect of the term, for both pleasure and the production of slave labour for the household, the so-called *vernae* (home-born slaves) (Rawson 2003, 95–97; Todman 2007; Laes 2010, 265–266; George 2013, 168–169; Lenski 2013, 129–130; on *vernae* specifically, see Herrmann-Otto 1994).

21. Lincoln further helpfully point to the distinction between "the authority of those who are 'in authority' (e.g., political leaders, parents, military commanders) and that of those who are 'an authority' (e.g., technical experts, scholars, medical specialists)" (1994, 3–4). Obviously, our example here falls into the latter category. See also the definitions of authority in Furedi 2013, 5–10, as well as Furedi's overall survey of the concept of authority through different historical periods.

Figure 5.4 Terracotta relief of a surgeon from Tomb 100. Ostia Museum, inv.no 5204. Archivio Fotografico del Parco Archeologico di Ostia Antica.

Although the upper parts and the left side are damaged, the scene is still identifiable. The relief is divided into two halves. On the left side two people in short tunics sit facing each other; the person on the left has an instrument in his right hand and is reaching towards the bared leg of the person on the right, whose leg is placed in a basin. On the right-hand side of the relief there is a depiction of an enlarged box containing scalpels and other surgical instruments pertaining to the occupation of the person depicted on the far left. He has been identified as a physician or surgeon and the figure presumably represents Scribonia Attice's husband, Marcus Ulpius Amerimnus (Calza 1940, 250; D'Ambra 2006, 79). The basin most probably signifies that the patient is having his leg bled or operated on, and the box of sharp implements, which is enlarged in order to underline its importance within the depiction, further confirms this interpretation. In a similar manner to the careful composition and symbolic elements of the midwife-relief, the surgeon-relief is clearly crafted to convey not only the occupational identity of the deceased person, but also his professionalism and undisputed authority within the medical profession.

A similar iconography is displayed on a slightly later marble sarcophagus reportedly found at Ostia and thus presumably from one of the city's necropoleis (Figure 5.5; Metropolitan Museum, inv.no. 48.76.1). Here, the deceased is seated on a low chair holding an open scroll in his hands and is dressed in a tunic and *himation*. The figure is thus represented in the style of a philosopher, and this in turn conveys his learned character. Next to him is an open cabinet which contains more scrolls and also a basin that is similar to the one illustrated on the relief from Tomb 100. Furthermore, on top

Figure 5.5 Sarcophagus of a doctor from Ostia, with detail below. Metropolitan Museum 48.76.1.

of the cabinet we see an open case containing various surgical tools;[22] this case is depicted in precisely the same manner as the open box on the relief of Tomb 100. Along the top of the sarcophagus and down each side of the central scene runs an inscription in Greek which condemns any subsequent burials in the sarcophagus as well as offering an explicit statement of the penalty for such violations: a fine payable to the treasury in Portus as well as eternal punishment (McCann 1978, 139). Unfortunately, the lid of the sarcophagus is not preserved and it has been suggested that the identity of the deceased was most likely stated here, as no such information is given on the sarcophagus itself (McCann 1978, 139). However, the style of dress and the Greek inscription indicate that he could have been one of the many physicians with a Greek cultural background who came to Italy to make a career.[23] Extensive study of ancient medicine seems to confirm that there were vari-

22. For identifications of the various surgical tools, see McCann 1978, 138.

23. See, for example, Cruse 2004, 56–60; Nutton 2004, 157–170.

ous attitudes regarding the social status and perception of doctors and other medical professionals, including midwives, in the Roman world, ranging from mistrust and plain ridicule to respect and admiration.[24] These attitudes naturally varied over time, and geographical as well as cultural and social factors played a decisive role in the diverse perceptions of these professions. While the terracotta reliefs of Tomb 100 seem to communicate to an audience who valued a simple and honest professional practice, the physician's sarcophagus has a different, more sophistically staged agenda: the image of the man on the sarcophagus pertains to the tradition of the learned philosopher-physician. This type of medic frequently features in ancient literary sources and is generally regarded, at least in the period of the high Empire, with respect and acknowledgement of his traditional Greek medical education and professional authority.[25] Some doctors who attended the households of the elite and even the Imperial family were highly esteemed and praised for their skills, and they must have made a rather comfortable living (Nutton 1992, 45–47). Nonetheless, a common feature of many Greek doctors would have been a slave background. They were often trained in the household of their master, and many freedmen continued to practice their trade after manumission (Nutton 1992, 38–40).

The Ostia sarcophagus not only aspires to a certain learned, prestigious side of the practice of medicine, it also makes an economic statement on behalf of its owner. Although scholars have discussed the economic means required to purchase a sculpted marble sarcophagus widely, it seems certain that such a final resting place was reserved for the well-to-do. Ben Russell even suggests that, for some, a decorated marble sarcophagus would have required the investment of a lifetime of savings (2011, 122–123). The final resting place of our physician certainly conveys strong messages of high social status and significant economic means, gained through a successful career and professional competence.

However, when comparing the sarcophagus with the reliefs from Tomb 100, it is important to underline the crucial difference in terms of the dis-

24. See, for instance, Pleket 1995; Nutton 1992; 2004; Cruse 2004, 194–196. On the social status of midwifes in the Greek world, see, for example, Demand 1995; Laes 2010, 2011. The medical profession, apart from midwifery, seems to have been almost exclusively male-dominated; however, see Künzl 1995 for funerary evidence of female physicians who, according to the various instruments found with them, practiced surgery and dentistry.

25. On the divergent perceptions and attitudes towards Greek medics in Italy, see Nutton 2004, 157–170. The scepticism about and low opinion of Greek medics—notably expressed by Cato the Elder and Pliny the Elder—is further explored in Cruse 2004, 56–60. The fascination with and increased influence of Greek culture in the upper echelons of Roman society in the second century AD must have helped to mitigate the previous negative attitudes to a certain extent (Nutton 1992, 45).

play context and, therefore, the difference also in the audience for which the communications were intended. The reliefs on the tomb façade were designed with distinct exterior motivations, communicating to a wide and diverse public audience of passers-by. The sarcophagus, on the other hand, was destined for placement inside a tomb complex, where a rather limited audience would have viewed it and interacted with it.[26] Thus, the physician's sarcophagus was designed, purchased and functioned within a much narrower and decidedly private context than the façade reliefs. Juxtaposing the reliefs and the sarcophagus it would, at first glance, seem that there is an obvious discrepancy between the depictions of the well-to-do Ostian physician, staging himself in a learned Greek context through his elaborate marble sarcophagus, and the much simpler and cruder terracotta figures at work on Tomb 100. There are, of course, economic differences in the choice of material. The terracotta reliefs must have had a significantly lower production cost than the carved marble sarcophagus. But is this discrepancy best explained by different social milieus—the well-to-do city doctor from Ostia versus the simple midwife and doctor from the freedman/slave milieu of Portus? Probably not; plenty of finely carved marble sarcophagi and funerary sculptures have been found in the tombs at Isola Sacra (Calza 1940, 190–247), and compelling evidence from Tomb 29 combines the two genres of terracotta reliefs and carved marble sarcophagi.[27] An elaborately carved marble sarcophagus inscribed with the names of the owners—Verius Euhelpistus and his wife—was found inside this tomb complex and several terracotta reliefs depicting scenes from a smith's workshop adorn the façade (D'Ambra 1988). The style and execution of the terracotta reliefs are very similar to those of the reliefs on Tomb 100. The figures are simple, the tools of the trade depicted are large and emblematic in character, and there are traces of red and blue paint (Calza 1940, 251–253; see D'Ambra 1988, 91–93 for an extensive description). This combination of the terracotta reliefs on the façade and the carved marble sarcophagus as a private burial container inside the complex demonstrates that the two genres could be carefully staged in the same context. Rather than seeing them as representative of different social groups with different economic means, the rationale for their individual use may be explained by the fact that they were designed for different purposes. The outward communication on the façade called for a stylistic expression that was different to that of the private commemoration of the sarcophagus. The simple façade, with its brickwork and titulus inscription, called for a simple and easily legible visual programme; the

26. Birk 2013, 34–39 discusses the (in)visibility of sarcophagi and their audiences.

27. For the tomb see Baldassare *et al.* 1996, 137–142.

private and more intimate interaction with a sarcophagus could convey complex and even personal portrayals, whilst the accompanying lengthy inscriptions demanded that viewers had the ability to read. The terracotta reliefs and the carved sarcophagi may thus be seen as expressions of different standards of representation in different contexts, as suggested by D'Ambra (1988, 91), and, we may add, they may be aimed at different audiences. So, for the audience to whom Scribonia Attice communicated the defining characteristic of her deceased husband, Marcus Ulpius Amerimnus, a doctor was most probably best defined through his ability to engage in direct contact with his patients, through actual treatment and concrete surgical procedures. The book scrolls and philosophical connotations of the sarcophagus might have meant less to the couple in terms of their everyday health concerns and struggle for survival. The simple visual representations of midwife and surgeon, both depicted hard at work undertaking their daily tasks, functioned as strong media though which the intended message could reach a wide public audience, some of whom would have had limited reading ability, if any at all. Following D'Ambra (2006, 79), it can be concluded that these reliefs were not shop signs put up to increase business but strong visual messages advertising something much more long-lasting: the carefully constructed representation of Scribonia Attice and her husband for eternity as authoritative experts in their professional fields.

Despite the different audiences of the visual communications of Scribonia Attice, Marcus Ulpius Amerimnus and the Ostian physician, there can be no doubt that the claims to occupational authority via depictions on both reliefs and sarcophagi were a means to promote an imposing defining characteristic of the deceased. Although we have no finds from inside Tomb 100, there is nothing to suggest that Scribonia Attice could not have commissioned an elaborately carved marble sarcophagus for herself and her husband to be displayed in the privacy of the tomb. However, the depiction of the authoritative relationship between midwife/doctor and their patients was an exclusively exterior design which served to emphasize the social standing, status and personal identity of the deceased broadly within the local community.

Occupational authority and the household

The visual representation of individuals rooted in occupational authority was already a long-standing tradition in the Roman funerary sphere at this time,[28] but the terracotta reliefs from Isola Sacra seem to have been a spe-

28. The most famous of such monuments is probably the mid to late first century BCE tomb of the baker and contractor Eurysaces near the Porta Maggiore in Rome (see Petersen 2006, 84–120 for a comprehensive and persuasive analysis).

cial feature of this particular necropolis (some ten in total are preserved: Calza 1940, 247–256). Apart from the midwife and surgeon reliefs, there are depictions of craftsmen and tradesmen at work, such as the previously mentioned smith or ironmonger, depictions of grinding machines, from a mill or bakery, and depictions of vendors of water, wine and oil in amphorae (Calza 1940, 251–256; D'Ambra 1981; 1988; Zimmer 1982; on the amphorae, see Gil 2008).[29] There is also a depiction of a boat with a helmsman, a coxswain and three men working the oars (Calza 1940, 254); it is, however, more difficult to say whether this particular scene should be interpreted as a more general symbol of the harbour milieu of Portus or a specific reference to the occupational identity of the tomb owner (boat owner, maritime tradesman, etc.).[30] The same is true of examples of similar scenes on sarcophagi, such as a piece found in Tomb 90 with depictions of ships in the harbour and a busy bar (Calza 1940, 203–205). A sarcophagus of one Titus Flavius Trophimas, reportedly found in Ostia, however, seems to be a thematic parallel to the physician's sarcophagus. The deceased is named in the titulus inscription as skilled in all arts, *panmousos*, and on either side of the inscription reliefs represent, on the left, two men at work practising their crafts of shoemaking and rope making and, on the right, musicians/dancers—perhaps Trophimas in the role of an initiate of the goddess Isis (Giuliano 1981, 148–150; Van Keuren 2009, 198; also Van Keuren et al. 2011, 165). The two friends who dedicated the sarcophagus to Trophimas thus found it fitting not only to commemorate their friend in words and images but also to make a statement about their own professional lives and identities as craftsmen. In doing so, they communicated through a visual language which employs generic representations of occupational authority; the objects symbolizing the crafts (shoes in the making and on exhibition in a shop—an authoritative space—as well as the depiction of professional remedies and equipment for the manufacture of rope) lend authority to the representations and thus to the individuals in question.

29. References to similar occupations are found in the epigraphic material from the Via Laurentina necropolis at Ostia, albeit not illustrated through terracotta reliefs (Heinzelmann 2000, 114). At Ostia's more prominent necropolis, the Porta Romana cemetery situated along the Via Ostiense, claims for occupational status and authority are laid down in epitaphs through proclamations of political or religious office (Heinzelmann 2000, 115). However, amongst the considerable sample of epitaphs from Isola Sacra itself, only very few mention the occupation of the deceased: ἀρχιατρός (chief physician), *coactor* (tax collector), *medicus* (physician), *scrib(a) aedilic(ius)* (clerk to a magistrate) and *tabell(arius)* (messenger) (Helttula 2007, 389).

30. D'Ambra 1988, 97–99; see also Blazquez Martinez and Garcia-Gelabert Perez 1991 on depictions of harbour life from Ostia and Portus.

However, if we want to consider how allusions to authoritative objects and images could be used as claims to occupational authority, it might be of relevance to distinguish between skilled or technically demanding occupations and unskilled labour. An authoritative position would probably be harder to establish and uphold if just about anyone could perform the tasks in question. Lincoln (1994, 4) writes of "asymmetrical relations," which we may see as a prerequisite for the establishment of occupational authority in that an expert must offer a convincingly professional product or service which a customer, patient or client could not (or decided not to) offer, acquire or produce themselves. Thus, not all statements of occupational *identity* met in funerary material will necessarily be a reflection of claims to occupational *authority*. Internally within the boundaries of the lower social classes, especially amongst slaves, occupational references could be obvious media for manifestations of status and social identity, but also means of establishing the individual's rightful membership of a group/household (Joshel 1992, 85–91; Borbonus 2014, 127–128). Thus, in a number of large *columbaria* from Rome, primarily used by serving members of early Imperial and elite households, there seems to have been a clear tendency to articulate one's occupational role in a funerary epitaph in order to legitimize one's position as a fully-fledged member of a particular household (Joshel 1992, 100–105; Borbonus 2014, 117). At the other end of the social ladder, work and occupational titles could be instruments employed by the elite to label a person as being of a low social status, as persuasively argued by L. Petersen (2006, 2). The need to make a living based on labour, rather than on inherited family wealth, defined an individual's place amongst the lower social classes—a sharp contrast to an elite life spent free of (manual) labour in the bath complexes and on the political stage (see also Joshel 1992, 63–69).

Yet, occupational references were not the only way in which aspects of social status and authority could be conveyed in tomb contexts. Returning to Tomb 100 at Isola Sacra, the epitaph of Scribonia Attice allows us to study the mechanisms by which patrons could exercise (authoritative) power over members of their *familia*. First and foremost, the power of the patron was clearly formulated in the concept of the dedication; here the patron could decide who to include in the exclusive group which was allowed burial within the monument. Membership of this group was based on the private decisions of the patron, but could be consolidated through authoritative standard phrases and juridical as well as religious threats. The naming of specific individuals who were allowed burial in Scribonia Attice's monument (her husband, her mother, Diocles and their freedmen/women as well as their descendants) was a very direct way of exercising power over both the monument and the family. In this particular case, Scribonia Attice further used her position as patron to punish two specific individuals, Panarato and Prosdocia, who apparently had disobeyed their mistress so badly and irrevocably that her final powerful response was their exclusion from burial and their public shaming carved into stone for eternity.[31] Scribonia Attice also used a standard phrase—"This monument will not pass to the heirs"—to conclude the epitaph. The composition of the phrase and the popularity it enjoyed not only within the local context of the Isola Sacra necropolis (Helttula 2007, 392) but widely throughout the Roman Empire should probably be seen as a common reaction of patrons who were faced with the potential loss of authority and control over their tombs after their death. If a patron had not made a legal will as a precaution against such circumstances or feared that a will would not be respected in the long term, the authority of a standardized juridical announcement on the façade of the tomb may have served to calm his/her concerns; the fact that it was seen as a necessary precaution on such a large scale points to the fact that tomb ownership and the authority of the original patron were often not respected and upheld.[32] Further means of trying to uphold control through the medium of epitaphs were the threats, both juridical and religious, which served to protect the tomb as well as the deceased. The inscription on the sarcophagus of the Ostian physician is a fine example of this. The inclusion of both a pecuniary penalty payable to the city authorities as well as a curse threatening the violator with eternal punishment demonstrates the powerful communicative qualities of the epitaph.

Conclusion

The Roman "deathscapes," the necropoleis, were firmly rooted in the urban spaces of their cities and thus closely connected with the world of the living. As busy, bustling places full of activities and people at all hours, necropoleis were arenas well suited for claims to authority and status manifestations between various individuals and groups of the local community. Tombs were ideal media through which relatives could represent and commemo-

31. This is one of the only examples in the material from Isola Sacra of this kind of exclusion from burial of specifically named individuals (Helttula 2007, 398). However, similar instances are known e.g. from Pompeii, see Williams 2012, 260–266 for a compelling analysis of the tomb of Publius Vesonius Phileros who evidently fell out with his friend Marcus Orfellius Faustus and took to measures of publically naming and shaming him on the funerary monument which was originally erected in commemoration of both of them.

32. There are plenty of examples of tombs being sold on to or taken over by strangers, as well as heirs who made extensive changes to monuments after the death of the patron (for example Tombs 75/76 at Isola Sacra: Baldassare 1996, 89–92; Hope 2009, 172–173; Williams 2012, 268–275).

rate the deceased (in real or manipulated terms). Taking as a point of departure a case study of Tomb 100 in the Isola Sacra necropolis near the harbour city of Portus, the present chapter argues that the design of this second century tomb, notably the decoration and dedicatory inscription on the façade, was carefully crafted in order to bring the patron of the tomb complex, Scribonia Attice, and her family into the limelight of the local community in terms of social status. Through the careful composition of the decorative reliefs on the façade of the tomb, Scribonia Attice produced a condensed expression of self-representation firmly rooted in references and claims to occupational authority. She further cemented the status of the family and their undisputed place in the local community by also including the professional credentials of her husband. Their professions as midwife and doctor/surgeon must have made them well-known to many members of local society and their tomb complex ensured that the widest possible audience could relate to the overall message of the tomb through text (the epitaph) and/or the visual programme (the reliefs). In comparison, the physician's marble sarcophagus from Ostia spoke to a different, more private audience; the representation of the learned philosopher-doctor, which conveys his Greek cultural background through his dress, book scroll and inscription in Greek, linked itself to Roman elite households of the time where a Greek cultural background was often seen as a marker of intellectual superiority and high culture. In this way, both monuments were successful in staging the deceased in authoritative positions aimed at the local contemporary community as well as at a more closed circle of relatives and friends, and, importantly, for posterity. Furthermore, the epitaphs and inscriptions demonstrate the means by which patrons could exercise authority over members of their *familia* and/or broader society. The inclusion within the tomb complex—or exclusion—of certain members of the household was a powerful tool to single out and reward or punish specific individuals, as the epitaph of Scribonia Attice demonstrates. This powerful position was not only based on the private decisions of the patron but was consolidated through juridical standard phrases as well as religious threats.

In a society such as that of Rome, where freed slaves and members of the lower classes had virtually no means of gaining significant political influence or power, laying claim to authority through occupation was within the reach of the educated or skilled individual. Work was also a means by which to enhance social status within one's own social circles or those of the lower classes of the local community. Staging oneself in an authoritative position could thus produce a significant consolidation of the social status of both the individual and the family in contemporary society, and for posterity.

References

Alfayé, S. 2009. "Sit Tibi Terra Gravis: Magical-religious practices against restless dead in the ancient world." In *Formae Mortis: el tránsito de la vida a la muerte en las sociedades antiguas*, edited by F. M. Simón, F. Pina Polo and J. R. Rodríguez, 181–216. Barcelona: University of Barcelona.

Baldassarre, I. *et al.* 1996. *Necropoli di Porto. Isola Sacra.* Rome: Istituto poligrafico e Zecca dello Stato, Libreria dello Stato.

Birk, S. 2013. *Depicting the Dead: Self-Representation and Commemoration on Roman Sarcophagi with Portraits.* Aarhus: Aarhus University Press.

Blazquez Martinez J.M. and M.P. Garcia-Gelabert Perez. 1991. "El transporte maritimo segun las representaciones de los mosaicos romanos, relieves y pinturas de Ostia." *Lucentum* 9–10: 111–121.

Bodel, J. 2000. "Dealing with the dead: Undertakers, executioners and potter's fields in ancient Rome." In *Death and Disease in the Ancient City*, edited by V. M. Hope and E. Marshall, 128–151. London: Routledge.

Bodel, J., ed. 2001. *Epigraphic Evidence: Ancient History from Inscriptions.* London/New York: Psychology Press.

Borbonus, D. 2014. *Columbarium Tombs and Collective Identity in Augustan Rome.* Cambridge: Cambridge University Press.

Calza G. 1940. *La Necropoli del Porto di Roma nell' Isola Sacra.* Rome: Istituto di Archeologia e Storia dell' Arte. La Libreria dello Stato.

Campbell, V.L. 2008. "Stopping to Smell the Roses: Garden Tombs in Roman Italy." *Arctos* 42: 31–43.

Cruse, A. 2004. *Roman Medicine.* Stroud: Tempus.

D'Ambra, E. 1981. *A Work "Ethic" at Ostia: the Isola Sacra reliefs*, UCLA. Thesis (M.A.).

———. 1988. "A myth for a smith: A Meleager sarcophagus from a tomb in Ostia." *American Journal of Archaeology* 92(1): 85–99.

———. 2006. "Imitations of life: Style, theme and a sculptural collection in the Isola Sacra necropolis, Ostia." In *The Art of Citizens, Soldiers and Freedmen in the Roman World*, edited by E. D'Ambra and G.P.R. Métraux, 73–90. Oxford: Archaeopress.

Demand, N. 1995. "Monuments, midwives and gynecology." In *Ancient Medicine in its Socio-Cultural Context*, edited by P. J. van der Eijk, M. Horstmanshoff and P. Schrijvers, 275–290. Amsterdam: Rodopi.

Dierichs, A. 2002. *Von der Götter Geburt und der Frauen Niederkunft.* Mainz: Philip von Zabern.

Ewald, B.C. and P. Zanker 2012. *Living with Myths: The Imagery of Roman Sarcophagi.* Oxford: Oxford University Press.

Feraudi-Gruénais, F. 2003. *Inschriften und "Selbstdarstellung" in stadtrömischen Grabbauten.* Rome: Quasar.

Fowler, C. 2013. "Identities in transformation: Identities, funerary rites, and the mortuary process." In *The Oxford Handbook of the Archaeology of Death and Burial*, edited by L. Nilsson Stutz and S. Tarlow, 511–526. Oxford: Oxford University Press.

French, V. 1987. "Midwifes and maternity care in the Roman world." In *Rescuing Creusa: New Methodological Approaches to Women in Antiquity. Helios Special Issue*, edited by M. Skinner, 69–84. Lubbock TX: Classical Association of the Southwest.

Furedi, F. 2013. *Authority. A Sociological History*. Cambridge: Cambridge University Press.

George, M. 2013. "Cupid punished: Reflections on a Roman Genre Scene." In *Roman Slavery and Roman Material Culture*, edited by M. George, 158–179. Toronto: University of Toronto Press.

Gil, P.O. 2008. "Identificación de dos locales de distribución de vino y aceite en relieves de Isola Sacra (IPO A 169A=ISLIS 305; IPO A 169B=ISLIS 306)." *Espacio, Tiempo y Forma, Serie II, Historia Antigua*, 21, 2008, 235–254.

Giuliano, A., ed. 1981. *Museo Nazionale Romano. Le Sculture*, 2. Rome.

Graham, E.-J. 2005. "Dining al fresco with the living and the dead in Roman Italy." In *Consuming Passions: Dining from Antiquity to the Eighteenth Century*, edited by Maureen Carroll, D. M. Hadley and Hugh Willmott, 49–65. Stroud: Tempus.

———. 2006. *The Burial of the Urban Poor in Italy in the Late Roman Republic and Early Empire*. Oxford: Archaeopress.

Heinzelmann, M. 2000. *Die Nekropolen von Ostia—Untersuchungen zu den Gräberstraßen vor der Porta Romana und an der Via Laurentina*. Munich: F. Pfeil.

Helttula, A., ed. 2007. *Le iscrizioni sepolcrali latine nell'Isola Sacra*. Rome.

Herrmann-Otto, E. 1994. *Ex ancilla natus: Untersuchungen zu den "hausgeborenen" Sklaven und Sklavinnen im Westen des Römischen Kaiserreiches*. Stuttgart: Steiner.

Hope, V. M. 2009. *Roman Death: Dying and the Dead in Ancient Rome*. London/New York: Continuum.

———. 2011. "Remembering to Mourn: Personal Mementos of the Dead in Ancient Rome." In *Memory and Mourning: Studies on Roman Death*, edited by V. M. Hope and J. Huskinson, 176–195. Oxford: Oxbow.

Hope, V. M. and J. Huskinson, eds. 2011. *Memory and Mourning: Studies on Roman Death*, Oxford: Oxbow.

Joshel, S. R. 1992. *Work, Identity, and Legal Status at Rome. A Study of the Occupational Inscriptions*. Norman: University of Oklahoma Press.

Kampen, N. 1981. *Image and Status: Roman Working Women in Ostia*. Berlin: Mann.

Künzl, E. 1995. "Ein archäologisches Problem: Gräber römischer Chirurginnen." In *Ancient Medicine in its Socio-Cultural Context*, edited by P. J. van der Eijk, M. Horstmanshoff and P. Schrijvers, 309–319. Amsterdam: Rodopi.

Laes, C. 2010. "The educated midwife in the Roman Empire: An example of differential equations." In *Hippocrates and Medical Education*, edited by M. Horstmanshoff, 261–286. Selected Papers Presented at the XIIth International Hippocrates Colloquium, Universiteit Leiden, 24–26 August 2005. Leiden: Brill.

———. 2011. "Midwives in Greek Inscriptions in Hellenistic and Roman Antiquity." *Zeitschrift für Papyrologie und Epigraphik* 176: 154–162.

Lenski, N. 2013. "Working Models: Functional Art and Roman Conceptions of Slavery." In *Roman Slavery and Roman Material Culture*, edited by M. George, 129–157. Toronto/Buffalo/London: University of Toronto Press.

Lincoln, B. 1994. *Authority*. Chicago, IL: University of Chicago Press.

McCann, A. M. 1978. *Roman Sarcophagi in the Metropolitan Museum of Art*. New York: Metropolitan Museum of Art.

Nutton, V. 1992. "Healers in the Medical Market-place: Towards a Social History of Ancient Medicine." In *Medicine in Society: Historical Essays*, edited by A. Wear, 15–58. Cambridge: Cambridge University Press.

———. 2004. *Ancient Medicine*. London: Taylor and Francis.

Ogden, D. 2001. *Greek and Roman Necromancy*. Princeton, NJ: Princeton University Press.

———. 2002. *Magic, Witchcraft, and Ghosts in the Greek and Roman Worlds. A Sourcebook*. Oxford: Oxford University Press.

Olson, K. 2008. *Dress and the Roman Woman: Self-Presentation and Society*. London: Routledge.

Petersen, J. H. 2010. *Cultural Interactions and Social Strategies on the Pontic Shores. Burial Customs in the Northern Black Sea Area c. 550–270 BC*. Aarhus: Aarhus Universitetsforlag.

———. 2014. "Openness and "closedness" in Roman tomb architecture: Tomb E1 of the Via Laurentina necropolis at Ostia as a case study." In *ARID* (*ANALECTA ROMANA INSTITUTI DANICI*), XXXIX 2014, 27–48.

Petersen, L. H. 2006. *The Freedman in Roman Art and Art History*. Cambridge: Cambridge University Press.

Pleket, H. W. 1995. "The Social Status of Physicians in the Graeco-Roman World." In *Ancient Medicine in its Socio-cultural Context*, edited by P. J. van der Eijk, M. Horstmanshoff and P. Schrijvers, 27–34. Amsterdam: Rodopi.

Porter, A. J. 2016. "Compassion in Soranus' Gynecology and Caelius Aurelianus' On Chronic Diseases." In *Homo Patiens: Approaches to the Patient in the Ancient World*, edited by G. Petridou and C. Thumiger, 285–303. Leiden: Brill.

Rawson, B. 2003. *Children and Childhood in Roman Italy*. Oxford: Oxford University Press.

Rawson, B., ed. 2010. *A Companion to Families in the Greek and Roman Worlds*. Oxford: Wiley/Blackwell.

Russell, B. 2011. "The Roman sarcophagus 'Industry': A reconsideration." In *Life, Death and Representation: Some New Work on Roman Sarcophagi*, edited by J. Elsner, and J. Huskinson, 119–147. Berlin: Walter de Gruyter.

Sørensen, T. F. 2010, "A saturated void: Anticipating and preparing presence in contemporary Danish cemetery culture." In *An Anthropology of Absence: Materializations of Transcendence and Loss*, edited by Bille, M., F. Hastrup and T. F. Sørensen, 115–130. New York: Springer.

Tarlow, S. 1999. *Bereavement and Commemoration: An Archaeology of Mortality*. Oxford: Wiley/Blackwell.

Todman, D. 2007. "Childbirth in Ancient Rome: From traditional folklore to obstetrics." In *Australian and New Zealand Journal of Obstetrics and Gynaecology* 47(2), 82–85.

Toynbee, J.M.C. 1971. *Death and Burial in the Roman World*. Baltimore, MD: Johns Hopkins University Press.

Van Keuren, F. 2009. *The Marbles of Three Mythological Sarcophagi at RISD and of Other Sarcophagi Found in Central Italy* (with L. P. Gromet). In *KOINE: Mediterranean Studies in Honor of R. Ross Holloway*, edited by D. Counts and A. Tuck, 187–206. Oxford: Oxbow.

Van Keuren, F., D. Attanasio, J. J. Hermann Jr., N. Herz, and L. P. Gromet. 2011. "Multimethod analyses of Roman sarcophagi at the Museo Nazionale Romano, Rome." In *Life, Death and Representation: Some New Work on Roman Sarcophagi*, edited by J. Elsner and J. Huskinson, 149–188. Berlin: Walter de Gruyter.

Williams, C. A. 2012. *Reading Roman Friendship*. Cambridge: Cambridge University Press.

Zimmer G. 1982. *Römische Berufsdarstellungen*. Berlin: Archaeologische Forschungen, 12.

About the author

Jane Hjarl Petersen is Associate Professor at the University of Southern Denmark in classical archaeology. In 2010 she was the cofounder of the research network AVADIN (http://artefact.saxo.ku.dk/) concerned with the study of materiality of identities and their negotiation across and beyond the Mediterranean region. Currently undertaking a research project on Death and Identity in Ostia—A study of funerary material and cultural diversity in the port city of Rome, she has a keen interest in field work and has participated in excavations and field projects in Italy, Cyprus and the Black Sea region. Among her main areas of research are Material culture studies, Burial archaeology, Interactions between culturally diverse population groups, Identity and gender studies, and Terracotta and coroplastics studies.

— 6 —

The Resurrection of the Body: Authoritative Creed, Materiality, and Changes in Popular Belief in Denmark in the Eighteenth and Nineteenth Centuries

Martin Rheinheimer

This paper analyzes visual and written materials which indicate some of the interesting changes that the authoritative, Christian doctrine of bodily resurrection underwent in modernity. These materials document a growing gap between the authoritative creed and people's beliefs, which cannot, I argue, be attributed solely to intellectual changes, but which was also highly reliant on changes in material living conditions and medical and hygienic progress. The paper suggests that the belief in the resurrection of the body was quite firm in the general population even in the eighteenth century—the century of the Enlightenment, but that it faded towards the end of the nineteenth century due to changes in the material life conditions, such as medical progress and a decline in child mortality. My sources are gathered from the predominantly Lutheran former Duchy of Schleswig, and particularly from northern Friesland, and consist of personal letters, sermons, and visual sources such as church paintings and gravestone images. By means of selected examples, I investigate what the authoritative dogma of belief in the resurrection of the body meant to ordinary people. I trace the causes of this belief, and I discuss why it faded towards the end of the nineteenth century.

The Apostles' Creed

In the Apostles' Creed, Christians profess that they believe in "the resurrection of the body, and life everlasting." This is a translation of the final parts of the Latin original: "Credo in Spiritum Sanctum, sanctam Ecclesiam catholicam, sanctorum communionem, remissionem peccatorum, carnis resurrectionem, vitam aeternam." Today, in a secularized, scientific world, in all likelihood only a few Christians believe in this officially authoritative profession of bodily resurrection in a literal sense, or in senses which are in alignment with official theological teachings on the subject. The idea of a firm belief in the creed of the resurrection of the body makes it difficult for us to understand people of earlier centuries. However, we have to remember that in addition to official religion, unofficial concepts and practices have invariably existed alongside the authoritative texts and views (McGuire 2008, 19–44). In medieval and early modern times, belief was not necessarily literal, and naturally it could differ from person to person. A famous example is Ginzburg's miller who had his own opinions about religion and belief (Ginzburg 1980). In this paper, I will discuss visual and written materials which indicate some of the interesting changes that the idea of bodily resurrection underwent in modernity. These materials document a growing gap between the authoritative creed and people's beliefs, which cannot, I argue, be attributed solely to intellectual changes, but which was also highly reliant on changes in material living conditions and medical and hygienic progress.

So, what *did* people believe? Some written and visual sources offer information in this regard. In the following, I want to show that the belief in the resurrection of the body was quite firm in the general population even in the eighteenth century—the century of the Enlightenment. To this end, I will use some examples from the former Duchy of Schleswig, and particularly from northern Friesland. The duchy was then in a personal union with the Kingdom of Denmark and, with the exception of a few very small minorities, purely Lutheran by confession. By means of the examples, I investigate what the belief in the resurrection of the body meant to people in their everyday lives. I will trace the causes of this belief, and reflect on why it faded towards the end of the nineteenth century. I have deliberately chosen examples of people who are not educated theologians in order to document the piety of ordinary people. A surprising number of testimonials of such people exist, but researchers have not yet analysed them.

Before we delve into the examples, we need to establish an understanding of how people imagined life after death historically. Afterwards, I contextualize my investigation by examining people's faith within the context of the broader demographic and social historical developments of the eighteenth century, before I move on to a closer look at specific death experiences and how they were managed during this era. Here, the question arises of how and to what extent the beliefs of specific individuals were shared with the general population. To that end, I look at selected visual sources such as paintings in churches and images on gravestones which illustrate the resurrection and key ideas about life after death. The analysis of visual material can help illustrate not only key developments in people's beliefs historically, but also how central faith doctrines were disseminated and changed. Finally, I will discuss why the belief in the resurrection of the body seems to disappear in the nineteenth century. In this study, visual culture is especially important as source material, because images acted as media for religious beliefs which were—for a certain time period—predominant and authoritative, after which they again disappeared.

The afterlife

Historically, the idea of an eternal life in heaven after death has had an enormous influence on understandings of life on earth in Western Europe. The current, finite life was, in comparison to eternity, brief. Therefore, it was seen as crucial to make sure that one went to heaven, so as not to have to spend eternity in hell. The troubles and sufferings of earthly life, including the death of close relatives, were seen as small and easily endured from the perspective of eternity, if eternal bliss beckoned in heaven. Plausibly, doubts about the power of God stemming from the poor circumstances of life on earth—injustice, suffering and death—disappeared in the face of the idea of the resurrection of the body.

The belief in the resurrection of the dead has changed several times across the centuries. Although death has often been treated from an ethnological point of view, the religious aspects have, in historical studies, often been reduced to a focus on death rituals, usually the funeral (best known is Ariès 1977, but cf. e.g. also Kragh 2003). Typically, historical investigations have focused on cemeteries and gravestones. Faith and eternal life are issues which have not regularly been the object of historical research. An exception is Colleen McDannell's and Bernhard Lang's history of heaven (McDannell and Lang 1988). Other scholars have done important research on special periods of time. Peter Brown has offered insights on early western Christianity, and Jacques Le Goff wrote a famous book on the birth of purgatory in medieval times (Le Goff 1984; Brown 2015; cf. also Bremmer 2002).

In most periods of history, Christians have imagined that eternal life would take place in the presence and proximity of God after death and Last Judgment. In the eighteenth century, however, many people believed in a bodily resurrection, as the Apostles' Creed suggests. They therefore imagined that they would meet their departed loved ones again in the afterlife. This understanding goes back to Augustine (McDannell and Lang 1988, 61). The Protestant reformers believed that there would be a reunion in heaven, but suggested that marriage and family would lose their meaning there, in the presence of God (McDannell and Lang 1988, 154–155,

178–180). According to Colleen McDannell and Bernhard Lang, these views of life after death prevailed until "the 18th century ushered in the modern heaven with its emphasis on the nearness of the next world to this one, its material character, and its acceptance of human love and progress." They continue: "With the nineteenth century came the apex of the anthropocentric heaven. A wide variety of preachers, theologians, poets, and popular writers depicted heaven as a social community where the saints meet their relatives and friends. The union of God and the soul after death gave way to the union of the lover and the beloved. Ideas of productive work, spiritual development, and technological progress contributed to the completeness of the other-worldly society" (McDannell and Lang 1988, 356).

The primary media in which these ideas—and concomitantly the authoritative text of the dogma—were communicated and disseminated in Northern Europe were oral (sermons), written (letters, books of devotion) and visual (gravestones, wall and ceiling paintings in churches). Examples of such media can be seen in the churches of Møgeltønder and Ubjerg where paintings show how the dead physically rise from their graves at the Final Judgment. Both church paintings date from the first half of the eighteenth century. Before we look more closely at selected examples, we need to look at the social conditions of the eighteenth century, and that means, above all, the demographic structures.

Child mortality

Until the nineteenth century, the infant mortality rate was very high. Throughout Western Europe between fifteen and twenty-five percent of children died within their first year. Another ten to fifteen percent of children died before the age of ten. Between a third and forty percent of the population thus died in childhood, and up to a quarter already as infants. There were regional differences, but the overall picture is quite uniform (Knodel 1988, 35–69; Gehrmann 2000, 142–148; Johansen 2002, 63–66; Løkke 1998, 119–124; Wrigley *et al.* 1997, 214–280). Also later in life, mortality remained high as relatively young people died from infections and epidemics and many women died in childbirth.

In seafaring regions, the high mortality at sea must be added. Here, often as many as twenty percent of the men died in shipwrecks, accidents or diseases (Rheinheimer 2016a, 174–175). Families never knew whether the provider would return from his trip and the sailor did not know whether his wife and children would still be alive when he came home, because many women died in childbirth, and epidemics snatched whole families away. In 1629, the first year of his duty on Amrum, the reverend Martin Flor had to bury 147 people who had died of the plague (Rheinheimer 2016a, 73). The absent sailors survived, but their wives and children were dead when they returned to the island.

Ipke Petersen (1744–1817) and his wife Angens (1747–1829) are exemplary with regard to such a situation. The couple lived on the little North Frisian island Oland, where they married in 1770. They were affected by the high mortality rate. Their first two children, Peter (I) and Vollig Christina (I), died one and a half and two years old in 1774 and 1776. The parents gave the same names to the next children. Later, two sons, Broder Frerck and Nahne Johannes, died of an epidemic in Malaga a few days apart in October 1803 at the age of only 21 and 19. The son Peter (II) died as a skipper in a shipwreck not far from Riga, probably on 6 October 1805, together with his mate, who also came from Oland. He was 25 years of age. Only one of the couple's six children survived the parents and gave birth to her own children, namely their daughter Vollig Christina (II), who married Frerk Paulsen in 1800; he was the son of the Oland captain Paul Frerksen. She died on the mainland in Loheide in 1848 (Rheinheimer 2016b, 25, 75).

How could the couple cope with all these misfortunes? The belief in the resurrection of the body, and the connected idea that one would meet one's relatives again in the afterlife probably made the death of young children and other close relatives easier to bear. Ipke and Angens offer an interesting example, because an exchange of letters and other writings of theirs has been preserved which document their feelings and reactions to death.

Mediating death experiences and beliefs: Treatises and letters

How could people cope with the early death of children? Private letters and treatises written by common people show that they functioned as media for religious reflection on authoritative beliefs and dogmas. The reverend Reinhold Ipsen, Angens' stepfather, expressed his condolences to the parents in a letter: "In fact, the decease of your small Ipke and Vollig Christina moved me deeply. However, this must be your greatest consolation that you can hope to find them again in heaven. At the death of my beloved little Broder, someone comforted me with the words: Reverend, we believe in the resurrection of the body and life everlasting, don't we? That was very awakening to me. It is really the best consolation. How God's ways are still wonderful" (Rheinheimer 2015, 40).[1] The belief in a life after death contributed to making the death of children and the hardships of life bearable.

What seems unbearable to us today, the death of small children, and the many sons, husbands, and lovers lost at sea, was easier to endure as a result

1. All translations in this paper are by the author, Martin Rheinheimer.

of the belief in the resurrection of the body. Therefore, in many seafaring regions people turned strongly to religion (Rheinheimer 2016b, 84). Ipke Petersen became a religious fanatic in the last years of his life, according to the church records. In the face of the intolerable, he sought refuge in faith. In the era of late pietism, on the island of Oland other people were religiously awakened, too. Among these we find the captain Paul Frerksen and his son Frerk who married Angens' and Ipkes' daughter Vollig Christina in 1800. They both wrote religious treatises on their awakening (Rheinheimer 2012, 63–65). When his two sons died in 1803, Ipke wrote a long religious treatise, too. Here he reinterpreted the death of his two sons in 1803 as an "experience of grace." In December, he wrote: "With the death of two of my beloved sons at once; oh Father, Father, this is a painful blow you have made for your children. May earth and every creature mourn for the loss of my dear children! But this must be so to the honour of your Creator; we had them dear and precious and would have liked to keep them, but you had them even dearer, my Father; therefore, we hope and believe confidently because you are present everywhere. You have accepted them for their faith, for Christ's will accept them in grace, and let them come to rest according to your promise Isa 57, v. 1. So rest in your chambers, sweethearts. We will come to you soon" (Rheinheimer 2016b, 78). Faith gave Ipke the force to live on in the face of these misfortunes.

Health was a precarious matter in the eighteenth century. When Ipke wrote in a letter to his wife, "I close in a hurry and hope it finds you healthy and calm" (Rheinheimer 2016b, 111), this was a genuine and concrete concern. Angens had similar thoughts. In April 1792, when Ipke wrote—enthusiastically—that he had received a ship and had now become a skipper (captain), Angens brought him down to earth by straightening his priorities: "The thing dearest to me is that you have had a comfortable journey and that my love was and may remain healthy in spite of all blows. We are—thank God—all safe and sound." Only at the end of the letter she writes: "Well, my dear, I wish you a blessed and godly beginning when it has come so far that we can call our dear father a skipper" (Rheinheimer 2016b, 124–125).

It seems that Ipke foresaw the early death of his sons when he met two of them in Altona in June 1801: "Now we three are together in father's cabin. My Lord, let us healthily and happily come together once again" (Rheinheimer 2016b, 144).

In 1812, Ipke still wrote in terms of a "profession of faith" with respect to the death of his sons: "Our three deceased sons have assisted us childlike and in greatest obedience. That they now live with you in heaven, and reap your and our child's blessings, that we do not doubt, because we have referred them to you, Lord Jesus, you, the world's conciliator and God when sin and guilt pressured them. We have seen in their lifetime that you accepted them" (Rheinheimer 2016b, 80).

Ipke ponders on the eternal bliss: "I will prepare myself for death, lie down constantly in faith before the feet of Jesus, now at his crib, looking at him as Mary's and God's son, as my Saviour. I want to beg of him, Lord Jesus, because I am now concerned about the nobility of my soul that it may return to the bliss of when it was first created. I beg you, my pastor, act with eagerness, earnestness, and true thoughts to provide for my soul, Lord Jesus, I pray thee, [...] for my good holy birth, when it's your time, then bring my soul for your adopted office to God, to its first blessed origin of which it is needy" (Rheinheimer 2016b, 81).

These letters show how the belief in a life after death made the death of the children and the hardships of life bearable, and how the belief in the resurrection of the body was quite literal. So Angens wrote about the separation from her seafaring husband: "We are delighted that when this life is expired, we will, in the next life, ceaselessly live together in heavenly joy" (Rheinheimer 2016b, 128). Angens also imagined the eternal life after death very concretely as a physical meeting and reunion with her family. At the same time, the terror of not going to heaven and having to spend eternity in hell was great.

Visual culture and the resurrection

Another medium for dissemination of the belief about the resurrection of the dead was paintings. They made it possible to convey religious ideas and imaginations to people who could neither read nor write. In the paintings, the resurrection had to be personalized in order to be depicted.

In the Kingdom of Denmark and the Duchy of Schleswig we find many churches where the Last Judgment and the resurrection of the body are presented on medieval wall paintings. Images can be found in village churches, for example in Østerlars on Bornholm, in Elmelunde and Keldby on Møn, in Maria Magdalene in Djursland, but also in Broager and Süderlügum in the Duchy of Schleswig. We also find such representations in the Church of the Holy Spirit and St John's Church in Flensburg or in the cathedral of Schleswig. Later, famous artists of European art history adopted the scene. In 1499–1502, Luca Signorelli painted the fresco "La resurrezione della carne" in the cathedral of Orvieto. Most famous is, surely, Michelangelo's Last Judgement in the Sistine Chapel which the artist finished in 1541.

In the eighteenth century, the scene became popular again. On the mainland of western Schleswig, we find large ceiling paintings depicting the Last Judgment with the resurrection of the dead in two village churches near Tønder, i.e., in the churches of Møgeltønder (1737) and Ubjerg (1747) (Moltke and Møller 1957, 361–362, 377). In these pictures, the dead rise physically from their graves to be sentenced to heaven or hell. The same motif can be seen on two large paintings in the Old Church (1735) and the New Church (1773) of Pellworm, an island close to Oland. On Pellworm, the local court was situated. So, it is very likely that Ipke Petersen has seen them (Figure 6.1).

The motif of the resurrection could also be applied to specific individuals. Thus, in the church of Oland, we find an epitaph for the skipper Ipke Paulsen which was painted around 1700. The image depicts Ipke Paulsen's shipwreck. Above the sinking ship (right) a cry is written: "Domine, serva nos, perimus" (Lord, save us, we are drowning). The crucified Christ answers: "Qui credit in me, vivet" (He who believes in me will live). At the top right, protruding from the clouds, an arm is holding a crown in its hand. Those

Figure 6.1 Final Judgment with the resurrection of the dead on a ceiling painting in Møgeltønder church (1737). Photo M. R.

who believe are saved and rewarded. The family of Ipke Paulsen kneels under Christ crucified. Here, both the living and the dead, marked with a cross, are represented as united in the belief in the resurrection of the dead (Brauer, Scheffler, and Weber 1939, 191–192). In this representation too, the resurrection of the body is implicit, because how else could the living and the dead both be present? Ipke and Angens, as well as the Pastor Reinhold Ipsen, knew this picture which so directly represents the physical resurrection, as it could be seen in their church every day, in a time otherwise poor in pictures. Reinhold Ipsen, like his father before him, had himself functioned as a reverend in this church (Figure 6.2).

This scene can also be found on gravestones.

Figure 6.2 Epitaph for skipper Ipke Paulsen in Oland church (circa 1700). The deceased is depicted with his wife and all his living and deceased children. Photo M. R.

Gravestones and ideas of salvation

On the North Frisian Islands, many gravestones with long inscriptions and pictures have been preserved from the seventeenth, eighteenth and nineteenth centuries. The biography of the deceased is usually placed in the context of salvation history, and the resurrection of the body is commonly mentioned. On the island of Amrum we find numerous examples. The gravestone of Hark Olufs (1708–1754) is an interesting example. Hark Olufs probably converted to Islam during his captivity in Algiers (Rheinheimer 2001), but nonetheless the following text is written: "God grant the / body a happy / resurrection at the last day" (Quedens 2009, 42).[2] Again, the resurrection of the body is explicitly mentioned.

At the end of the inscription on the gravestone of Knudt Knudten (1712–1761) we find the following expression of an implicit confidence in the resurrection of the body: "Therefore stop mourning / Soon we find each other again" (Quedens 2009, 96). Such expressions seem genre-bound and formulaic, but at the same time they reflect individual life situations and express individual beliefs. The gravestone of Kerrin Erken (1728–1749) likewise proclaimed the hope of a reunion in heaven. Kerrin had died at childbirth at an age of only 21 years, and her daughter followed her into the grave a few weeks later. The bereaved widower summarized his grief in words and had them carved on the gravestone: "O moaning sorrow / when faithful hearts separate / Here lies the trunk and the branch / the mother with the child / My consolation is that I find them / in heaven again" (Quedens 2009, 120).

On the gravestone of Andres Fink (1678–1738) and his wife Marret, we find an image of the resurrection. The stone is 148 cm high and 74 cm wide. On the front, the crucified Christ is depicted over the family (11 people). The inscription says:

"The blood of Jesus Christ cleanses us from all our sins // I. N. R. I. // Here the bones expect / a happy resurrection of / late skipper Andres Finck, so / born on Amrom Ao. 1678 20 May, entered in / matrimony with Marret Tückis / there in 1705, in lasting marriage / together begotten 7 children as 4 sons / and 3 daughters, of whom 3 sons and 2 daugh/ters are already gone into the blessed eternity. / Died Ao. 1738 3rd Decem. / of his age 60 years 7 months and 13 days / as well as his wife / Marret Andresens / so born Ao. 1679 21 July / died. Ao. 17—of her age /—years—months / I. S. G. G. I. [Their souls God is merciful.]" On the reverse, a Wadden Sea ship is shown moving towards the right. The inscription says: "As a skipper I have sailed / many years and a long time / with people, also merchant goods / to the

2. Again, as with all translations in this paper, the translation is by the author, Martin Rheinheimer.

Elbe, Weser and elsewhere / on the way also endured / much concern day and night / on the sea and on the beaches / to rest God has brought me / Andres Finck / Ao. 1740" (Quedens 2009, 60–63).

The picture on the gravestone calls to mind Ipke Paulsen's epitaph. Similarly, the couple and their nine children (five boys and four girls) are depicted on the gravestone. This raises doubts as the inscription talks about only seven children. The explanation is that the children originated from two marriages (Rheinheimer 2010, nr. 134. 5). The first marriage is not mentioned on the gravestone with a single word. The children of the first marriage are thus concealed in the text, but shown on the picture. The first wife, Ehlen, had died in 1704 and had left Andres Fink as a widower with two young children. The following year, he married his second wife Marret, and the third child was born already in August 1705. Later, the descendants "forgot" to add the date of the death of the first wife on the gravestone. This shows that the relationship among stepchildren and stepparents could be quite difficult in practice.

Since some of the children had died before others were born, they had not all lived at the same time. They could first meet each other after their bodily resurrection, as shown on the picture. To illustrate this, the crucified Christ is shown above them and a skull and bones lies in front of them. The inscription also says that "the bones expect a happy resurrection." As people might wonder whether they deserved it at all, a logo above the picture states: "The blood of Jesus Christ cleanses us from all our sins." Thus, there were no obstacles to a bodily resurrection.

On this gravestone, the reunion in heaven also highlights a problem—that the deceased had been married twice. A resurrection of the bodies would thus mean that he would have two wives in heaven at the same time—which would make him a bigamist. Therefore, only the second marriage is mentioned on the inscription. The children from both marriages stand under the resurrected Jesus, but only the second wife is depicted. What is the matter with the first? Is she denied resurrection at the final judgment in order to solve the problem of two marriages in heaven?

This issue was mostly a problem for theologians. The widow in the former example tried to solve it by omitting the first wife. However, this was not always the solution to the problem. On the more northerly island of Rømø, gravestones can be found on which both wives are depicted beside the deceased, and this was obviously not a problem for the bereaved. The gravestones of Peder Jørgensen Bundes († 1771), Laust Laussen († 1753), Peder Laustsen and Niels Pedersen Alheyt († 1768) are fine examples (Falk 1988, 34–35, 74–75, 78–79, 80–83). This shows that understanding the

Figure 6.3 Gravestone of Andres Fink († 1738) at Amrum cemetery. Here the deceased is shown with his second wife only, but all of his nine children from both of his marriages are depicted. Photo M. R.

situation of the one husband and the two wives in eternity as a real problem was mainly a result of the personal belief of Andres Fink's widow—it was she who had the stone erected (Figure 6.3).

On the island of Föhr, gravestones depict the resurrection of the body in a very concrete way. For example, the gravestone of Catrina Boyens (1715–1747) shows the deceased standing on a cloud and saying goodbye to her husband who is standing next to three daughters and a son, while she is welcomed by Christ in front of the heavenly Jerusalem (Lüden 1984, 58–59). Another gravestone from Föhr shows the Final Judgment. Under a depiction of the heavenly Jerusalem, Jesus stands as judge in the clouds, and below him an angel is placed between the chosen and the damned. This gravestone was, like the others, carved in the eighteenth century, but its original inscription has been abraded, and the person for whom the gravestone was once produced is not known anymore. Under the picture the following words are preserved: "Jesus Christ himself, God's son / Will open me the door to heaven / lead me to eternal life" (Lüden 1984, 128—my translation). As we can see here, even the heavenly Jerusalem was imagined physically. In Boldixum, on the island of Föhr, the beautiful gravestone of whaling commander Hay Jürgens (1708–1771) and his wife shows his now rigged off vessel on the left and the heavenly Jerusalem in the clouds on the right.

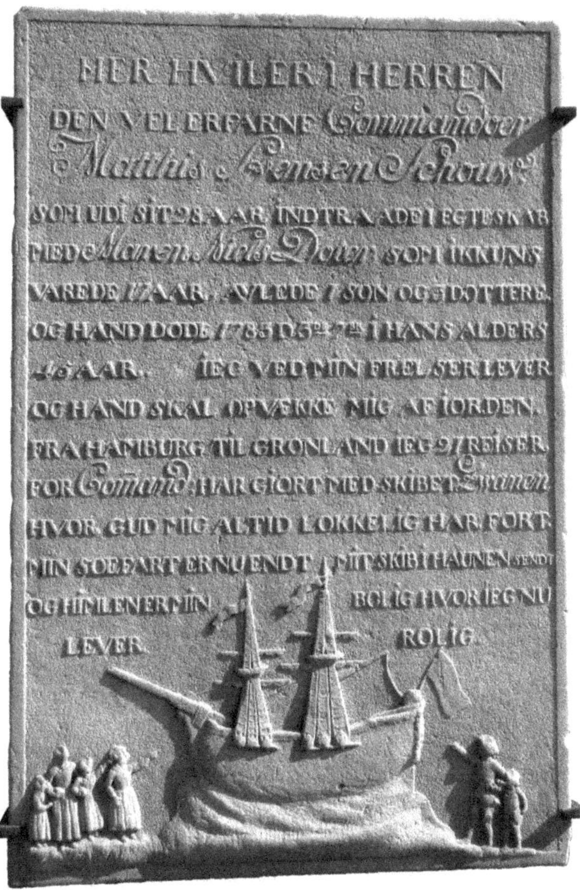

Figure 6.4 Gravestone of Matthis Svensen Schouw († 1783) at Rømø cemetery. Here the deceased is shown with this son to the right, and his wife and their three daughters to the left. Photo M. R.

Above it is written: “The last journey went to heaven / from this vile turmoil of the world“ (Lüden 1984, 82–83).

On the gravestone of whaling commander Matthis Svensen Schouw (1738–1783) on Rømø, the beginning of the inscription reads: “I know my saviour lives / and he will wake me up from earth.” At the end the inscription says “My voyage is now over, my ship is sent to harbour, and heaven is my residence, where I now live quietly.” Under this inscription, his ship is depicted. On the left, his widow and three daughters are waving, on the right he and his son wave (Falk 1988, 56–57—my translation). Again, all are displayed simultaneously alive, which plausibly indicates a belief that they are all in heaven or will be there in the future (Figure 6.4 and Figure 6.5).

Figure 6.5 Gravestone of Peder Laustsen at Rømø cemetery. Here the deceased is shown with his two wives and five children. Photo M. R.

Changes since the end of the nineteenth century

This sort of belief in the resurrection of the body began to change rapidly and disappeared towards the end of the nineteenth century. Usually, this development is understood in the context of the Enlightenment and the theological response. Thus, the quest for the historical Jesus from around 1750 questioned the reality of the resurrection of Jesus (for instance J. F. Bardt in the late eighteenth and Schleiermacher in the early nineteenth century).

The changing tides can already be perceived in the doubts of the enlightened and educated reverend Reinhold Ipsen, who had to be reminded of the core of the faith by a parishioner. “At the death of my beloved little Broder, someone comforted me with the words: Reverend, we believe in the resurrection of the body and life everlasting, don’t we? That was very awakening to me. It is really the best consolation. How God’s ways are still wonderful” (Rheinheimer 2015, 40). Actually, as a trained theologian and reverend, Reinhold Ipsen should have known this better than an ordinary parishioner. But perhaps exactly for that reason, he no longer believed in a physical resurrection of the body.

However, for the general population there was another reason: the decline in mortality, especially child mortality. The decline came about at the same time as the belief in the resurrection of the body waned and disappeared. The decline in infant and child mortality began in Germany and Denmark around 1890. It fell rapidly to its current rate which is below 0.5 percent (Johansen 2002, 184–190; Løkke 1998, 119–124). The hygienic and medical progress was accompanied by a change in attitude. The high infant and child mortality rates were no longer accepted as given by God; it was now seen as a duty for society, parents and doctors to solve this social, hygienic and medical problem (Løkke 1998, 464). As the constant threat of death was diminished, beliefs that helped to cope in the face of the death of one’s family were not required to the same extent anymore.

Coinciding with the demographic transitions, the Enlightenment brought new concepts of identity: the nation state and scientific thinking. Darwin’s theory of evolution and the idea of the descent of man from apes questioned the Bible as such, creating doubt about its literal truth. If the myth of creation was no longer valid, perhaps the doctrine of the resurrection of the body was also wrong, or, at least, it needed to be understood in a different way.

At the same time, changes in the school system took place. Since the Reformation, the catechism, hymns, and the Bible had been the main textbooks. Reading and writing were primarily taught in order to enable people to read the Bible. According to Luther, a person’s faith was based on the reading of the Bible and this was a prerequisite for going to heaven.

Around 1800, the school system was reformed. This only took place slowly. History and science did not enter the curricula of primary schools until the mid-nineteenth century. At the end of the nineteenth century, church and state were separated in Germany, as in Catholic France. Even though religion was still a teaching subject in Germany, the schools now came under state supervision (Geißler 2013, 51, 125–126, 203; Appel and Coninck-Smith 2013–2015, vol. 1–3). These changes in the school system were a prerequisite for a broader decline in the belief in authoritative Christian dogmas, as well as for their reinterpretation and new attributions of meaning. Of course, the belief in the resurrection of the body did not completely disappear everywhere; some groups did preserve it, in others it was re-interpreted, spiritualized, etc., even if the general picture is one of decline.

The high mortality rate, especially of children, but also of sailors, thus formed part of the reasons behind the decline in and transformations of the modern belief in the resurrection of the body. When mortality declined, this belief disappeared too, or was transformed radically. The prevailing social-material conditions were the cause of the change of key, authoritative Christian dogmas. People were able to cope with the social conditions because faith created a hope for the afterlife. We can observe similar connections already in the early days of Christianity. In the times of the persecutions of Christians, church fathers like Irenaeus imagined that a new life after death awaited the martyr. To him, heaven was "the glorified material world" (McDannell and Lang 1988, 67; cf. 48–53). This was one way to cope with the persecutions from a minority position and to endure martyrdom. This belief changed with the decline of the persecutions, and Irenaeus was barely read for many years. In the nineteenth century, he was, however, rediscovered, and in Denmark, N.F.S. Grundtvig (1783–1872) translated his book on the resurrection of the body and the eternal life (Grundtvig 1855)—at a time when the faith began to change again.

References

Appel, Charlotte and Ning de Coninck-Smith, ed. 2013–2015. *Dansk skolehistorie. Hverdag, vilkår og visioner gennem 500 år.* 5 volumes. Aarhus: Aarhus Universitetsforlag.

Ariès, Philippe. 1977. *L'homme devant la mort.* Paris: Seuil. (English edition: *The Hour of Our Death.* New York: Vintage Books, 1982).

Brauer, Heinrich, Wolfgang Scheffler and Hans Weber. 1939. *Die Kunstdenkmäler des Kreises Husum.* Berlin: Deutscher Kunstverlag.

Bremmer, Jan N. 2002. *The Rise and Fall of the Afterlife.* London: Routledge.

Brown, Peter. 2015. *The Ransom of the Soul: Afterlife and Wealth in Early Western Christianity.* Cambridge, MA: Harvard University Press.

Falk, Fritz Joachim. [1988]. *Gamle kommandørsten på Rømø i ord og billeder.* Skærbæk: Foreningen "Venner af Rømøs Natur".

Gehrmann, Rolf. 2000. *Bevölkerungsgeschichte Norddeutschlands zwischen Aufklärung und Vormärz.* Berlin: Berlin Verlag Arno Spitz.

Geißler, Gert. 2013. *Schulgeschichte in Deutschland. Von den Anfängen bis in die Gegenwart.* 2nd edition. Frankfurt am Main: Peter Lang.

Ginzburg, Carlo. 1980. *The Cheese and the Worms: The Cosmos of a Sixteenth-Century Miller.* London: Routledge & Kegan Paul.

Grundtvig, N.F.S., trans. 1855. *Om Kiødets Opstandelse og det evige Liv af Biskop Irenæus.* Kjøbenhavn: Møller.

Johansen, Hans C. 2002. *Danish Population History 1600–1939.* Odense: University Press of Southern Denmark.

Knodel, John E. 1988. *Demographic Behavior in the Past: A Study of Fourteen German village Populations in the Eighteenth and Nineteenth Centuries.* Cambridge: Cambridge University Press.

Kragh, Birgitte. 2003. *Til jord skal du blive ... Dødens og begravelsens kulturhistorie i Danmark 1780–1990.* Aabenraa: Museumsrådet for Sønderjyllands Amt.

Le Goff, Jacques. 1984. *The Birth of Purgatory.* Aldershot: Scholar's Press.

Løkke, Anne. 1998. *Døden i barndommen. Spædbørnsdødelighed og moderniseringsprocesser i Danmark 1800 til 1920.* København: Gyldendal.

Lüden, Walter. 1984. *"Redende Steine": Grabsteine auf der Insel Föhr.* Hamburg: Christians Verlag.

McDannell, Colleen and Bernhard Lang. 1988. *Heaven: A History.* New Haven, CT: Yale University Press.

McGuire, Meredith B. 2008. *Lived Religion: Faith and Practice in Everyday Life.* Oxford: Oxford University Press.

Moltke, Erik, and Elna Møller. 1957. *Danmarks kirker. Sønderjylland, XXI. Tønder Amt.* København: G.E.C. Gads Forlag.

Quedens, Georg. 2009. *Im Hafen der Ewigkeit. Die alten Grabsteine auf dem Amrumer Friedhof.* 3rd edition. Amrum: Jens Quedens Verlag.

Rheinheimer, Martin. 2001. *Der fremde Sohn. Hark Olufs' Wiederkehr aus der Sklaverei.* Neumünster: Wachholtz Verlag.

———. 2010. *Geschlechterreihen der Insel Amrum 1694–1918.* Amrum: Verlag Jens Quedens.

———. 2012. "Nordfriesische Seeleute in der Amsterdamer Handelsfahrt." *Zeitschrift der Gesellschaft für Schleswig-Holsteinische* Geschichte 137: 31–77.

———. 2015. "Briefe des Querner Pastors Reinhold Ipsen an seine Oländer Verwandten." *Rundbrief des Arbeitskreises für Wirtschafts- und Sozialgeschichte Schleswig-Holsteins* 115: 27–44.

———. 2016a. *Die Insel und das Meer. Seefahrt und Gesellschaft auf Amrum 1700–1860.* Stuttgart: Franz Steiner Verlag.

———. 2016b. *Ipke und Angens. Die Welt eines nordfriesischen Schiffers und seiner Frau (1787–1801).* Stuttgart: Franz Steiner Verlag.

Wrigley, E. A., R. S. Davies, J. E. Oeppen and R. S. Schofield. 1997. *English Population History from Family Reconstitution 1580–1837*. Cambridge: Cambridge University Press.

About the author

Martin Rheinheimer is a Professor of Maritime and Regional History and the Head of Department of the Department of History at the University of Southern Denmark. He holds a Dr. phil. in medieval history and a Dr. habil. in early modern history. In the last years he has published books on the maritime history of the North Sea islands, most recently: *Die Insel und das Meer: Seefahrt und Gesellschaft auf Amrum 1700–1860*, Stuttgart: Steiner (2016); *Ipke und Angens: Die Welt eines nordfriesischen Schiffers und seiner Frau (1787–1801)*, Stuttgart: Steiner (2016).

— 7 —

Myth, Materiality, and Book of Mormon Apologetics: A Sacred Text and its Interpreters

Olav Hammer

The Book of Mormon, first published in 1830, presents a detailed account of the migration of several groups from the ancient Near East to the Americas, and how these groups became the ancestors of the Native Americans. The description of these migrations fits well with common early nineteenth-century beliefs about the origins of the indigenous populations of America, but contradicts in numerous ways the scientific consensus that emerged roughly a century ago. Key apologists have constructed a range of arguments for the literal truth of the Book of Mormon account. This paper examines the structure of a number of common apologetic arguments, and shows how interpretive commentary can project new meanings on a canonical text.

"I told the brethren that the Book of Mormon was the most correct of any book on earth..."

(Joseph Smith, quoted in the Introduction to the Book of Mormon)

The materiality of the past and the authority to interpret it[1]

In 1830, Joseph Smith published the Book of Mormon, a text purportedly translated from an ancient record engraved on golden plates, describing the fortunes of various peoples of Near Eastern origin that populated the Americas: the Nephites, Lamanites, Mulekites, and Jaredites.[2] The Jaredites were first, migrating across the ocean shortly after the Tower of Babel inci-

1. This paper is a highly condensed version of a discussion of Mormon interpretations in my forthcoming monograph on alternative archaeology with the working title *Alternative Archaeology: Modern Myths of the Distant Past.*
2. It would be very cumbersome to qualify each passage that relates what the Book of Mormon says, or what a particular apologist has written, with expressions such as "purportedly" or "according to the sources." The quasi-factual language employed in many places in the present chapter in no way implies that I am addressing, much less endorsing, the truth claims of those sources.

dent. Much later, on the eve of the Babylonian captivity, other groups travelled to the New World. They spread out over the land, split into opposing factions, created cities, fought battles, and came to a downfall in cataclysmic wars. The survivors of the last of these conflicts are among the ancestors of the Native Americans. The Book of Mormon account of these peoples is studded with descriptions of particular geographical sites, names of people and places, reports of wars, and indications of their material culture and way of life. This alternative history of the ancient Americas has throughout Mormon history been taken at face value by the vast majority of Latter-Day Saints. At the same time, the Book of Mormon account would seem to contradict most of what non-Mormon researchers have been able to document about American prehistory. Outside the Mormon community, the idea that the Nephites created vast cities or that the Lamanites were among the forefathers of the Native Americans is universally rejected.

Faced with such massive opposition, how can Mormons assert with utter conviction that the Book of Mormon is correct? Fundamentally, the answer has to do with Mormon beliefs concerning continuing small-scale revelations. It is commonly claimed that prayer will result in an answer from God, an inner certitude that the message of the Book of Mormon is true. This belief in the power of prayer is in part grounded in a self-referential passage, where the reader is exhorted to ask God with a "sincere heart" if the account is true (Moroni 10:4):

> And when ye shall receive these things, I would exhort you that ye would ask God, the Eternal Father, in the name of Christ, if these things are not true; and if ye shall ask with a sincere heart, with real intent, having faith in Christ, he will manifest the truth of it unto you, by the power of the Holy Ghost.

This claim is reiterated in the Introduction to the text of the Book of Mormon. Nowhere in this brief prelude to the Book of Mormon is there any mention of finding material evidence for the historical narrative. Rather, "We invite all men [sic!] everywhere to read the Book of Mormon, to ponder in their hearts the message it contains, and then to ask God, the Eternal Father, in the name of Christ if the book is true."

Such exhortations to find validation of the Book of Mormon through prayer notwithstanding, there have been countless attempts by members of the Mormon community to answer questions about the empirical claims of the text by discussing potential links between the world within the text and material evidence from fields such as archaeology, anthropology, DNA analysis, and paleontology. This apologetic literature asserts the authority of its authors to elucidate both the "true" significance of material objects and material geographical features, and the "real" meaning of relevant Book of Mormon passages. Bruce Lincoln (1994) suggests that authority occupies a middle ground between coercion on the one hand and rational persuasion on the other. As will become apparent, Mormon apologetic discourse appears significantly closer to the rational persuasion end of this continuum. Evidence is presented, references are quoted, and counterarguments are defused. What makes this literature an example of authoritative discourse rather than of rational argumentation, is that it is only treated as plausible by Mormon religious insiders.

Nothing in the literature for and against the historicity of the Book of Mormon suggests that authority figures on either side are making any serious dent in the arguments of their opponents. Rather, the import of particular data is judged on the background of the naturalistic or religious world view that each side already holds, while that world view is conversely understood to be strengthened by the specific data adduced. This method of drawing conclusions and assessing claims within a given milieu and within a shared paradigm is closely related to a common hypothesis-testing heuristic, Bayesian inference.

On differential standards of rationality and Bayesian inference

Thomas Bayes' (1701–1761) main claim to fame is the development of a mathematical equation used to evaluate the probability of an event, given the background knowledge that one already has. An informal, non-mathematical version of Bayes' approach to probability is used by all of us in assessing new evidence in relation to our background assumptions about how the world works. Whether we are conscious of it or not, we judge evidence in relation to the beliefs we already hold. Suppose competent, trustworthy witnesses assure us of the following:

1. Our next-door neighbor was observed walking down the sidewalk of a busy street in our home town
2. Actor Tom Cruise was observed walking down the sidewalk of a busy street in our home town
3. Swami X was observed levitating six feet above the sidewalk of a busy street in our home town

Proposition 1 seems completely believable, because our background assumptions tell us that it is an utterly everyday experience that people walk on sidewalks, and that we can run into our neighbors unexpectedly. Proposition 2 is rather less believable, because we also assume that the super-famous rarely venture out into public space, given that their privacy would be invaded by untold numbers of paparazzi and gawkers. Perhaps our witness saw somebody with an uncanny resemblance to the famed actor? Proposition 3 would by many be rejected completely, because most of us assume that the force of gravity affects even the saintliest of swamis. Perhaps our witness saw an illusionist, somebody who performed a trick, hoping that passers-by would prove willing to pay him a tip for a picture?

A different set of background assumptions, of course, radically alters the believability of all three propositions. If we are absolutely sure that our neighbor was on vacation on the other side of the globe, statement 1 could be rejected as utterly implausible. If we knew that Tom Cruise was in town to shoot a new film, statement 2 suddenly seems much more plausible. And if we became fervent adherents of the religious movement headed by swami X, and were convinced that he had perfected techniques that enabled the control of mind over matter, it would seem completely plausible that our dear guru had indeed been spotted, suspended in mid-air.

Although the difference is not easy to pinpoint, the shift in probability is different in cases 1 and 2 compared to 3. A concept of rationality, shared by very many people, but notoriously hard to define with any precision, accounts for the revised opinion in the first two cases. Nearly everybody will find it utterly commonsensical that the next-door neighbor cannot be simultaneously relaxing on an atoll in the Maldives and strolling down the main street of our hometown. The case with the levitating swami, however, is radically different. Our life-long experience of the effects of gravity on the human body conspires to make us accept that we cannot lift ourselves off the ground merely by willpower. The willingness of our witness to make an exception for swami X, and our willingness to accept this as true, depend on socialization into the world view of a particular group and is acceptable only to other members of that group.[3]

Religious socialization, in particular, is about providing adherents with background assumptions that will affect their acceptance (or lack thereof) of new information. If we are convinced that Joseph Smith really was a prophet who by means of divine inspiration translated the Book of Mormon from an ancient text in Reformed Egyptian that had been engraved on golden plates, the existence of the Jaredite people is readily accepted. If the Book of Mormon mentions that the Jaredites had elephants, the lack of any material remains of elephants in the archaeological finds is not a counterargument

3. The concept of widely shared rationality and its hard-to-define border vis-à-vis its "irrational" counterpart resemble the so-called demarcation problem between science and "pseudo-science" in the philosophy of science (cf. Hansson 2017). It should be stressed that rationality as envisaged here is a much broader phenomenon, one that is tacitly accepted by us all and set aside only in particular settings, especially in religious contexts.

against the Book of Mormon, but a minor anomaly in search of a solution. It remains an open question whether the Jaredites were Olmecs, and whether the mysterious elephants might have been mammoths that survived well beyond the date generally assumed for the extinction of this species, but these are mere details that interested Mormon intellectuals can debate with each other and with outsiders.

Social processes and historically contingent events—the rise to power of institutions, the persuasive abilities of individual thinkers, structures that confer authority—rather than mere "facts" play major roles in determining precisely what background assumptions get accepted within a given community, and what gets defined as "irrational." The fact that a small group of Mormon writers backs up the claims of the Book of Mormon confers plausibility even for Mormons who are willing to accept the Book of Mormon narrative with little or no further argumentation, because they were raised within the Church. They know that there is incontrovertible evidence, even if they may be hard pressed to explain exactly what this evidence consists of.

The emergence of a scientific account of New World prehistory

Before the emergence of a scientific discipline of archaeology, a major focus of interest in the prehistory of the New World was the earthen mounds found in great quantity in the eastern half of the North American territory.[4] Controversy was rife regarding the origins of these mounds, and throughout most of the nineteenth century, proponents of the theory that the mound builders were the ancestors of the Native Americans were pitted against those who were adamant that a different and more "civilized" people must have built them.

Who were the mound builders, in the view of those who saw them as a different people than the present-day Native Americans? The most common theory connected them with the Lost Tribes of Israel. Many mounds contained human remains, while others had been used as fortifications. Taken together, this could be understood as evidence of the wholesale slaughter of the mound builder race by the Indians. Only when modern archaeological methods such as controlled excavations began to be used in the 1880s, the theory of the mound-builder race was finally discarded. The final nail in the coffin of the story of the superior, vanished race is usually attributed to the publication of a massive study by Cyrus Thomas of the Bureau of Ethnology (Thomas 1894).

4. For a survey of pre-scientific views of the Native Americans, see Wauchope 1962. On the mound builder myth, see Silverberg 1969. On the relationship of archaeology with widespread conceptions of Native Americans, see McGuire 1992.

Once the idea was firmly in place that the diverse peoples in the New World were the descendants of the same ancestors as those of the mound builders, not the survivors in a war against culturally superior Israelites, the question of the ultimate origins of the Native Americans still remained. Where did the first people to colonize the Americas come from, and when did this take place? Up to the late nineteenth century, writers on the origins of the Native Americans often formulated theories that presupposed that the native populations had come to the Americas via transoceanic voyages.

Until the early twentieth century, it was still generally thought that humans had arrived in the Americas no earlier than 4000 BCE. In 1926, stone projectile points found near Folsom, New Mexico, showed that humans had been present since the Pleistocene. In the early 1930s, Pleistocene stone tools were found at sites near Clovis, also in New Mexico. Soon after these first discoveries, new sites with similar stone points were found from southern Canada to Central America, and the Clovis culture came to be regarded as the first wave of humans to have settled the New World. In order to explain these findings, the Land Bridge Theory, i.e. the theory that Native Americans came from Asia via the Bering Strait, became the dominant hypothesis in the 1930s. When radiocarbon dating was developed by Willard Libby in 1949 (and increasingly refined, beginning in the 1960s, by taking into account the varying levels of ^{14}C in the atmosphere over time), the early remains of the Clovis culture were dated to roughly 13,500 years ago. This early date matched the available archaeological finds, the evidence of an ice age land bridge across the Bering Strait that could serve as a transport route, and the fact that linguistic diversity in the Americas is so great that common ancestral languages must have been spoken many thousands of years ago. The model of settlement that saw the Clovis people as the first humans in the New World was the reigning orthodoxy for several decades. In recent years, mounting evidence of even earlier migrations has pushed back the date of arrival of the first humans. This does not, however, weaken the dominant position of the Land Bridge paradigm, which is considered by the vast majority of researchers to be solidly supported by archaeological evidence, anthropology, and DNA analysis.[5]

The Book of Mormon account can easily be harmonized with pre-scientific nineteenth-century theories, but departs radically from the current scientific paradigm. The increasing distance between the scientific mainstream and scripturally-based mythological accounts is familiar also from

5. The fundamental tenets of the Bering Land Bridge hypothesis and its historical development can be found in any sufficiently recent account of American prehistory. For a useful textbook-level introduction with numerous references to the very substantial literature, see Adovasio and Pedler 2005.

a Protestant context, but the range of responses from various Protestant denominations has been much broader, with very literalist interpretations at one end, and very liberal ones at the other. The LDS Church, as Armand Mauss (1994) has argued, withdrew from the American intellectual mainstream, and has insisted on the literal truth of the Book of Mormon narrative. Significant apologetic efforts are deployed to support this literalist position.

Apologetics in two modes

Mormon apologetic texts can proceed along two analytically distinct, albeit in practice often intermingled, paths. One the one hand, there is literature of a reactive kind, which addresses the critical points raised by skeptics. On the other, there is a sizeable corpus of writings that more independently attempts to present a compelling picture of the identity of the Nephites or Jaredites, using clues from both the canonical texts of Mormonism and the archaeological record to describe how and where they lived. A small number of authors have produced the bulk of this literature. The following presentation will first outline the main virtuoso defenders of Mormonism. Then, some standard defenses against skeptical questions will be listed, together with some of the attempts to provide evidence for the historicity of the Book of Mormon by linking events mentioned there to the archaeological record.

Apologetic activists and their institutional setting

Like most other movements, Mormonism counts a small number of people who produce the intellectually-oriented apologetics, and a much larger group of adherents who, at most, read and assimilate the results published by the elite. A perusal of the biographies of some of the most widely cited members of this literati class of apologists shows that there are common denominators among them.[6]

Milton Reed Hunter (1902–1975) received a PhD in history from the University of California, Berkeley in 1935.[7] Hunter was cofounder of a major apologetic institution, the New World Archaeological Foundation, affiliated since 1961 with Brigham Young University (BYU). Hugh Nibley (1910–2005) graduated from University of California, Los Angeles (UCLA), with a disserta-

6. The list contains only a sample, and there are dozens of other writers who are or were active in journals, on websites and other channels of publication. I have somewhat impressionistically chosen to mention authors whose publications are most voluminous and/or are frequently referred to as seminal thinkers by other LDS sources.

7. For biographic data, see Anon. 1975. "Elder Milton R. Hunter Dies," *Ensign* August 1975, online at https://www.lds.org/ensign/1975/08/news-of-the-church/elder-milton-r-hunter-dies?lang=eng. All websites cited in this chapter were checked and active on November 10, 2015.

tion on a Classics topic quite unrelated to Mormon doctrine. He was a professor at BYU from 1946 until his death, for the last 20 years as emeritus. Max Wells Jakeman (1910–1998) received a PhD from University of California, Berkeley, with a dissertation on the history of the Yucatan Peninsula. He joined the faculty at BYU in 1946, where he founded the archaeology department, and became regarded by many as the "father of Book of Mormon archaeology."[8] John L. Sorenson, born 1924, holds a PhD from UCLA, and is professor emeritus of anthropology at BYU. Daniel C. Peterson received his PhD in Near Eastern Languages and Cultures from UCLA, and is professor of Islamic Studies and Arabic at BYU.[9] William J. Hamblin (b. 1954) received his PhD from the University of Michigan in 1985, and is Professor of History at BYU.

A distinct pattern emerges from these thumbnail accounts. Most of the highly active apologetic authors obtained advanced degrees from secular institutions, and were thereafter recruited to faculty positions at BYU. Originally called Brigham Young Academy, Brigham Young University was founded in 1875, with the purpose of fusing every branch of learning with a Mormon religious ideology.[10] The strongly religious agenda is in force also today. Everybody at the university, i.e. faculty, administrative staff, and students, is expected to "voluntarily live the principles of the gospel of Jesus Christ," which in this case includes the "restored Gospel," i.e., the canonical LDS scriptures.[11] Teaching is infused with the same agenda: "All students at BYU should be taught the truths of the gospel of Jesus Christ."[12]

BYU has under its aegis several institutions with an apologetic mission. A network or institution that for many years was of central importance in the defense of the Book of Mormon was the Foundation for Ancient Research and Mormon Studies or FARMS. This network was founded by John W. Welch in 1979. Welch became part of the BYU faculty in 1979, but only in 1997 did FARMS merge into BYU, on the invitation of LDS president Gordon B. Hinckley and others. Over the next years, FARMS merged with the Center for the Preservation of Ancient Religious Texts (CPART), the Middle Eastern Texts Initiative (METI), and the Laura F. Willes Center for Book of Mormon Studies. The joint body in 2006 changed its name into the Neal A. Maxwell Institute for Religious Scholarship, or Maxwell Institute for short.

8. See Anon. 1998. "Memorial: Max Wells Jakeman (1910–1998)" in *Journal of Book of Mormon Studies* 7(1): 79.
9. See mormonscholarstestify.org/151/daniel-c-peterson-2
10. See the BYU website yfacts.byu.edu
11. http://registrar.byu.edu/catalog/2015-2016ucat/GeneralInfo/HonorCode.php
12. http://registrar.byu.edu/catalog/2015-2016ucat/AboutBYU/Mission.php

In its capacity as an umbrella organization, the Maxwell Institute promotes an ideologically very wide range of scholarship, from the entirely non-religionist to writings that are decidedly apologetic. The mission statement of the Maxwell Institute (of which a brief extract is quoted here) attempts to have it both ways. Some phrases are clearly religionist in tone, while others emphasize the academic rigor of its scholars:

> Above all, we seek to embody the qualities of what our namesake has called the "disciple-scholar." As an institute of religious scholarship, our work is informed by the highest standards of academic study as well as by the principles of our own faith. [...] As Elder Maxwell put it: "For a disciple of Jesus Christ, *academic scholarship is a form of worship*."[13]

Although much of the apologetic argumentation surrounding the Book of Mormon is found in popularized media such as websites, the top-echelon venues for publishing such materials are the journals and books that appear under the aegis of the Maxwell Institute and other religious institutions. The primary journal in this regard is the *Journal of Book of Mormon Studies*, founded in 1992 and now run by the Maxwell Institute. The journal's guidelines steer a middle course between disinterested and religionist scholarship: the usual academic approaches (historical, literary, etc.) should be applied to the Book of Mormon, but "inspirational or devotional elements flow naturally from scholarly analysis."[14]

Unsurprisingly in the modern age, considerable apologetic work is also carried out on websites affiliated with or sympathetic to the LDS Church. The websites of the institutions mentioned above, and in particular Brigham Young University and its affiliated institutes, contain numerous apologetic statements. Another site with very rich contents of a similar nature is Fairmormon.org. In 1997, the Foundation for Apologetic Information and Research (FAIR) was founded to provide apologetic responses to questions about Mormonism. In 2013, FAIR changed its name to FairMormon.[15] The FairMormon site is run by volunteers, and has no official link to the LDS church, although the materials on the site support the doctrines of Mormonism. Interestingly, the official site of the Latter-day Saint Church, Lds.org, is not a primary place to look for writings of this kind, since the Church has no official position on precisely how the link between narrative and history on the ground is to be construed.

13. Emphasis in the original. http://mi.byu.edu/moving-forward-2014/

14. Publications.maxwellinsitute.byu.edu

15. On the background of https://www.fairmormon.org/, see http://blog.fairmormon.org/2013/08/23/fair-has-new-nameshaken-faith-syndrome-updated/?utm_source=feedburner&utm_medium=feed&utm_campaign=Feed%3A+fairldsblog+%28FAIR+Blog%29

Defending the Book of Mormon against perceived anachronisms

A host of books and websites attempts to debunk the perceived anachronisms and seemingly impossible details in the Book of Mormon story. Mormon apologists have responded in an equally voluminous written output. As is often the case with debates between skeptics and believers, a standard set of topics has developed over time, with both sides repeating the same arguments with few variations (cf. Hammer 2007, 391–392). This section will briefly survey a selection of stock topics, and will focus especially on the Mormon response.

Potential technological anachronisms of the Book of Mormon

The Book of Mormon refers several times to objects made of steel and other metals. Following the Book of Mormon's own chronology, the first swords of steel to be mentioned were crafted by a Jaredite king by the name of Shule (Ether 7: 9). Skeptical authors have objected that steel was unknown at the time Shule supposedly lived. One apologetic response has been to look in the literature for evidence that at least some iron objects had been manufactured in the Near East in that early period, presupposing that these metal objects, or the knowledge of how to manufacture them, were brought along to the New World.[16]

Steel is also mentioned in 2 Nephi 5: 15 and Jarom 1: 8, this time in lists of materials in use among the Nephites. Although Mormon chronology places this period at a much later date than Shule, steel was, according to mainstream scientists, still unknown in the New World. Precisely when steel was in use depends on the definition one gives the word "steel." Meteoric iron could for instance have a composition that, technically speaking, makes it steel. It has also been suggested that Joseph Smith translated a term that actually refers to "bronze" as "steel," influenced by a King James Version passage that has the same inaccurate translation (Hamblin and Merrill 1990, 346–347).

Book of Mormon references to the natural world

1 Nephi 18 tells the story of the journey of Lehi's group to the New World. They arrive in verse 23, and in verse 25, as they journey "in the wilderness," they find "beasts in the forest of every kind, both the cow and the ox, and the ass and the horse, and the goat and the wild goat." Yet, these are all animals that, according to scientific consensus, were absent in the New World. A common suggestion in Mormon literature is that the people who had just

16. For a range of apologetic arguments, see Roper 1996, 1997, 1999; Hamblin and Merrill 1990; See also Jeff Lindsay's apologetic website at jefflindsay.com/LDSFAQ/FQ_metals.shtml#laban.

arrived classified unfamiliar species by giving them familiar names. The cattle could have been bison, deer, or Baird's tapir.[17] The goats could also have been a different species, for instance deer.[18]

Horses are not only part of the list in 1 Nephi 18: 25, but are also briefly mentioned in various other narratives spanning in internal chronology from Jaredite times (Ether 9: 19) to a fairly late date in Nephite culture (3 Nephi 3: 22). Mainstream scholarship on the evolutionary development of horses asserts that modern horses are the last remaining species of a once much larger family, Equidae, the earliest specimens of which date back 5 million years. Numerous species lived in North America, but they had all died out roughly 12,000 years ago, either because of climate change or because they were hunted. Horses only returned to the Americas when they were brought from the Old World.

One way to account for the presence of horses in the Book of Mormon is to suggest that the word could be a translation of a term in Reformed Egyptian that was expanded to denote a different species than the domesticated equine we call "horse" (cf. Sorenson 1985, 295). A common suggestion in the apologetic literature is that the horses may have been tapirs. Michael Ash presents arguments for why this identification makes sense of the scriptural passages.[19] Horses and tapirs share some key characteristics: their digestion and the shape of their foot, both of which figure prominently in the classification of animals in the Mosaic Law (thus in classificatory terms presumably overruling the fact that tapirs are much smaller than horses). Book of Mormon "horses" are never mentioned in connection with riding or combat, and Ash surmises that they may have been kept as a source of food and may have pulled chariots. Since the wheel was unknown in the New World, "chariot" may also be a rough translation of something else, perhaps a travois. Since there is no evidence that tapirs were ever domesticated, they may perhaps just have been "associated" with travois, i.e. with their meat loaded on these means of transportation as a supply of food. Another common suggestion (to which we will return below) is that mainstream science is simply wrong, and that there were actually horses in the period when the Jaredites and Nephites are supposed to have lived in America.

Finally, a claim that has received its share of critical as well as apologetic attention is that there were elephants among the Jaredites. There is only one single mention of them, in Ether 9: 19:

17. See en.fairmormon.org/Book_of_Mormon/Anachronisms/Animals/Cattle

18. See en.fairmormon.org/Book_of_Mormon/Anachronisms/Animals/Goats

19. http://www.fairmormon.org/perspectives/publications/horses-in-the-book-of-mormon

> And they also had horses, and asses, and there were elephants and cureloms and cumoms; all of which were useful unto man, and more especially the elephants and cureloms and cumoms.

Leaving aside the mysterious cumoms and cureloms, nothing else is said of these elephants than that they lived in Jaredite times, i.e. in the second half of the third millennium B.C. in emic chronology. That allows apologists to assert that they could have been mammoths. Scientific accounts date the extinction of this species to around 10,800 radiocarbon years before present, either as a result of extensive hunting by Clovis people, climate change, or both (the literature is vast, see Haynes 2002; bibliography in Grayson). Mormon literature argues that pockets of these animals survived long past that time, and that the memory of them is in fact so recent that several Native American tribes tell of large animals with trunks.[20]

Superimposing the Book of Mormon on the material world

Besides defending the Book of Mormon against criticism of the kind presented above, apologetic literature typically attempts to make the events of the text plausible by superimposing the narrative of the Book of Mormon onto the material evidence. Two major ways of doing so are, firstly, to attempt to correlate the events preceding the departure of Lehi with places and events in the ancient Near East and, secondly, to try to anchor events and places mentioned in connection with the life of various post-emigration Book of Mormon peoples with sites in the Americas. Near Eastern matches are presumably easiest to make, since critics and apologists agree on at least a number of basic issues: some place names can be correlated with real-world sites, some people are known from historical records, and some cultural traits described in the book correspond to what is known from the Ancient Near East. Much more fraught with difficulty is the attempt to superimpose Book of Mormon details with facts on the ground in America: none of the names, people or events in the book can be read off the historical record, but need to be projected onto the landscape. The attempts to do so will occupy the remainder of this chapter.

Most early writers assumed that the migrants from the Old World populated the entire American continent, a gigantic land mass that was empty when they arrived (Sorenson 1992, 9). If there were other people already living in the Americas when first the Jaredites and then Lehi's people arrived, the Book of Mormon would seem to be utterly silent about them. Not only that: Ether 2: 5 explicitly has the earliest settlers, Jared and his flock, go "into that quarter where there had never man been." Similarly, for the

20. A summary of such arguments can be found at http://en.fairmormon.org/Book_of_Mormon/Anachronisms/Animals/Elephants

descendants of Lehi's group, a literal reading of 2 Nephi 1: 8–9 is that the land was kept empty for them (emphasis added):

> 8. And behold, it is wisdom that *this land should be kept as yet from the knowledge of other nations*; for behold, many nations would overrun the land, that there would be no place for an inheritance.
>
> 9. Wherefore, I, Lehi, have obtained a promise, that inasmuch as those whom the Lord God shall bring out of the land of Jerusalem shall keep his commandments, they shall prosper upon the face of this land; and *they shall be kept from all other nations, that they may possess this land unto themselves.*

This reading received a boost by being supported by Apostle Orson Pratt, who in an 1866 edition of the Book of Mormon added geographical locations in footnotes, and regarded the entire American hemisphere as part of Book of Mormon geography (Sorenson 1992, 14, 141–142). The golden plates, in Pratt's view, came from the hill Cumorah in upstate New York, and this was also the scene of the final battle between Nephites and Lamanites (Sorenson 1992, 9).

Rank and file members of the Church seem to have continued to accept the idea that the entire Western hemisphere was the setting of the Book of Mormon, while Mormon literati were open to discussing various models with different geographical scopes. An idea disseminated at the time, that presupposed a continent-wide dispersal of the Nephites and Lamanites, was that Lehi had landed in Chile. This view was some years later elaborated by James A. Little and Franklin D. Richard in their book *A Compendium of the Doctrines of the Gospel* (1882) (Sorenson 1992, 19). Nevertheless, many attempts at finding geographic correlations coexisted, and the Church took no official position (Sorenson 1992, 15–16). One of these competing readings of the book located events in a much more restricted geographical setting, in Mesoamerica. In 1841, John Lloyd Stephens published *Incidents of Travel in Central America, Chiapas and Yucatan*, a book that fascinated many American readers with its description of ancient peoples in Mesoamerica.[21] The existence of writing and other signs of advanced civilizations seemed to corroborate the picture painted in the Book of Mormon of a literate culture reaching the New World and building large cities there. Among Mormons, the effect was what a recent study has called "modifications within the traditional hemispheric framework" (Roper 2015, 209). An elaborate version of this Mesoamerican model would, in the contemporary period, become dominant among Mormon intellectuals.

The most in-depth argumentation for the Mesoamerican model can be found in the work of John L. Sorenson. Many other Mormon writers have

21. For a recent discussion (by a religious insider) of the importance of Stephens' books for early LDS understandings of Book of Mormon geography, see Roper 2015.

fleshed out further details or supported the model, but Sorenson's work remains the primary reference. Sorenson's own reflections on the presuppositions for his work allow readers to see how his corpus of writings reflects an apologetic agenda, yet presents itself as an unbiased exploration. The apologetic aim of the work comes across clearly in the Foreword by Leonard J. Arrington, Truman G. Madsen and John W. Welch, who (*An Ancient American Setting*, x, [AAS][22]) tell how LDS scholars have compared "Book of Mormon materials with the practices of *other* ancient religious peoples" (emphasis added). Knowing about the context of the Book of Mormon peoples and events would both allow Church members to find the message more powerful, and spread the word more effectively to others. Rational investigation of the Book of Mormon in this perspective functions as added support for beliefs that are already firmly held.

Sorenson's own guiding question is equally revealing: "*How* did the Book of Mormon events happen?" (AAS xvi, emphasis added). In order to answer this question, Sorenson asserts that one needs to take all geographical mentions in the Book of Mormon into account, be an expert in Mesoamerican conditions (Sorenson 1992, 209), including rates of travel, terrain, and ecological factors, "purge our minds as far as possible of preconceptions" (Sorenson 1992, 210), use information from the entire book, and subject the theories that one creates to constructive criticism. Because the records were penned by people who had firsthand knowledge or based their reports on the firsthand knowledge of others, all data need to be assumed to be coherent and to make sense (Sorenson 1992, 215). What an outsider reads as myth is thus taken so seriously as historical data, that Sorenson even defuses a scripturally-based counterargument against his approach by means of a scriptural argument. Since the face of the whole earth changed with the crucifixion of Christ (as recounted in 3 Nephi 8), perhaps that has made Mesoamerica before the cataclysmic event impossible to recognize for somebody living after it took place? But Mormon and Moroni lived after the catastrophe and had no problems identifying the ancient sites (AAS 45).

Not all elements of the narrative are to be interpreted equally literally, according to Sorenson. On the one hand, words in the text that can be interpreted topographically (up, down) mean precisely that. From the land of Nephi to the land of Zarahemla, one travels "down," a textual detail that should correspond to an actual topography (Sorenson 1992, 215). On the other, the very act of translating a text introduces "imprecisions" that can account for problems such as the seeming anachronisms listed above. Most

22. Due to the large number of references to Sorenson 1985, the abbreviation AAS (for *An Ancient American Setting*) will be used in the remainder of this chapter.

importantly for an attempt to map Book of Mormon geography onto a New World setting, Sorenson assumes that directional terms such as north and south can be very imprecise (AAS 216).

Armed with these basic presuppositions, the Book of Mormon can be perused for clues. The narrative takes place in an hourglass isthmus separating two lands (AAS 6), where the southern part is "nearly surrounded by water" (Alma 22: 32). Furthest to the south was the land of Nephi, whereas Zarahemla lay closer to the isthmus. The Book of Mormon region of Bountiful is the southern part of the isthmus itself. The next territory to the north thereof is Desolation. The Land of Moron comes just north (Ether 7: 6). North of Desolation but along the east coast lies a wet land. Beyond those regions the geography remains hazy (AAS 6). The dimensions of this territory can be judged from the time it took people to get from one place to another. A problem is, of course, that these transportation times can vary enormously. The mention of distances between various locations does preclude a setting covering the entire continent: the distance from Nephi to Zarahemla would have been merely roughly 180 miles (AAS 12), and the whole stretch of land where all Book of Mormon events take place should be no more than 450-500 miles from one end to the other (AAS 14). Numerous topographic details show that the region was hilly or mountainous, with an eastern lowland area, a much less extensive western shore, and a major river identified in the Book of Mormon as Sidon (AAS 23–27). There are signs of a tropical climate: endemic fevers are mentioned (Alma 46: 40), as is moist heat on the eastern shore (Alma 51: 33, 52: 31, 62: 35). The population must have been large, and at least some people were literate.

What part of the Americas does all of this point at? The only isthmus that fits the bill, says Sorenson, is the Tehuantepec area. Mesoamerican cultures in that region rose and declined in a chronological pattern that, for Sorenson, fits the internal chronology of the Book of Mormon. The rise and fall of the Olmec fits Book of Mormon descriptions of the Jaredites (AAS 116–119, see especially the table on p. 118). The emergence of new high cultures in the area fits descriptions of the situation of the People of Lehi and their descendants, the Nephites and Lamanites (p. 125–137, see table on p. 135).

Once the basic geography has been legitimated, the next task is to carry out a more detailed comparison between details of the text and specific facts of Mesoamerican geography and culture (AAS 49). There are some constraints in carrying out this task, since The Book of Mormon is a lineage history (AAS 50–56), and by implication everything else assumes marginal importance. Furthermore, large portions of the time-span are compressed into very few pages or even lines, and the book does not have much to say about day-to-day life. The clues offered by the text are examined in great and complex detail, and occupies a very considerable portion of Sorenson's book. One single example will illustrate how the author goes about doing this (AAS 175–182).

Mosiah, chapters 7 and 11 to 17, tells of the prophet Abinadi, who according to the internal chronology of the Book of Mormon lived around 150 BCE, during the reign of a king by the name of Noah. At this time, the Nephite ruling elite governed the land from the city of Lehi-Nephi. Like so many other prophets in the Book of Mormon, Abinadi visits the court, calls for the locals to repent, and prophecies of the coming of Jesus. And like the messages of many other prophets, Abinadi's call goes unheeded. After a lengthy trial, Abinadi is sentenced to death. One man, Alma (often referred to as Alma the Elder), is convinced of Abinadi's message, and ultimately becomes a prophet in his own right, at first secretly gathering around him a group of believers.

In order to escape the oppression of King Noah, Alma and his followers in Mosiah 18 retreat to a place referred to as the waters of Mormon and located next to a forest. Mosiah 18: 5 explains that the site had a fountain of pure water. A baptismal scene in 18: 14 indicates that the water was a sufficiently sizeable body for the converts to be "buried" in it. Other passages that mention these waters add to the impression of a quite large body: its waters later submerge a city (3 Nephi 9: 7), and joined "the borders of Mormon" (Alma 21: 1). Indirect textual evidence, finally, suggests that it lay in the direction of Zarahemla. King Noah eventually discovers the whereabouts of the renegade group and sets out to crush them. Alma receives a divine revelation, and flees out into the wilderness with his flock, once again in the direction of Zarahemla. They arrive at a place that they give the name Helam, where they construct a settlement by the same name. Mosiah 23:4 identifies Helam as a site where there also was pure water.

Already at this point, there are a number of details that Sorenson can match with conditions on the ground. The city of Lehi-Nephi has already for other reasons been identified with the Guatemalan site Kaminaljuyu, and Zarahemla is placed west to northwest thereof. Drawing a line in the right cardinal direction, and calculating roughly how long travel may have taken in the Guatemalan terrain, the nearest sufficiently large body of water can be located that could correspond to the waters of Mormon. Sorenson finds Lake Atitlán a good candidate. The lake is bordered by trees, which fits the description of a forest. Continuing in the same direction and calculating once again what distance might be involved, taking the local topography into account, Sorensen (AAS 180) feels confident that two possible locations for Helam can be identified in the Rio Blanco Valley. This site is later in the

Book of Mormon narrative converted into a city, so an archaeological structure in each possible location needs to be located, that might fit the bill. Sorensen provides suggestions, and notes that one site at Malacatancito is "of Nephite age" (AAS 182).

Besides such ostensible geographical matches, apparent similarities in culture play an important role in Sorenson's argument. A few examples of his argumentation will suffice.

a. Mesoamerican temples were built on similar principles as Ancient Near Eastern temples such as that of Solomon: there were various spaces with different degrees of sacredness, and steps leading up to the space where sacrifices were conducted (AAS 143).
b. In both places, settlement patters were typically an area inhabited by people who used a particular ceremonial complex as religious center, and lived in homes dispersed among the fields (AAS 159).
c. The class-borne stratified society described in the Book of Mormon fits the centralized chiefdoms of the Mesoamerican area. (AAS 164). Both societies had a specialized priestly class that wielded considerable power (AAS 206–209).
d. Politics and religion were in both cases completely integrated (AAS 165).
e. The religion of the locals, i.e. people who were not swayed by the message of prophets, was structurally similar. Sorenson characterizes this as magical, subjugating nature to the needs of humans, and containing rites of passage and shamanistic healing (AAS 217–218). Sorensen's view of religion is evolutionistic, in that the Nephite prophets attempt to lift these "Baalist" peoples to "gospel-level faith" (218).
f. Pyramid towers displayed the prestige of the local society and had religious connotations, as did the ziggurats of Mesopotamia (AAS 172–173).
g. The methods of warfare were similar (AAS 261–264). The weapons described in the Book of Mormon were similar to Mesoamerican ones, thick cloth was used as protective armor, military leaders headed their own lineage groups, and standards or flags identified each such group.
h. The Book of Mormon is repeatedly concerned with the nefarious influence of secret societies. Such institutions are well documented from around the world, including Mesoamerica (AAS 300–309). The Franciscan friar Bernardino de Sahagún tells of *nahualistas*, members

of such secret brotherhoods who were "trained in black magic after undergoing severe initiation" (AAS 301). Sorenson's explanation for the existence of such coteries is hyperdiffusonist: common historical origins, rather than shared social processes, explain the ubiquitous presence of secret, initiatory groups (AAS 305).

i. Quetzalcoatl functions structurally as an amalgam of Yahweh (as deity of rain and fertility) and Christ (AAS 326–333). Quetzalcoatl was associated with the symbol of a shell, which apparently was a resurrection symbol for the Aztecs (AAS 328). Sorenson suggests that the entire topic requires much more research (AAS 329–330).

j. Finally, one of the more complex arguments deals with Nephite chronology (AAS 270–274). Book of Mormon chronology links with Biblical chronology in various ways, e.g., by the birth of Jesus mentioned in both canonical texts. From Lehi's departure to the year of Christ's birth, the Book of Mormon allots 600 years (3 Nephi 1:1). Both events, in turn, are in emic chronology linked to other dateable events, set roughly 593 years apart. This minor discrepancy makes sense, according to Sorenson, if one assumes that the Nephites reckoned years in the way the Mayans did, as a 360-day *tun* without the five unlucky days.

Interpretive authority and the management of anomalies

Mormon sources refer to the work of Sorenson and his colleagues as thoroughly persuasive. Nevertheless, authority over scriptural interpretation and archaeological fact based on the strategies presented above turns out to be an unstable commodity. Any attempt to project a Book of Mormon account onto a specific geographical location and the material evidence of the past encounters problems and anomalies that apologists and critics will fight over. Four such challenges to the authority of the proponents of the Mesoamerican model will be briefly considered.

Cardinal directions

The identification that the Mesoamerican model makes between Book of Mormon geography and the area around the Tehuantepec isthmus needs to resolve one very basic issue. This land bridge area runs roughly east to west, but the Book of Mormon account speaks of a north-south axis. The "north" of the Book of Mormon must be roughly 60 degrees away from the north indicated by a compass. Sorenson's *An Ancient American Setting for the Book of Mormon* devotes considerable effort to defusing this potential critique (a substantial section carries the subtitle "Directions in the Book of Mormon," AAS 38–42). His proposed solution is based on the fact that quite a few languages have words for directions different from our cardinal points, and Hebrew supposedly did too (AAS 38–39). Thus, it should occasion no surprise that a text translated from a language radically different from English should preserve a very different set of terms for directions than those automatically assumed by English-language readers. Other apologists have argued that Book of Mormon directions make eminent sense in the light of Mesoamerican systems of directionality.[23]

The two hills Cumorah

The presupposition that the present-day Hill Cumorah is the same place as the location mentioned in the Book of Mormon was a correlation first made by Oliver Cowdery (Hamblin 1993, 172). The impression is surely reinforced by the annual pageant performed at the hill in upstate New York. A play shown on this occasion depicts Joseph Smith's encounter with the golden plates and some of the events related in the book.

Proponents of the limited, Mesoamerican geography model are faced with the question of how the plates recording a battle at a site in Mesoamerica could have been found by Joseph Smith in a hill several thousand miles away. Apologists cite scriptural evidence: Mormon 6: 6, on their reading, states that the hill Cumorah where the final battle stood cannot have been the same as where the golden plates were buried.[24] Furthermore, according to the Book of Mormon (Mormon 6: 11–15) at least 230,000 people died in battle at the Hill Cumorah. Even this battle was only one-tenth the size of that which took place at the same site when, according to Ether 15: 2, nearly two million Jaredites were slaughtered. The hill in Palmyra, New York, seems an unlikely candidate for events of such magnitude.

A site for the Book of Mormon hill proposed by adherents of a Mesoamerican setting is Cerro de Vigia, in Veracruz, Mexico. Palmer (1981) asserts that this hill fits the descriptions in various scriptural passages best. The problem that for them stands in need of an explanation is not the existence of two distinct Cumorahs, but rather the immense distance between them. Moroni would, on this interpretation, have transported the golden plates, for many years and across half a continent, as a single individual among presumably hostile tribes. The explanation given for this is that Moroni had thirty-five years to carry the plates from Mexico to New York (AAS 44–45). Although quite an accomplishment, Mormon apologists insist

23. See the detailed discussion in Gardner 2013.

24. The passage is, however, hardly unequivocal: "I made this record out of the plates of Nephi, and hid up in the hill Cumorah all the records which had been entrusted to me by the hand of the Lord, save it were these few plates which I gave unto my son Moroni."

that it is far from impossible. A ship-wrecked sixteenth century sailor, David Ingram, reportedly took eleven months to walk from Tampico, Mexico, to the Saint John River by the border between Maine and Canada.[25]

The Zelph incident

In 1834, Joseph Smith led a militia group from Kirtland, Ohio to Jackson County, Missouri. On June 3, they stopped at the bank of the Illinois River and retrieved some skeletal remains and an arrowhead that had been buried in a mound. Several people who had been part of the group (but not Joseph Smith himself) several years later wrote that Joseph had received a vision that identified the bones as the remains of a Lamanite warrior named Zelph. A traditional hemisphere-wide reading of the Book of Mormon is compatible with finding interred Lamanite bones in Illinois. It would, however, be a problem if the events narrated in the Book of Mormon had all taken place in Mesoamerica. A common apologetic strategy is to deploy source-critical arguments to destroy the credibility of the witness reports.[26]

DNA Controversies

By far the most serious challenge to any attempt to match myth and materiality is the emergence in recent decades of DNA analysis. The development of increasingly sophisticated understandings of how the genetic record works would seem to undermine the theory of even partial Near Eastern origins for Native Americans.[27]

Mormon apologists, unsurprisingly, fight back. An unsigned article with the title "Book of Mormon and DNA Studies," dated January 31, 2014, is posted on the LDS Church's website.[28] The arguments in this text can be summarized as follows: Like the results of any science, those of genetics are tentative. Since one cannot know anything about the genetic makeup of Book of Mormon peoples, geneticists would presumably not know what to look for. DNA analysis can therefore neither prove nor disprove the Book of Mormon account. The Church website does, however, disavow the traditional reading of the Book of Mormon and implicitly supports Sorenson's work. Early LDS members may have assumed that the Jaredites, Mulekites, and Lehi's people

25. For further details, see the article by Michael R. Ash in the Feb 28, 2011 issue of *Deseret News*, online at http://www.deseretnews.com/article/705367606/How-Moroni-and-the-plates-may-have-made-it-to-Hill-Cumorah.html?pg=all

26. See Godfrey 1989 for a detailed attempt to show that Joseph Smith probably never made the comments regarding Zelph that are attributed to him.

27. See Southerton 2004 for a sustained effort at undermining the Book of Mormon historiography by arguments from genetics.

28. https://www.lds.org/topics/book-of-mormon-and-dna-studies?lang=eng

came to an empty continent, but the Book of Mormon never actually says so. If the migrants from the Ancient Near East were just a tiny fraction of the total population, their genetic imprint may be impossible to find.

The details of DNA analysis are highly technical and the literature can seem impenetrable to non-specialists. The Mormon position thus receives considerable rhetorical support by the fact that a small number of geneticists who are LDS Church members with, arguably, Ugo A. Perego as the most prominent, defend the historicity of the Book of Mormon. Interestingly, the position defended by Perego and colleagues (cf. Perego and Ekins 2014) is not that DNA analysis in any way supports the Book of Mormon historiography, but merely that the jury continues to be out, and that genetics is not equipped to answer the question whether the groups of ocean-crossing migrants described in the Book of Mormon really existed.

Defending the faith: The apologetic genre and Book of Mormon historiography

This chapter began by outlining the difference, posited by Bruce Lincoln, between rational argumentation, the deployment of authority, and the use of force. The apologetic works that have been used as primary sources are surely seen by Mormons as paragons of rational argumentation, so what makes it reasonable to categorize them as examples of authoritative discourse? This section will attempt to show that most apologetic sources are constructed in ways that closely emulate rational argumentation as understood by most academics, but that they differ in significant ways from this norm precisely because they are examples of apologetic discourse, and thus rely on the background assumptions of the recipient in order to be perceived as plausible defenses.

Literary critic Gérard Genette (1997) uses the term paratext to describe the sundry materials that, together with the text *sensu stricto*, make up a publication. The title, author's name and professional titles, cataloging information, text and images on covers and flaps, dedications, mottoes and preface, endorsements by peers, the quality and binding of the finished book, publisher's flyers, and interviews with the author are just a few of these accompanying items. The effect of the paratext is to nudge the reader toward a particular interpretation of the text: as a solid academic work, as a set of speculative hypotheses, as a mass-market popularization, and so forth. A sample of books and articles written by major apologetic authors and published through LDS-related channels shows how the paratext makes much of this literature, and especially more recent titles, resemble either mainstream academic scholarship, or popularizations thereof. They exude an aura of objective investigation. These texts come with a battery of footnotes or endnotes providing sources for their claims. They refer to archaeological excavations, philological details, and genetic evidence. They present carefully structured refutations of their opponents' views. As material objects, publications emerging from LDS milieus are presented within covers that look very much like those of scholarly books, mention the academic degree of their authors on the front cover, have endorsements printed on the back, are illustrated with photographs, maps, tables, and graphs that look very much like their counterparts in mainstream academic publication, mention peer-review procedures on their websites, and so forth.

Yet, apologetic works, despite the academic paratext, are constructed quite differently than mainstream non-confessional academic publications. Scholarly credibility comes from abiding by such norms as using the available secondary literature in a source-critical vein, giving due consideration to conflicting opinions, and quoting any given source fairly so that the original intention of the author is preserved. Institutionalized mechanisms, ranging from peer reviews to critical discussions by other scholars, contribute to detecting breaches of these scholarly norms. From a very early stage, students are socialized into a style of thinking and writing that builds on such academic virtues. Apologetic literature has other aims, and is rooted in historical genres such as forensic rhetoric, with very different characteristics. The primary function of apologetic literature is to persuade, and it can do so by seeking allies in perhaps unexpected sources, suppressing or ridiculing dissenting voices, and quoting selectively. A few examples can illustrate how Mormon apologetic texts do precisely that.

Sorenson's choice of references is extremely eclectic, ranging from works with academic publishers, such as the widely-reviewed and favorably received *Man across the Sea* by Carroll L. Riley (1971), the "standard scholarly work on transoceanic voyaging" (AAS 112), to the von Däniken-like pseudo-archaeological author Barry Fell, who although he "makes serious errors" has nevertheless written books that "constitute a challenge yet to be examined carefully and explained adequately by conventional scholars" (AAS 80).

The Book of Mormon has much to say about the influence of secret societies. As we have seen, John L. Sorenson notes that such secret societies are found around the world, and attributes a common historical origin to them (AAS 305). To support his argument, Sorenson refers to "historian" Nesta Helen Webster (1876–1960). Sorenson does not mention that Webster was actually a far-right conspiracy theorist and anti-Semite, who in the early 1920s became a believer in the Illuminati (see Lee 2005). Her thoroughly conspiracist book, *Secret Societies and Subversive Movements* (1924), is used several times as a source, even on "Jewish... secret groups" (AAS 306).

The Book of Mormon claim that there were horses in the Americas in Jaredite and Nephite times, i.e., in relatively recent pre-Columbian history, goes against the scientific consensus but is nevertheless supported by referring to various non-LDS writers. M.F. Ashley Montague supposedly supported both the existence of horses and mammoths in North America during that epoch. Montague, one might add, wrote books on topics such as race and gender equality, and does not appear to have had any particular expertise in the field of prehistoric New World fauna.[29] Furthermore, references to his statements seem always to be mediated by other Mormon authors, and in particular *The World of the Book of Mormon* by Paul R. Cheesman, an author whose apologetic texts have been reviewed unfavorably even by other LDS-affiliated scholars.[30] A second reference is to Yuri Kuchinsky, whose work on pre-Columbian ponies is published in *North American BioFortean Review*[31], an online publication that appeared from 1999 to 2006 and was dedicated to cryptozoology. A third is to an article on the extinction of megafauna in America published in *Science* (Martin 1973). Sorenson correctly states that Martin saw no theoretical reason why pockets of horses could not have survived the Pleistocene, but does not inform his readers that Martin immediately thereafter notes that there is no evidence that horses did in fact survive.

Just as support is welcome even from dubious or antiquated sources, critical voices are unwelcome, and sources of criticism are usually discredited. Examples of this strategy are easy to find. There are apologetic texts which use ad hominem or sarcastic language when describing opponents, characterize them as anti-Mormon, or cast doubt on their professional qualifications. A particularly glaring example concerns Thomas Stuart Ferguson, once a significant source of inspiration for those who wished to find links between the Book of Mormon and Mesoamerican archaeology, but who is now something of a persona non grata. After having co-founded the New World Archaeological Foundation and written books defending Mormonism by referring to archaeological findings, considerable evidence suggests that he lost his faith, and became convinced that the quest for archaeological confirmation was futile. After his death, a book describing his personal deconversion (Larson 1997) appeared. Ferguson never disaffiliated from the Church, either because he did not wish to cause his family and friends too much emotional pain, or because he found that the Church as a social

29. See the New York Times obituary for Montague at http://www.nytimes.com/1999/11/29/us/ashley-montagu-94-anthropologist-and-popular-author.html

30. See the dismissive review on the Brigham Young University website https://ojs.lib.byu.edu/spc/index.php/MSR/article/viewFile/34203/32028.

31. Vol 2, no. 3, issue #5, online at http://www.strangeark.com/nabr/NABR5.pdf

institution had many positive aspects, even if he no longer believed in its teachings. The apologetic site fairmormon.org goes to great lengths to present Ferguson as a very minor figure in Mormon scholarship, and a cynical man with dubious morals.[32]

Even in questions where there is very nearly a scientific consensus, it will usually be possible to locate a few dissenting voices. If one peruses a very vast literature, includes old or obscure publications in one's search, and lists as important evidence opinions that have been voiced at any point over the last century or more, the odds of finding textual evidence to support an unorthodox view is all the greater. As a method of arguing, the mention of minority views but silencing the near-consensus is ubiquitous in persuasive rhetoric of secular as well as religious kinds.[33]

Asserting religious authority in the contemporary period

As we have seen, the historical narrative in the Book of Mormon matches the presuppositions of early nineteenth century audiences, but is seriously challenged by advances over the last century and a half in disciplines as diverse as anthropology, archaeology, genetics, and linguistics. In the face of such challenges, individuals with the requisite training and a loyal commitment to the Mormon story attempt, in the words of Bruce Lincoln (1994, 4) to "produce consequential speech, quelling doubts and winning the trust of the audiences whom they engage" (Lincoln 1994, 4). Doing so has made apologists engage with opponents on the latter's turf. Rather than contenting themselves with the suggestion that sincere prayer will result in an inner feeling of certitude, Mormon writers construct both defensive arguments and proactive claims that the story in the sacred text can be superimposed on what is known about pre-Columbian America.

The defensive arguments can be reduced to two types. Firstly, the Book of Mormon is assumed to be a translation of a text in a foreign language, composed by people who were confronted with an environment they did not have the vocabulary to describe. Perhaps the supposedly anachronistic items are merely rough and easily misunderstood labels: cattle and horses could have been tapirs. Secondly, it is argued that controversial and putatively anachronistic items mentioned in the Book of Mormon really did exist in the New World, and that conventional archaeologists overlook this fact. Horses, it is claimed, did not die out in a distant prehistoric epoch, but were present when Book of Mormon peoples arrived on the scene. The proactive arguments, i.e.

32. http://en.fairmormon.org/Question:_Was_Thomas_Stuart_Ferguson_an_archaeologist%3F

33. In secular contexts, one need but think of climate skeptics, holocaust deniers, 9/11 conspiracy theorists, and tobacco lobbyists as examples of discourses where a tiny dissenting minority is promoted as "the other side of the issue."

those that match the scriptural account with the landscape and cultures of Mesoamerica, produce a fine-grained map of southern Mexico and Guatemala with Jaredite, Nephite, and Lamanite names superimposed on them.

To outsiders, such attempts to assert the authority of a particular reading of scriptural mythology over the scientific consensus come across as tendentious, but in a sense the hand of these Mormon intellectuals has been forced. In the contemporary period, the rhetorical force of science is unparalleled. Numerous religions have therefore attempted to find an ally in science, or at least emulated its external characteristics,[34] and Mormon writers have been part of that historical trend. Broadly speaking, mainstream scientific investigation of the distant past is characterized by the deployment of particular methods of research (such as controlled excavations, pollen analysis, dendrochronology, DNA analysis, and so forth), by the acceptance of core tenets that to the scientific community appear to be massively supported (e.g., the Land Bridge Hypothesis or the approximate date of extinction of various North American mammals), and by historically well-established institutional factors (including publishing in non-denominational peer-reviewed journals).[35] Few if any of these elements were in place when Joseph Smith had the Book of Mormon printed in 1830, but all of them have over time assumed paramount importance and present massive stumbling blocks for a wider acceptance of the Mormon account of the past. Adopting the specific characteristics of scientific investigation would risk radically undermining the Book of Mormon narrative. Sidestepping science entirely may appeal to religious insiders, but would undermine its broader credibility, as well. Hence, Mormon intellectuals have responded to the challenge by deploying their own methods (scriptural exegesis, reinterpretations of archaeological evidence), tenets (the complete accuracy of the Book of Mormon), and institutional structures (faith-based research institutions and faith-promoting publications), and have used such science-like strategies in order to arrive at conclusions that they deem satisfactory, but are shared by few if any outsiders to the Church. What one side finds to be compelling empirical evidence of the historical accuracy of the canonical text, the other side sees as the construction of *ad hoc* hypotheses. Socialization into a Mormon or a secular world view will ensure that the Bayesian inferences of LDS Church members and secular readers are vastly different, as are their views of who is an authority and what constitutes authoritative discourse. Hence, secular and Mormon discourses concerning

34. For cases studies illustrating this fact, see the numerous examples in Lewis and Hammer 2011.

35. This threefold characterization of the scientific mainstream is inspired by the discussion in Asprem 2015.

the past become radically incommensurable, a fact noted also by Mormon authors (e.g., Hamblin 1993, 197).

The official position of the LDS Church is that the historical veracity of the Book of Mormon is a matter of faith and personal revelation. As we have seen, the text itself suggests that an inner certitude as the result of heart-felt prayer, rather than empirical investigation, can settle the matter. A top-echelon leader of the LDS Church, serving directly under the President, Apostle Dallin H. Oaks, voices an official opinion in his statement that "It is our position that secular evidence can neither prove nor disprove the authenticity of the Book of Mormon" (Oaks 2001, 239). Nevertheless, key members of the Mormon intellectual community assert that the evidence is in their favor. Ultimately, this has far-reaching effects on what constitutes authoritative discourse, making Mormon readers of the book simultaneously open to having their view confirmed and immune to any empirically-based disconfirmation.

References

Adovasio, J.M. and David Pedler. 2005. "The peopling of North America." In *North American Archaeology*, edited by Timothy R. Pauketat and Diana DiPaolo Lauren, 30–55. London: Blackwell.

Asprem, Egil. 2015. "Dis/unity of knowledge: Models for the study of modern esotericism and science." *Numen* 62: 538–567.

Gardner, Brant A. 2013. "From the East to the West: The problem of directions in the Book of Mormon." *Interpreter: A Journal of Mormon Scripture* 3: 119–153.

Genette, Gérard. 1997. *Paratexts: Thresholds of Interpretation.* Cambridge: Cambridge University Press.

Godfrey, Kenneth W. 1989. "The Zelph Story." *BYU Studies* 29: 32–56.

Grayson, Donald K. 2007. "Deciphering North American Pleistocene extinctions." *Journal of Anthropological Research* 63: 185–213.

Hamblin, William J. 1993. "Basic methodological problems with the anti-Mormon approach to the geography and archaeology of the Book of Mormon." *Journal of Book of Mormon Studies* 2: 161–197.

Hamblin, William J. and A. Brent Merrill. 1990. "Swords in the Book of Mormon." In *Warfare in the Book of Mormon*, edited by Stephen D. Ricks and William J. Hamblin, 329–351. Salt Lake City: Deseret Book Co.

Hammer, Olav. 1997. "New Age religion and the sceptics." In *Handbook of New Age*, edited by Daren Kemp and James R. Lewis, 379–404, Leiden: Brill.

Hansson, Sven Ove. 2017. "Science and pseudo-science." In *The Stanford Encyclopedia of Philosophy* (Summer 2017 Edition), edited by Edward N. Zalta. https://plato.stanford.edu/archives/sum2017/entries/pseudo-science/.

Haynes, Gary. 2002. "The catastrophic extinction of North American mammoths and mastodonts." *World Archaeology* 33: 391–416.

Hoskisson, Paul Y., ed. 2001. *Historicity and the Latter-day Saint Scriptures.* Provo, UT: Brigham Young University Religious Studies Center.

Larson, Stan. 1997. *Quest for the Gold Plates: Thomas Stuart Ferguson's Archaeological Search for the Book of Mormon.* Salt Lake City: Freethinker Press.

Lee, Martha F. 2005. "Nesta Webster: The Vice of Conspiracy." *Journal of Women's History* 17: 81–104.

Lewis, James R. and Olav Hammer, eds. 2011. *Handbook of Religion and the Authority of Science.* Leiden: Brill.

Lincoln, Bruce. 1994. *Authority: Construction and Corrosion.* Chicago, IL: University of Chicago Press.

Martin, Paul S. 1973. "The discovery of America." *Science*, New Series 179: 969–974.

Mauss, Armand. 1994. *The Angel and the Beehive: The Mormon Struggle with Assimilation.* Urbana: University of Illinois Press.

McGuire, R. H. 1992. "Archeology and the first Americans." *American Anthropologist* 94: 816–836.

Oaks, Dallin. 2001. "The historicity of the Book of Mormon." In *Historicity and the Latter-day Saint Scriptures,* edited by Paul Y. Hoskisson, 237–248. Provo, UT: Brigham Young University Religious Studies Center.

Palmer, David. 1981. *In Search of Cumorah.* Bountiful, UT: Horizon. Special collection.

Perego, Ugo A. and Jayne E. Ekins. 2014. "Is decrypting the genetic legacy of America's indigenous population key to the historicity of the Book of Mormon?" *Interpreter: A Journal of Mormon Scripture* 12: 237–279.

Roper, Matthew. 1996. "Eyewitness descriptions of swords in the Book of Mormon." *Journal of Book of Mormon Studies* 5: 150–158.

———. 1997. "On cynics and swords." *FARMS Review of Books* 9: 146–158.

———. 1999. "Swords and 'cimeters' in the Book of Mormon." *Journal of Book of Mormon Studies* 8: 34–43, 77–78.

———. 2015. "John Bernhisel's gift to a prophet: Incidents of travel in Central America and the Book of Mormon." *Interpreter: A Journal of Mormon Scripture* 16: 207–253.

Silverberg, Robert. 1969. *Mound Builders of Ancient America: The Archaeology of a Myth.* Greenwich, CT: New York Graphic Society.

Sorenson, John L. 1985. *An Ancient American Setting for the Book of Mormon.* Salt Lake City, UT: Deseret Books.

———. 1992. *The Geography of Book of Mormon Events: A Source Book.* Provo, UT: The Foundation for Ancient Research and Mormon Studies.

Southerton, Simon. 2004. *Losing a Lost Tribe: Native Americans, DNA and the Mormon Church.* Salt Lake City, UT: Signature Books.

Thomas, Cyrus. 1894. Report on the mound explorations of the Bureau of Ethnology. *12th Annual Report of the Bureau of Ethnology for 1890-1891.*Washington: Smithsonian Institution.

Wauchope, Robert. 1962. *Lost Tribes and Sunken Continents: Myth and Method in the Study of the American Indians.* Chicago, IL: University of Chicago Press.

About the author

Olav Hammer is Professor of the Study of Religions at the University of Southern Denmark, Odense, Denmark. His three main research areas concern 'alternative' religion in Europe, alternative archaeology as modern myth-making, and issues of rhetorical legitimation in the history of various religious traditions. Recent publications include *Western Esotericism in Scandinavia* (Leiden: Brill 2016, edited with Henrik Bogdan), the *Brill Handbook of the Theosophical Current*. Leiden: Brill 2013; and *Cambridge Companion to New Religious Movements* (Cambridge: Cambridge University Press 2012, both of the preceding edited with Mikael Rothstein).

III

Authority, Media and Modern Identity Politics

— 8 —

Between Progress and the Frontier: Authority and Mob Violence in The Gonzales Inquirer at the Turn of the Twentieth Century

Anne Magnussen

At the turn of the twentieth century, Anglo Texans dominated the town of Gonzales, Texas, at all levels regarding political, socio-economic and cultural features. According to the local newspaper's coverage of Gonzales life, the county's legal, political and cultural institutions represented an authority that was only implicitly racially defined, but that nevertheless was unquestionably Anglo Texan. Building on Hanna Arendt's definition of authority and applying a narrative approach as the main methodological tool, I describe how The Inquirer defined authority within the framework of a narrative of progress and in relation to two other co-existing narratives, a Southern narrative and a frontier narrative. The progress narrative can be seen as part of the important social, economic and demographic changes that the region went through at the time, changes that challenged Anglo Texan dominance on several levels. In this chapter I study this process by using a specific conflict that involved ethnicity, violence and power. In June 1901, Gregorio Cortéz was accused of killing the Gonzales County Sheriff Richard Glover, and I use this case as a prism through which I study how mob violence seriously challenged The Inquirer's progress narrative and the idea of Anglo Texan authority. I analyze how the newspaper tried to overcome the conflict between the high level of violence against African Texans and Mexican Texans and the idea of Anglo Texan authority. The Inquirer ultimately failed to do this, and as a perspective on the analysis, I discuss how the progress narrative was reshaped over the succeeding years.

On June 12, 1901, Gregorio Cortéz allegedly shot and killed Richard Glover, the sheriff of Gonzales County in central Texas. Cortéz escaped, but on June 22 after a manhunt that involved hundreds of people he was caught in southern Texas. Cortéz was brought to the Gonzales County Jail at the beginning of July to await prosecution for three murders, including that of the Gonzales sheriff. One month later, the case against Cortéz for the murder of Sheriff Glover was still pending, but he was sentenced to 50 years in penitentiary for the murder of another man. As a reaction to the sentence, a mob gathered outside the jail and demanded that the interim sheriff, F.M. Fly, handed over Cortéz. Without success the mob tried to break down the door and after a while they left. The local newspaper *The Daily Inquirer* (and its weekly edition, *The Gonzales Inquirer*) followed the events closely, from the killing of Glover and throughout Cortéz' flight, his capture and the first court case against him.

Even though the mob did not succeed in getting to Cortéz, the risk of a lynching was real. This was spelled out on the front page of the *San Antonio Express*, which stated "An Attempt Made to Lynch Gregorio Cortez." (*San Antonio Express,* August 12, 1901, 1). Mob violence was not unusual at this time, and even though the precise extent of this kind of violence is difficult to ascertain, William D. Carrigan and Clive Webb have documented 20 mortal cases in Texas within the period leading up to the Glover/Cortéz case (1880–1900). However, according to the two scholars this figure only represents "a fraction of the actual number of Mexicans lynched" (Carrigan and Webb 2013, 5). At the turn of the century in Texas mob violence typically ran along racial lines, and the absolute majority of the victims of mob violence were either African Texan or, as Cortéz Mexican Texan, and the perpetrators were usually Anglo Texan or *white* (Carrigan 2004, 132–161). The mob at the county jail hid their faces, but there are no indications that they were anything but white either.

The Cortéz/Glover case offers several interesting conflicts for an analysis of the questioning of authority. An obvious example would be the confrontation between Cortéz and the sheriff. In this paper, however, I focus on how Anglo Texan behaviour undermined the authority of the legal system as it did for example when the mob turned up at the Gonzales County Jail. With the Cortéz/Glover case and other cases as examples, I will argue that mob violence not only questioned the Gonzales institutions' authority, but also the idea that authority was nature-given or unquestionably Anglo Texan.

Anglo Texans dominated Gonzales and Texas at all levels with regard to political, socio-economic and cultural features. According to *The Inquirer*'s (daily and weekly) general coverage of Gonzales life, the county's legal, political and cultural institutions represented authorities, which were only implicitly racially defined, but which nevertheless were unquestionably Anglo Texan. The city and county leadership and administration were entirely Anglo Texan; the business and cultural activities described in the newspaper were those of Anglo Texan families, and when Mexican Texans or African Texans were mentioned, they were marked clearly as such. *The Inquirer* defined Anglo Texan dominance within a narrative of progress according to which Gonzales' institutions were fully developed and their status and decisions generally respected.

This chapter is a study of how *The Inquirer* reacted when the Cortéz/ Glover case challenged this Anglo Texan institutional authority. As one of the town's key promoters of Anglo Texan authority, *The Inquirer* tried to overcome the conflict between authority and violence in its coverage of the Cortéz/Glover case. As will be apparent in the analysis below, this was no easy task. After a short introduction to the conceptual framework and literature, including the relationship between authority and (extralegal) violence, I analyse how *The Inquirer* defined authority within the framework of the progress narrative and in relation to two other co-existing narratives, a *Southern* narrative and a *frontier* narrative. As the second part of the analysis, I will discuss how *The Inquirer* grapples with the presentation of the Cortéz/Glover case.

Conceptual framework and literature

According to Hannah Arendt, authority is "unquestioning recognition by those who are asked to obey," which means that a person or an office with authority requires neither coercion nor persuasion to remain in authority (Arendt 1970, 45). Bruce Lincoln draws on Arendt's definition when describing the relationship between authority and force:

> [I]f force is actually used, or if threats of force are made with anything less than extreme delicacy (a delicacy that insures deniability), authority risks being perceived as a fig leaf of legitimacy that conceals the embarrassment of naked force. And when authority operates (and is seen to operate) on pain and fear rather than on trust and respect, it ceases to be authority and becomes (an attempt at) coercion. (Lincoln 1994, 6)

When power is made visible through the use of violence, it no longer represents authority. The fact that the Anglo Texan mob recurred to threatening with extralegal violence against Cortéz therefore undermined the idea of institutional authority. Raúl Rodriguez Guillén refers to mob violence, or more specifically to lynching, as a type of force that questions authority. Writing about recent cases of lynching in Mexico, Rodriguez Guillén argues that generally speaking, the exemplary character of lynching "is a step backwards with regards to the institutionalization of authority; it represents a return to the law of the strongest, not of the fairest, calling into question the judicial system as a whole" (my translation, Rodríguez Guillén 2014, 176). In the specific context of central Texas at the turn of the century, mob violence activated references to the *frontier* narrative, which was a dominant narrative in Texas for a considerable part of the nineteenth century.

As indicated, the concept of narrative is used as an analytical tool. Drawing on Arendt's definition of authority, Frank Furedi argues that "[a]ssumptions on authority are informed through cultural narratives about how a community perceives the past, its institutions and the uncertainties it faces" (Furedi 2013, 13; Bal 2009, 225–229). Narratives shape ideas, values and behaviour, which lends a dominant narrative a particular power as it highlights some groups and values and marginalizes—or silences—others (Trouillot 1995, 26–27).

In the case of *The Inquirer*'s coverage of Gonzales life, Mexican Texans and African Texans played no active role, and if anything, they functioned as the counter image to the dominant Anglo American community. In this way, the narrative of progress that *The Inquirer* promoted did not have to be defined explicitly according to race and ethnicity; it was an unquestioned state of affairs.

A similar focus on the Anglo Texans as the unquestioned protagonists was present also in traditional accounts of Texas history. The people who belonged in Texas, the real *Texans,* were defined according to race (white) and ethnicity (European), and other ethnic or racially defined groups played the roles of antagonists or the Other. The defining period and event in traditional accounts were the Anglo American Immigration into Texas from the 1820s and the Texas revolution at the beginning of the 1830s (Barker 1969; Lack 1991; Magnussen 2016). This changed especially from the 1980s with a new generation of scholarship that introduced an explicit focus on other ethnic groups and the relationship between them and the Anglo Texans. Studies of Mexican Texans were especially numerous, but also studies of African Texans began to emerge (Barr 2009; Campbell 1989; Stewart and de León 1993; Montejano 1987; Zamora 1993). Studies often focus on the violent nature of ethnic and racial interaction, including studies of mob violence (Carrigan 2004; Carrigan and Webb 2013). With these studies, race and ethnicity became a key focus, and with specific relevance for this paper, *whiteness* studies have gained much traction since the beginning of the 1990s, although focused less specifically on Texas. David Roediger draws attention to the central fact that race is a socially constructed category that is reproduced and modified over time, which means that the meanings attached to being white also change (Roediger 2008, xi–xii; Jacobson 2012). Inspired by *whiteness* studies, this paper differs from many of the studies of ethnic conflict and interaction in Texas because of its focus on conflicting narratives within the Anglo Texan or white community, and not primarily in relation to other ethnic or racially defined groups. Hereby it offers Gonzales as a case with regards to bigger questions concerning race, ethnicity and power at the time in central Texas. This paper also draws on other studies of the Cortéz case and of the press in Texas (Limón 1994; Mertz 1974; Paredes 1958; Walraven 1999; Kökény 2004).

With the choice of terminology, i.e. Anglo Texans, African Texans and Mexican Texans, I differentiate between three groups of Americans according to their ethnicity. I use Mexican Texan as a reference to all persons of Mexican descent living in Texas, not taking into account whether they were US or Mexican nationals. The groups were of course far from as homogenous as the general terms indicate, and each group represented considerable differences with regards to origins, citizenship and socio-economic status. At the turn of the century, the general ethnic distinction nevertheless shaped discourse and behaviour in Texan society. In accordance with Roediger mentioned above, race is understood as a social construction, with the distinction between black and white as the main distinction. Anglo Texan and *white* are used as synonyms in this paper, as are African Texan and *black*. At the turn of the century it was not unusual to see Mexican Texans defined as a third race (*Mexican*), but the group was also often included with African Texans in a common category of *Coloreds*.

The topic of terminology with regards to race and ethnicity in the US is no simple matter, and any choice comes with its own drawbacks. For this paper, I have found the above categories the most adequate, but the possibilities and consequences of any choice are many (Carrigan and Webb 2013, xiii; Gómez 2007, 12–13; McDonald 2007, 165; Montejano 1987, 10–11; Orozco 2009, 10–12; Stewart and de León 1993, xiv–xv). Mob violence and lynching are central terms in this study, but their definition and reference to the historical events are far from simple (Carrigan 2004, 10). I use "extralegal violence" as the overarching term for any use of violence committed outside of the legal system. "Mob violence" defines extralegal violence committed by a group of people, and following Carrigan, lynching is "a summary execution committed by a self-appointed group without regard for established legal procedures" (Carrigan 2004, 10).

New times in Gonzales

From 1880 to 1920, Texas went through important social, economic, and political changes. Since Texas' independence and succeeding US statehood in the 1830s and 1840s, cattle and ranching had dominated in central Texas, including in Gonzales county, but with the arrival of the railroad and new methods of irrigation, the region was fast turning into a region of more labour intensive agriculture, such as cotton production, wheat, fruit and vegetables. The development created a new demand for agricultural labour and the region saw a considerable increase in immigration from Mexico and from other parts of the US (Montejano 1987, 106–128; US Census, Gonzales, Texas 1880, 1900).

In 1882 Gonzales had its first railroad branch, which connected the town to the main railway between the coast and the mainland. The town was already the administrative and legal centre of the county, but helped along by the railroad connection it also became an important commercial and small-scale industrial centre for the region. The turn of the century saw the creation of new production sites, including a cotton oil mill and a cotton mill, as well as the expansion of an existing brick yard and a lumber yard (Vollentine 1986, 99–119).

Along with the development in agriculture, commerce and production, the town's population grew from 1641 people in 1890 to 4297 in 1900 (US Census, Gonzales, Texas 1900; Vollentine 1986, 94). Gonzales was urbanized with hotels, bars and more shops, but also with graded streets, sidewalks, and the expansion of electricity, water supply and the sewage system. Local authorities also tried to regulate behavior in downtown Gonzales through legislation and registration (Gonzales City Council Minutes 1899–1905).

Part of the urbanization process was the development of more, and more stable, institutions such as schools and churches. Neighbourhoods and institutions were segregated; there were separate schools for white and black children, and from 1899 there was also a so-called Mexican school (*The Gonzales Inquirer* (abbreviated *GI*), May 4, 1899, 8). The Anglo Texan population lived within the town's original 49 blocks and with the population increase it expanded eastwards. The African Texan neighbourhood was located around the railroad station to the north of downtown and expanded further north and northeast. As the Mexican Texan population was relatively new in Gonzales, a separate neighbourhood was only beginning to take shape close to the river and some of the town's small industries.

Segregation meant marginalization and generally the Mexican Texan and African Texan areas in town were marginalized not only in space, but also with regard to the standard of amenities. However, segregation also meant concentration and size and opened for a strengthening of the ethnically defined institutions, including more and new possibilities with regards to community based positions of responsibility and power. This was seen especially in relation to the African Texan community's schools and churches. Although less well-established, a similar process seemed to be underway also within the Mexican Texan community.

Until the 1880s, the racial dynamics in Gonzales had followed that of the US South, and a Southern narrative had dominated with a clear relationship of power between the *white* and *colored* communities. At the turn of the century, this dynamic had become less straight-forward due to at least three factors relating to demographic change. The new presence of a Mexican Texan community was one factor, and another was a bigger, but also more independent and visible African Texan community. A third factor was that with the population growth, the white population had become more heterogeneous. Whereas most of the white community of the 1880s had roots in the US south, a considerable part of the newcomers came more or less directly from Europe or from other parts of the US (US Census, Gonzales, Texas 1880, 1900, 1910).

These three changes challenged Anglo Texan dominance as defined by the Southern narrative. *The Inquirer*'s strengthening of a narrative of progress with Anglo Texans as the natural and only heroes can be seen as an effort to insist on Anglo Texan authority in the face of these race- and ethnically related changes. The study of *The Inquirer*'s coverage of the Cortéz/Glover case is an analysis of what happened to Anglo Texan power in Gonzales in a period of societal change. More specifically, I analyse how *The Gonzales Inquirer* tried discursively to insist on Anglo Texan authority in the face of the use of violence in the Cortéz/Glover case.

Narratives of the frontier, of the south, and of progress

In 1853 two Anglo Texans, S.W. Smith and D.S.H. Darst, founded *The Gonzales Inquirer.* It was the main—and for most of the town's history only—Gonzales newspaper (Vollentine 1986, 134). There were a few efforts to establish African Texan and German Texan newspapers, but they did not last beyond a maximum of a couple of years (*GI*, June 4, 1953; Vollentine 1986, 135). *The Inquirer* sympathized with the dominant party in the region, the Democratic Party, but it seldom made this explicit (an exception was *The Daily Inquirer* (abbreviated *DI*), September 17 1908, 2). Many of the points made in the analysis below are based on recurrent statements in the newspaper, but for practical purposes, only few specific examples will be mentioned in the references. As an Anglo Texan newspaper it primarily brought articles and notes about its own community, and whenever African Texans or Mexican Texans were mentioned, they were marked by their race. This was the case in news stories, on jury and tax lists, and with many references to schools and churches (Magnussen 2009). The *unmarked* community was Anglo Texan and on the few occasions that they were actually marked, it was as white and as part of distinctions between for example White and Negro schools and teachers (*GI*, Aug. 9 1900, 2).

Similar to other Texan newspapers during the late nineteenth and early twentieth century, *The Inquirer* played an important role in the community, not only by offering information and news, but also by shaping readers' values, behaviour, and sense of community. The role of the editor was that of "an interested participant in the history that moves about him" (*GI*, June 4, 1953), and editors were often very specific in their appeals to the readers for example to keep downtown Gonzales clean or to contribute to investments in local small-industry projects or in infrastructure (*GI*, June 22, 1899, 6; *GI*, March 5, 1903, 5). Also on a more general level the editors' choice of article subjects and comments on local, regional and national events fed into what I have called the narrative of progress. This narrative was visible in other contexts too, for example in legal and political decision making, but *The Inquirer* was the medium that spelled it out most conspicuously and consistently.

The narrative of progress was relatively new at the turn of the century and it was part of broader developments and trends within the so-called Texas Progressive Era. The central efforts of the progressive era were political reform and anti-corruption measures, and its values related to science, education, industry, democracy and hard work. In Gonzales, the progress narrative emerged alongside two other already existing narratives that had influenced Anglo Texan identities over the bigger part of the nineteenth century, namely the frontier narrative and the Southern narrative. The two differed from the narrative of progress on several points, and one with specific relevance for this article is that the new progress narrative did not—as the other two did—explicitly include the use of violence as legitimate behaviour.

In his study of violence in seven central Texan counties (not including Gonzales) William D. Carrigan describes how historical memories of the frontier and of racial slavery were central to the continued use and legitimization of extralegal violence throughout the nineteenth century and the beginning of the twentieth century (Carrigan 2004, 18). Within the narrative framework used in this paper, the frontier narrative drew on memories about the dangerous life on the frontier before a legal system was in place, making the use of violence necessary to protect one's family. The Southern narrative, on the other hand, had as its foundation the relationship between slave and owner, and according to Carrigan, this relationship "undermined the formal legal system by informally handling the investigation, judgement and sentencing of many crimes" (Carrigan 2004, 13).

Both narratives had the Anglo Texan as the protagonist, and ethnicity and/or race defined their main conflicts with the Native American and the Mexican as the antagonist in the frontier narrative, and the African American in the Southern narrative. Carrigan sums up the violent characteristic of these narratives:

> Local memories of extralegal violence were powerful in central Texas. They encompassed rebellion against "despotic" Mexico, battles against "savage" Native Americans, repression of "carpetbagging" whites, and control of "beastlike" emancipated African Americans. (Carrigan 2004, 14)

In his analysis of mob violence, Carrigan does not include what I have called the narrative of progress. There may be several reasons for this, and one of them could be that it was not as explicit in any of the counties that Carrigan studied as it was in Gonzales and in *The Inquirer*. In any case, this narrative stands out from the other two as it completely ignores two features that are central to Carrigan's presentation of the frontier and the Southern memories, namely the use of violence and the references to the past, i.e. the nineteenth century. The frontier and Southern narratives shaped the future as a continuity of the past, while the narrative of progress defined itself in opposition to the past.

The frontier and Southern narratives could occasionally be seen in *The Inquirer*, especially the latter, with references to the South and primarily in relation to the African Texan population (*GI*, Dec 1, 1898, 2; *GI*, Oct 23, 1902, 4). However, they were both challenged, although in different ways, at the turn of the century. According to Frederick Turner, the frontier ceased to exist at the end of the nineteenth century as the Americans had reached the west coast, and also in *The Inquirer*, frontier values and behaviour were considered a thing of the past at the beginning of the twentieth century (Turner 1893). The Southern narrative had been present in Gonzales since the middle of the nineteenth century, and at the turn of the century Southern values continued to define the Anglo Texan community. This was no surprise as more than 50 percent of the Gonzales population were first or second generation immigrants from the US South (US Census, Gonzales, Texas 1880, 1900). With a more heterogeneous white population from especially the last 20 years of the nineteenth century, the Southern narrative was, however, if not questioned, at least harder to maintain as the dominant narrative. Also the industrialization and urbanization processes challenged this narrative as it changed the dynamics between blacks and whites and introduced a third group, the Mexican Texans.

Around 1900, *The Inquirer* promoted the narrative of progress that in many ways represented the progressive values of the time. The newspaper shared and contributed to the general optimism and confidence in a bright future that defined the ideas behind the Texas Progressive Era. According to

The Inquirer, the construction of a cotton mill in Gonzales in 1900 was exactly the kind of initiative that would secure Gonzales a bright future, and the newspaper's coverage eloquently described Gonzales' heroes of progress. In April 1901, the newspaper proclaimed in a headline and subtitle:

> INDUSTRIAL GONZALES IT IS. Fully Equipped Machine Shops to be Established, With Practical Men at the Head. Keeping Gonzales Money in Gonzales Will Build Up and Push the City Forward in the Industrial Race for Supremacy. (*GI*, April 18, 1901, 1)

The "practical men" were the narrative's heroes and even though they were not explicitly referred to as Anglo Texan or white, it was clear that they were. This could be seen for example in the newspaper's special sections on businesses and businessmen in Gonzales. As a case in point, in 1899 the newspaper printed a series of portraits of Anglo Texan businesses and businessmen, emphasizing their key role in Gonzales' development. Among the business men portrayed, several generations were represented, including some of the original settler families from the 1830s; the cattle and cotton families arriving in the 1850s; and quite a few newcomers including several German American families (*GI,* April 27, 1899, 1 and 3; *GI,* May 4, 11 and 18, 1899, 1). The business men's origins were often mentioned, but they were not explicitly referred to as white, although they all were.

The narrative focused on progress, finance and industry, but with an important twist: The Anglo Texan heroes worked primarily for the community and only secondly for personal gains. This was spelled out repeatedly in comments such as: "[...] there are things more to be considered than the mere piling up of money and more precious than high living. A man cannot be selfish and at the same time a good citizen" (*GI*, April 13, 1899, 7). And: "There is nothing more important to a town or of greater interest to a community than the display of public spirit in city improvement of all kinds. They are the evidence of a refined and progressive people" (*GI*, March 24 1904).

The progress narrative embraced all changes in the region and in Gonzales as entirely positive, including the many new shops and industries and the demographic growth. Bigger was by definition better, and the newspaper did not hold back for example when it came to comparisons between Gonzales and much bigger places such as Houston (*GI*, April 27, 1899). As will be apparent below, the progress narrative influenced and shaped values and practices with regards to race, ethnicity, and power relations, but it also pushed forward the business and industrial activities going on in Gonzales at the time. The construction of the cotton mill and the cotton oil mill as well as infrastructural improvements can be seen as examples of this.

The narrative of progress differed, as mentioned above, from the other two narratives with regards to its oppositional view of the past. This made it more useful when it came to unite the new heterogeneous, white population, not around a common past, but around a common future and a common skin colour. There was already a relatively big population of German descent in Gonzales, and at the end of the nineteenth century it only increased. To this should be added that the last decade of the nineteenth century saw more immigrants from Eastern Europe (US Census 1880, 1900). Even though the majority of Gonzales' white population belonged to protestant churches, there were small groups of Jews and (non-Mexican) Catholics (Frenzel 1999, 11, 57; *GI*, Jan 19, 1884, 3; *GI*, May 25, 1899, 5; *GI*, April 18, 1907; Vollentine 1986, 127).

Another basic difference was that race and ethnicity played a central role in both the frontier and Southern narratives, while these features did not seem to contribute at all to the progress narrative. As implied in the quotations above about selfish citizens, the (Anglo Texan) hero's main challenge was to overcome his own potential propensity *not* to contribute to the community. The conflicts did not emerge from racial or ethnic confrontations as in the first two narratives, but from within the Anglo Texan community —or more specifically—within (the Anglo Texan) man.

The fact that the progress narrative did not mark its heroes explicitly in terms of race or ethnicity, but as *citizens* or only by name, was central to the assumption of both belonging and authority. The Anglo Texans were citizens, while Mexican Texans and African Texans were defined first by their race and ethnicity, and only secondly, as belonging in Gonzales or by name. The narrative of progress can be understood as *The Inquirer*'s effort to shape the community's perception of the past and of the future. The narrative implied that the community, including its development and institutions, was Anglo Texan, and within the logic of *The Inquirer*'s progress narrative, Anglo American institutions represented the natural authority. An individual's skin colour, *whiteness*, pointed in and of itself to specific qualities, to a specific position in society and therefore to authority (Furedi 2013, 8; Roediger 2008, 3).

At the turn of the century in Gonzales, the narrative of progress worked in three directions. It tried to push The Anglo Texan community to develop Gonzales in commercial and industrial terms. Secondly, it was part of an effort to unite the new, bigger and more heterogeneous *white* community after the influx of new people. And as the third direction, it insisted that racially defined conflicts were no longer an issue, that they belonged to the past. However, race related conflicts and violence continued to be part of Gonzales, and at times it was impossible for *The Inquirer* to ignore it.

One of these times was when Gregorio Cortéz allegedly killed the sheriff of Gonzales County.

Rumour has it: Mob violence in Gonzales county

This paper focuses on *The Inquirer*'s coverage of the Glover/Cortéz case and not on the case itself, but a minimum of background information about the case will nevertheless be useful. According to the media coverage and the court papers, the case unfolded as follows. The events took off when Sheriff Morris of neighbouring Karnes County approached Cortéz and his brother outside their home, inquiring about a stolen horse. The situation escalated and when the Sheriff shot Cortéz' brother, Cortéz shot and killed Sheriff Morris and then ran off. From statements in court and in interviews it was clear that Cortéz believed that he acted in self-defence. When he nevertheless tried to escape it was because he doubted that he, a Mexican up against an Anglo, would be treated fairly by the justice system (*El Regidor*, December 23, 1909, 2; Abernethy *et al.* 1904, 5; District Court Files, Case No. 3256). He therefore looked up a friend, Martín Robledo, and asked him for help. Robledo lived on a small farm in Gonzales County. As soon as the news of Morris' death began to circulate, officials and citizens formed posses to look for the killer, and Sheriff Glover of Gonzales County was in charge of a posse that went to the house of the Robledo family. It is not entirely clear what happened in the confrontation between the posse and the group at Robledo's house, but what is known is that Glover and another member of the posse, Henry Schnabel, were killed, and Cortéz and two other Mexican Texans connected to the Robledo family escaped. This marked the beginning of a three week long manhunt for Cortéz until he was finally caught and brought to Gonzales County Jail (Abernethy *et al.* 1904; *District Court, Gonzales*, Case No. 3264; *GI*; *DI*; *San Antonio Express*, June 1901; *El Regidor* 1909–1911).

During the manhunt the posses targeted *Mexicans*, killing three Mexican Texans and seriously wounding at least five, and probably all Mexican Texans living in central and south Texas were scared (Carrigan and Webb 2013, 175; see also Paredes 55–107; *El Regidor* 1909–1911; *San Antonio Express*, June 1901). Carrigan and Webb list two broad types of mob violence, one that "includes mobs that targeted and killed particular individuals for specific crimes or actions" and another, which is "the indiscriminate slaying of individuals based on group identity, such as being from Mexico" (Carrigan and Webb 2013, xii). The authors argue that they are not mutually exclusive, and the Glover/Cortéz case can be said to involve both. The mob at the county jail specifically targeted Cortéz, and even though the manhunt was focused on the search for one individual, it seemed to turn into a general search for Mexicans (*DI*, June 17, 1901, 1; *DI*, June 20, 1901, 1; *DI*, June 24, 1901, 1).

As part of their research on mob violence against Mexican Americans, Carrigan and Webb discuss the Cortéz/Glover case. They state that all the newspapers in the region covered the events closely, and that "wildly inaccurate newspaper stories fanned the fear and prejudice of readers, Cortéz mutating in the pages of the *San Antonio Express* into a marauding gang of murderers." (cited in Carrigan and Webb 2013, 174). On a more general level, they argue that

> [w]ith some honorable exceptions, English language newspapers in the American West responded to the lynching of Mexicans either by excluding coverage from their paper, or, when such incidents were already public knowledge, exonerating the actions of the mob. (Carrigan and Webb 2013, 114)

As will be apparent, *The Inquirer*'s coverage of the Cortéz/Glover case seemed to represent a more complex and partially contradictory attitude towards the specific events and to the use of violence. The contradictions emerged from the fact that the Cortéz/Glover case challenged some of the main characteristics of the progress narrative. For one, the case involved ethnicity as a central component, and furthermore, it made explicit Anglo Texan extralegal violence against the established institutions. *The Inquirer's* coverage of the Cortéz/Glover case represented it from two perspectives with regards to mob violence and authority. According to one perspective the newspaper condemned mob violence, and according to the other, it argued (although reluctantly at times) in favour of mob violence under special circumstances.

To begin with the former, the newspaper criticized mob violence, for example when it argued that it was "fortunate" that the mob failed in getting to Cortéz at the county courthouse (*DI*, August 12, 1901, 1; *GI*, August 15, 1901, 3). It also stated that "[a]t best the mob spirit is brave only in its frenzy or in the consciousness of its overwhelming numbers" (*DI*, August 14 1901, 1; *GI*, August 15, 1901, 1). In an uncommented quotation from another newspaper it considered that "Mobs are essentially cowardly" (*DI*, August 14, 1901, 1; *GI*, August 15, 1901, 1). *The Inquirer* also admired Sheriff Fly's role in the events and his defence of Cortéz with headlines such as "A Courageous Sheriff" and "Sheriff Fly's Nerve" (*DI*, August 12, 14, 1901, 1; *GI*, August 15, 1901, 1, 3). From this perspective, *The Inquirer* confirmed the values of the narrative of progress: Gonzales society was well beyond the *mob law* of frontier times and had well-functioning institutions that served the community—represented by the sheriff's office, the jail, and the county court.

The Inquirer nevertheless went to considerable lengths to modify what had taken place at the jail. In an effort to maintain that the Gonzales citizens respected its institutions and their authority, it did two—partially contradictory—things. The newspaper implied that the participants of the mob were not actually Gonzales citizens, and it described the mob as acting almost civilized. The former point was apparent in the choice of headline: "A Mob Pays Gonzales a Visit," which emphasized that the mob was an outside force; that it did not really have anything to do with Gonzales. Apparently, the people in the mob could not be recognized as they covered their faces, and some (including the new Sheriff Fly) argued that they had been from Karnes County, whose sheriff (Morris) had been killed in the confrontation that had started off the events (*DI*, August 12, 1901, 1; *San Antonio Express*, August 12, 1901, 1). With its choice of title *The Inquirer* distanced itself and Gonzales from the events: a mob could not belong in Gonzales. With the choice of subtitle: "ARMED, ORGANIZED AND DISCIPLINED, BUT NOT VIOLENT" (di aug 12, 14, 1901 1 / gi aug 15 1901 1, 3), the mob was described almost as a civilized group. At least, it maintained some of the key values of the narrative of progress, as they were organized and disciplined.

The Inquirer also tried to deny that Gonzales citizens were involved in mob violence in relation to the preceding manhunt. At one instance during the search for Cortéz, a posse thought it had caught him and the two men who had escaped with him from the Robledo house. In the confrontation, one of the men was killed and another seriously hurt. According to *The Inquirer*, it was an honest case of mistaken identity with nobody to blame (*GI*, June 20, 1901, 1). The incident was not described in any greater detail in the newspapers, but it is difficult to consider it anything but an example of extralegal violence. In the first days after Glover's death and Cortéz' escape, Texan newspapers brought notes about a mock-hanging in Gonzales of a Mexican Texan (*San Antonio Express*, June 16, 1901, 1; *El Regidor*, January 13, 1910, copy from 1901 coverage). *The Inquirer* mentioned the case a few days later as a rumour, while at the same time questioning that it had actually taken place:

> It was rumored yesterday that a Mexican was hung near Monthalia. An effort was being made to make the Mexican tell what he knew of the fleeing Mexicans and was kept hanging too long it was said. The rumor has not been corroborated and it is hoped will be found groundless (*DI*, June 17, 1901, 1).

Three days later, the newspaper commented on the same rumour again, and this time in a much more forceful way. Under the headline "Not True," *The Inquirer* vehemently denied the mock hanging and used capital lettering to emphasize the denial as it wrote "NO MEXICAN HAS BEEN HUNG IN THE COUNTY" in capital letters in the middle of the article (*DI*, June 20, 1901, 1). The explicit reference to Gonzales County is a parallel to the argument above that the mob at Gonzales Jail did not consist of Gonzales citizens.

Further on in the same article *The Inquirer* commented upon other violent incidents involving Mexican Texans. The newspaper recognized that two *Mexicans* had "met with death [...] while making a demonstration to resist arrest," but that none of them had been hung (*DI*, June 20, 1901, 1). Efforts to "resist arrest" may cover many things, but to speculate, a well-founded fear of mob violence one way or another may explain why a Mexican Texan resisted arrest during the time in question. These examples show that in comparison with at least some other Anglo Texan newspapers, *The Inquirer* tried to explain away mob violence relating to Gonzales citizens or the county, either by arguing that it was committed by non-Gonzales citizens or that it was not really mob violence. In this way the newspaper maintained its condemnation of mob violence. In *The Inquirer*'s representation of them, the specific incidents did not challenge the narrative of progress in any serious way, and neither the authority of Anglo Texan institutions.

The newspaper's efforts to deny or redefine extralegal violence did not keep for long. *The Inquirer* began arguing that while mob violence was wrong, it was understandable or even legitimate under specific circumstances. The first court case at Gonzales County Courthouse against Cortéz was for the killing of Henry Schnabel at the Robledo farm where both Schnabel and Glover died. It was a murder that according to the court papers was very difficult to actually pin on Cortéz (District Court Files, Case No. 3264). The sentence of 50 years in penitentiary seemed to be a compromise and was far from satisfactory for the people who were convinced that Cortéz deserved nothing short of a death sentence. To many, the courts made a serious mistake when it did not begin with one of the sheriff killings, as it was the general belief that they would have led to a death sentence (*San Antonio Express*, August 12, 1901, 1). *The Inquirer* included this viewpoint when the newspaper copied reports from other newspapers, for example from *Houston Post*, that stated "Mob violence is not to be excused but condemned, but still there are some extenuating circumstances" and one of these circumstances was when the justice system did not work properly (*Houston Post* in *DI*, August 14, 1901, 1). When the formalized justice system did not work, mob violence was the only way of securing that justice was done. *Bellville Times* was very explicit in its criticism of the Courts' decision to begin with the Schnabel killing, and the newspaper stated that that the Courts were:

> [...] inviting the mob—and if tomorrow a jail is found broken and a Mexican desperado discovered swaying from a telegraph pole somewhere in the volume of the gulf breeze, the world will know that Judge Lynch scored where the law made a goose egg. (*Bellville Times* in *GI*, Aug 15, 1901, 4)

Summing up *The Inquirer*'s two perspectives on extralegal violence, the first condemned mob violence and tried to distance Gonzales from it. It did not, in principle, damage the narrative of progress, but it was hard to maintain in the face of continued mob violence in the region. The second perspective, blaming the institutions, turned out to be more persistent and fed into a general debate of the time. As opposed to the former, this perspective activated the frontier narrative and seriously challenged the narrative of progress. One of the key elements of the narrative of progress was the belief in fully developed institutions, the authority of which was unquestioned. Mob violence, on the other hand, belonged to the frontier narrative and the necessity of taking the law into one's own hand because of the lack of well-functioning institutions. Within the framework of the frontier narrative, the Cortéz/Glover case also became an ethnically defined conflict. It became apparent that Anglo Texan power was based on violence, and not on an unquestioned Anglo Texan institutional authority as it was formulated within the narrative of progress.

The Inquirer went to great lengths to try to explain away actions that looked very much like rogue violence against Mexican Texans. Thereby the newspaper tried to insist on the Anglo Texans' civilized characteristics implied in the narrative of progress. It seemed to be a losing battle, though, as the narrative was challenged by mob law and strong frontier values pitting the Anglo Texan *Texans* against the Mexicans and legitimizing violence. The *Mexican* became a racialized actor, the villain, which seriously challenged the basic values of the narrative of progress and its focus on improving (white) community. With a reference to Lincoln's definition of authority, *The Inquirer*'s recognition that Anglo Texan extra-legal violence was understandable and could even be legitimized, basically questioned the progress narrative: "[...] when authority operates (and is seen to operate) on pain and fear rather than on trust and respect, it ceases to be authority and becomes (an attempt at) coercion" (Lincoln 1994, 6).

The frontier narrative was at least partially back in *The Inquirer* with the representation of racially and ethnically defined conflicts and a limited trust in the legal institutions. Almost ironically, it seemed that the frontier narrative and its mob violence almost solved one of the key challenges that *The Inquirer* implicitly tried to address with the progress narrative, namely the unification of the heterogeneous white population. Carrigan argues that mob violence actually strengthened the white community, when he states that "During the early twentieth century the growth of white solidarity, so important to the creation of large lynch mobs, reached its climax" (Carrigan 2004, 179). However, as described earlier, *The Inquirer* also saw the

Anglo Texan community of Gonzales as civilized far beyond frontier times and had big hopes for the future, economic development and expansion. In this context, a lack of trust in the institutions did not fit well. Based on the above analysis it could be argued that Gonzales had a crisis of authority at the beginning of the twentieth century, and over the following 20 years extralegal violence against both Mexican Texans and African Texans only increased in Texas generally, although without any equally spectacular incidents in Gonzales such as the Cortéz/Glover case (Carrigan 2004, 162–187).

It would require further studies to figure out how the question of authority evolved in Gonzales, but as part of the final remarks I discuss two different developments that could be taken into account in such studies.

Concluding remarks

Over the first 20 years of the twentieth century, two developments took place that had consequences for the question of authority in Gonzales and would be relevant to discuss in a broader study. One related to the modification in *The Inquirer* of the progress narrative, and the other to Mexican Texan and African Texan reactions against Anglo American dominance. In its coverage of Gonzales life after the Cortéz/Glover case, *The Inquirer* maintained many of the features from the progress narrative, but it combined them with strong historical references that created continuity and made race-related and ethnic conflicts part of the narrative.

One of the defining features of the progress narrative was the focus on the future in opposition to the past. This changed over the first 10–15 years of the twentieth century. Alongside the many articles and notes that fed into the progress narrative—similar to those mentioned above in the section on narratives—came more and more historical accounts, especially about the Texas revolution and Gonzales's specific role in it. Within the historical narrative of the Texas revolution, Gonzales had been "the Lexington of Texas" and the place of the "first shot of the Texas revolution," which were both references to the American revolution. This story was told repeatedly in *The Inquirer* during these years (*GI*, September 28, 1901, 4; *DI*, April 8, 1903, 2; *GI*, April 30, 1903, 6; *GI*, September 15, 1904, 8; Magnussen 2009). As part of a general US trend, women in Gonzales County established chapters of the historical associations, the Daughters of the Revolution of Texas (DRT) and the United Daughters of the Confederacy (UDC), and their activities were covered closely in the newspaper, not least their fundraising for monuments to the Texas revolution and to the Confederate Dead (Magnussen 2009).

This new historical focus is an interesting phenomenon for several reasons, including the question of gender, but specifically in relation to *The*

Inquirer's progress narrative, the activation of references to the Texas revolution and the Civil War made the ethnic and racially defined opponents visible again. History became part of the newspaper, but also of Gonzales as a place. The most conspicuous example was the placing of two historical monuments in 1910, one to the Confederate Dead and one to the Texas Heroes, on public squares in downtown Gonzales, next to the county courthouse.

The historical features did not oppose the progress narrative as the frontier narrative had done: instead, it supplemented it, and the monuments serve as a good example. They became part of the ordering and civilizing of downtown Gonzales, alongside the construction of sidewalks, electric lightening, and the rules against keeping pigs within the city limits. History transformed the lawless frontier times to parks and landscaping around historical monuments. *The Inquirer* continued to be a key promoter when it came to the redefinition of the progress narrative. When Gonzales won a price for "the cleanest town in Texas in her class" in 1912, *The Inquirer*'s coverage illustrates how the historical references had become part of the progress narrative. The newspaper argued that

> "Gonzales, The Lexington of Texas, Coming Into Her Own. Her Historical Importance Deserving of Further Recognition on the Part of Texas by the Appropriation of an Adequate Sum for the Establishment of a State Park Here. Truly Gonzales, the Lexington of Texas, is coming into her own. Another victory has been won, and Gonzales, routing disorder, rubbish, [...] as she routed Santa Anna's Mexican soldiers in years long gone, won the $300 prize and has taken her place as the cleanest town in Texas in her class."
>
> (*GI*, December 26, 1912, 1).

The Inquirer activated historical references (Santa Anna was the Mexican president and general in charge of the Mexican side in the wars for Texas independence in the 1830s) in its argument in favour of future developments of Gonzales, in this case a state park. In this way, historical significance came to legitimize future progress and civilization of Gonzales as a place. A key word in the quotation is that the conflict with the Mexicans had taken place "in years long gone." *The Mexican* was the historical enemy that did not belong in Gonzales. This must, of course, be studied in further detail, but it might be interesting to discuss whether this definition of the Mexican as the historical enemy was used to legitimize the continued discrimination and even violence against the Mexican Texans in the region.

The activation of the Civil War and the Confederacy arguably differed from the Texas revolution, as the Civil War led to the emancipation of the African American population, at least in principle. However, there are several memories of the Civil War of which one considers Southern white community as the moral victors, and therefore could be used in a similar way (Blight 2001; McMichael 2007, 95–96).

The definition of Gonzales as historical through the visibility of historical references—in public space and in *The Inquirer*—dissolved the opposition between the frontier and Southern narratives on the one hand, and the progress narrative on the other. It reinforced Anglo Texan dominance, and it might also be possible to argue that it strengthened authority structures within the Anglo Texan community. However, it also highlighted the battle lines of confrontation with the other two main ethnic communities, making it visible that Anglo Texan power was based on violence rather than authority.

This leads to another perspective, which would be relevant to include in further study, namely the development of African Texan and Mexican Texan counter narratives to Anglo American power. Both the African Texan and the Mexican Texan communities pushed back against the racial and ethnic hierarchy and the use of violence, and they did this through the construction of counter narratives, protests, and organizational structures (Carrigan 2004; Rosales 1999, 3–4).

The African Texan counter narrative placed race and the black-white relationship at the centre and used emancipation and the celebration of the end of slavery in 1865 as key features and events. As with most marginalized counter narratives it is not as easy to document this narrative as the Anglo Texan narratives (Trouillot 1995, 26–27). According to Carrigan, one of the African Texans' most effective protests against violence was to leave Texas, and there was a considerable emigration of African Texans from Texas to northern US states during the first 20 years of the twentieth century (Carrigan 2004, 170–172). Since the period of Reconstruction after the Civil War, African Texans had been politically active, and even though the actual means of influence were severely limited with segregation and disenfranchisement, they continued to try to organize (Atkins 1932; Hine 1979; Miller and Ulbig 2008). The first Texas chapter of The National Association for the Advancement of Colored People (NAACP) was formed in El Paso in 1915, and the organization worked in defence of African Texans in the judicial system, as well as to improve the conditions in the school system and more generally, to protest against segregation (Houston 2009, 510–511).

The history of the Anglo Texan efforts to racialize Mexican Texans as an inferior group stretched back to at least the beginning of the nineteenth century and references to Mexicans as a mixed or "mongrel" race (Campbell 2003, 131–132; Gómez 2007; Menchaca 2001). When Cortéz escaped after the confrontation with Sheriff Morris because he was afraid of mob violence, he drew on a Mexican Texan counter narrative that had the conflict between

Anglo Texans and Mexican Texans as its core. This narrative was present for example in the Mexican *corridos* that circulated in Texas, and it represented the Anglo Texans as violent, as cowards, and as lacking any human characteristics. This image was very far from the progress narrative's idea of the civilized and progressive citizen (Paredes 1958). Also the Mexican Texans began to organize in the early twentieth century, and the initiative behind for example the *Congreso Mexicanista* held in southern Texas in 1911 referred to discrimination in the educational system, but also very specifically to Anglo Texan violence against Mexican Texans (Magnussen 2013).

However, when it came to race, the Mexican Texan counter narrative was not as straightforward as the African Texan narrative. Especially the Mexican Texan middle class questioned the categorization of themselves as *colored*, and tried to insist on the fact that Mexican Texans were formally "white" according to the US Census lists (Foley 1997; Magnussen 2013; Overmyer-Velázquez 2013). The authority of Anglo Texan institutions was seriously questioned at the beginning of the twentieth century, and the Cortéz/Glover case exemplifies some of the fault lines when it came to race, ethnicity, and power.

References

Abernethy, B. R., Samuel Belden and J. R. Wooten. 1904. "Appeal from District Court, Colorado County. Brief for Appellant [Gregorio Cortéz]" *Court of Criminal Appeals of Texas*, Austin Term A.D. 1904.

Arendt, Hannah. 1970. *On Violence*. London: Penguin Press.

Atkins, J. Alston. 1932. *The Texas Negro and His Political Rights. A History of the Fight of Negroes to Enter the Democratic Primaries of Texas*. Houston, TX: Webster Publishing Company.

Bal, Mieke. 2009. *Narratology. Introduction to the Theory of Narrative*. 3rd ed. Toronto: University of Toronto Press.

Barker, Eugene C. 1969. *The Life of Stephen F. Austin, Founder of Texas, 1793–1836; a Chapter in the Westward Movement of the Anglo-American People*. Austin: University of Texas Press.

Barr, Alwyn. 2009. "Early organizing in the search for equality. African American Conventions in Late Nineteenth-Century Texas." In *Seeking Inalienable Rights. Texans and Their Quests for Justice*, edited by Debra A. Reid, 1–16. College Station: Texas A&M University Press.

Blight, David W. 2001. *Race and Reunion. The Civil War in American Memory*. Cambridge, MA: The Belknap Press of Harvard University Press.

Campbell, Randolph B. 1989. *An Empire for Slavery: The Peculiar Institution in Texas, 1821–1865*. Baton Rouge: Louisiana State University Press.

———. 2003. *Gone to Texas: A History of the Lone Star State*. Oxford: Oxford University Press.

Carrigan, William D. 2004. *The Making of a Lynching Culture. Violence and Vigilantism in Central Texas, 1836–1916*. Urbana and Chicago: University of Illinois Press.

Carrigan, William D. and Clive Webb. 2013. *Forgotten Dead. Mob Violence against Mexicans in the United States, 1848–1928*. Oxford: Oxford University Press.

Daily Inquirer, The, 1900–1905. Gonzales, Gonzales County, Texas.

District Court Files, Case No. 3256 (Final No. 3392) State of Texas Vs Gregorio Cortez. Charge: Murder, 1st Degree. Date 6-14-1901. Injured person: R.M. Glover. Filed 3rd of July 1901, Criminal Court, Gonzales. District Clerk's Office, Gonzales County Courthouse, Gonzales County, Texas

District Court Files, Case No. 3264, State of Texas Vs Gregorio Cortez. Indict for the murder of Henry Schnabel, July term, A.D. 1901. Criminal Court, Gonzales District Clerk's Office, Gonzales County Courthouse, Gonzales County, Texas.

Foley, Neil. 1997. "Becoming Hispanic: Mexican Americans and the Faustian pact with whiteness." In *Reflexiones 1997. New Directions in Mexican American Studies*, edited by Neil Foley, 53–70. Austin: CMAS Books, Center for Mexican American Studies, University of Texas at Austin.

Frenzel, Paul. 1999. *Historic Homes of Gonzales*. 5th ed. Gonzales: Reese's Printing.

Furedi, Frank. 2013. *Authority. A Sociological History*. Cambridge: Cambridge University Press.

Gómez, Laura E. 2007. *Manifest Destinies. The Making of the Mexican American Race*. New York: New York University Press.

Gonzales City Council Minutes, March 21, 1902, Vol. 3, p. 425; July 6 1905 Vol. 4, p 89-90. Gonzales County Records, Texas State Library and Archives Commission. Victoria College / University of Houston.

Gonzales Inquirer, The, 1898–1912; January 19, 1884; June 4, 1953. Gonzales County, Texas.

Hine, Darlene Clark. 2003 [1979]. *Black Victory: The Rise and Fall of the White Primary in Texas*. Columbia: University of Missouri Press.

Houston, Ramona. 2009. "The NAACP State conference in Texas: Intermediary and catalyst for change 1937–1957." *The Journal of African American History* 94(4): 509–528.

Jacobson, Matthew Frye. 2012. "Becoming Caucasian: Vicissitudes of whiteness in American politics and culture." In *Race and Immigration in the United States: New Histories*, edited by Paul Spickard, 131–147. London: Routledge.

Kökény, Andrea. 2004. "Construction of Anglo-American identity in the Republic of Texas as reflected in the 'Telegraph and Texas Register'." *Journal of the Southwest* 46(2): 283–308.

Lack, Paul D. 1991. "In the long shadow of Eugene C. Barker: The revolution and the republic." In *Texas through Time: Evolving Interpretations*, edited by Walter L. Buenger and Robert A. Calvert, 134–164. College Station: Texas A&M University Press.

Limón, José. 1994. *Dancing with the Devil*. Madison: The University of Wisconsin Press.

Lincoln, Bruce. 1994. *Authority. Construction and Corrosion*. Chicago, IL: The University of Chicago Press.

Magnussen, Anne. 2009. "New people, new historical narratives: When the Mexican-Americans came to Gonzales, Texas, at the turn of the twentieth century." *Diálogos Latinoamericanos* 16: 16–34.

———. 2013. "Belonging on the border: Mexican American strategies at El Primer Congreso Nacionalista, Texas 1911." In *Contested Places,* edited by Anne Magnussen, Peter Seeberg, Kirstine Sinclair and Niels Arne Sørensen, 135–153. Odense: University of Southern Denmark Press.

———. 2016. "Comics as historical source material: Race, ethnicity and power according to Texas History Movies." *Studies in Comics* 7: 99–125.

McDonald, Jason J. 2007. "Confronting Jim Crow in the 'Lone Star' capital: The contrasting strategies of African-American and ethnic-Mexican political leaders in Austin, Texas, 1910–1930." *Continuity and Change* 22(1): 143–169.

McMichael, Kelly. 2007. "'Memories are short but monuments lengthen remembrances': The United Daughters of the Confederacy and the power of civil war memory." In *Lone Star Pasts: Memory and History in Texas,* edited by Gregg Cantrell and Elizabeth Hayes Turner, 95–118. College Station: Texas A&M University Press.

Menchaca, Martha. 2001. *Recovering History, Constructing Race. The Indian, Black, and White Roots of Mexican Americans.* Austin: Texas University Press.

Mertz, Richard J. 1974. "'No One Can Arrest Me' the Story of Gregorio Cortéz." *The Journal of South Texas* 1: 1–17.

Miller, Worth Robert and Stacy G. Ulbig. 2008. "Building a populist coalition in Texas, 1892–1896." *The Journal of Southern History* 74(2): 255–296.

Montejano, David. 1987. *Anglos and Mexicans in the Making of Texas, 1836–1986.* Austin: University of Texas at Austin.

Orozco, Cynthia E. 2009. *No Mexicans, Women or Dogs Allowed: The Rise of the Mexican American Civil Rights Movement.* Austin: University of Texas Press.

Overmyer-Velázquez, Mark. 2013. "Good neighbors and white Mexicans: constructing race and nation on the Mexico-U.S. border." *Journal of American Ethnic History* 33(1): 5–34.

Paredes, Américo. 1958. *With His Pistol in His Hand.* Austin: University of Texas Press.

Regidor, El, 1909–1911, San Antonio.

Rodríguez Guillén, Raúl. 2014. "Crisis De Autoridad Y Violencia Social. Actores Políticos Y Sociales Frente a Los Linchamientos." In *No Nos Alcanzan Las Palabras. Sociedad, Estado Y Violencia En México,* edited by Gabriela Contreras Pérez, José Joaquín Flores Félix, Araceli Mondragón González and Isis Saavedra Luna. México, D.F.: Casa Abierta al Tiempo.

Roediger, David R. 2008. *How Race Survived US History: From Settlement and Slavery to the Obama Phenomenon.* London: Verso.

Rosales, Francisco Arturo. 1999. *Pobre Raza! Violence, Justice, and Mobilization among México Lindo Immigrants, 1900–1936.* Austin: University of Texas Press.

San Antonio Express, June–August 1901, San Antonio.

Stewart, Kenneth L. and Arnoldo de León. 1993. *Not Room Enough: Mexicans, Anglos, and Socio-Economic Change in Texas, 1850–1900.* Alburquerque: University of New Mexico.

Trouillot, Michel-Rolph. 1995. *Silencing the Past: Power and the Production of History.* Boston, MA: Beacon Press.

Turner, Frederick Jackson. 1893. "The significance of the frontier in American history." In *Annual Report of the The American Historical Association.* Chicago, IL: The American Historical Association.

US Census, Gonzales, Texas 1880, 1900, 1910, 1920. Microfilm, Center of American History, University of Texas at Austin.

Vollentine, Genevieve B., ed. 1986. *History of Gonzales County,* Vol. 1. Dallas: Curtis.

Walraven, Edward Lee. 1999. "Ambivalent Americans: Selected Spanish-language newspapers' response to Anglo domination in Texas, 1830–1910." Unpublished PhD thesis, Texas A&M University.

Zamora, Emilio. 1993. *The World of the Mexican Worker in Texas.* College Station: Texas A&M University Press.

About the author

Anne Magnussen is Associate Professor, PhD, at the Department of History, University of Southern Denmark. Her research typically involves a focus on public history, identity and ethnicity, using analytical strategies related to narrative and space/place. Articles related to the subject of the present study include "Comics as historical source material: Race, ethnicity and power according to Texas History Movies." *Studies in Comics* 7(1) (July 2016), 99–125, and "Belonging on the Border. Mexican American Strategies at El Primer Congreso Nacionalista, Texas 1911." In Anne Magnussen, Peter Seeberg, Kirstine Sinclair and Nils Arne Sørensen, eds. *Contested Places.* Odense: University of Southern Denmark Press 2013, 135–153.

— 9 —

Resisting the Silence: The Emergence of the Danish Jewish Congregational Magazine and its Reorientation of Communal Authority

Maja G. Zuckerman

Previous studies of Danish Jews have mainly focused on the social and cultural struggles between the East European immigrants, who arrived in Denmark from 1904, and the established Jewish community in the early decades of the twentieth century. However, I argue that a much more fundamental conflict was taking place within the community in the years preceding World War One, namely a struggle over the very definition of what Jewishness and what the Jewish community could and should entail, as seen in other European Jewish communities. The struggle was influenced by the appearance and the integration of a large group of Jewish immigrants but it was also a struggle that preceded their arrival and went beyond their presence. More precisely, it was a modern repetition of the old struggle over whether Jews belonged intrinsically to a global collective that spanned the emerging nation states, or, as the nineteenth century emancipatory dictum went, belonged as any other citizen to their respective nation-states with their Jewish faith as a private asset at the side. I look at this community struggle not via an analysis of the official channels and loci of politics per se—such as leadership, organisation or representation—but through unfolding and analysing how authoritative versions of Danish Jewishness were challenged through a medium, namely, the journal Jødisk Tidsskrift, which aspired to reconfigure the very foundation upon which this Jewishness was rooted. As I show in this analysis, through the mediation of the journal, that is, through the content of the articles, the design and format, as well as its distribution pattern, the Danish Jews began to be relocated within, and more closely tied to, a world Jewry and to an allegedly Jewish peoplehood. The journal challenged the Danish Jewish authorities and also attempted to reconfigure the very position from which these authorities could and should speak from in the future.

> How many of our Jews are interested in Jewish questions, in Jewish literature, history and culture, not to speak of Jewish politics? This lack of interest is seen most notably in the fact that our community never had an organ for Jewish questions; that the society, which occasionally numbered 4,000 members, has never felt the need of an organ, where the community's own affairs and Jewish affairs in general could be discussed. The few members who wanted to keep track of this field had to gain their knowledge via the foreign Jewish press, and the even fewer persons who have had something to say, were forced to keep quiet. ... With this issue, we begin a Danish journal for Jewish questions; it is clear to us that we mend a real lack, but not a common longing. (*Jødisk Tidsskrift*, April 5, 1907). [1]

So read the programmatic opening editorial of one of the first Danish-Jewish magazines, *Jødisk Tidsskrift*,[2] which was published for the first time on April 5, 1907.[3] The editorial was written by editor-in-chief Louis Herman Frænkel (1886–1935). In it he connected several issues that would come to dominate the magazine for the next year and a half and constitute a constant bone of contestation for the legitimacy and authority of the Danish Jewish leadership.[4]

As exemplified in the opening editorial, the magazine repeatedly accused the Danish Jews in general, and its leadership in particular, for its lack of Jewish knowledge and commitment to the Jewish cause. The Jewish community was described as lacking a social, cultural, historical, and political awareness of its own Jewish identity. Moreover, the Danish Jews were described as in need of a public sphere of their own due to their lack of assertiveness. The magazine claimed that the Jewish community did not discuss and develop essential matters about its own past, present, and future not only because of this lack of Jewish awareness but also due to the very absence of a community organ to promote the necessary knowledge and engagement. Instead, the magazine accused the local Jewish leadership

1. This and all subsequent translations from the Danish language are my own, unless otherwise stated.
2. Hereafter abbreviated JT.
3. Another bi-weekly magazine, *Mosaisk Tidende* (later *Mosaisk Samfund*) was actually launched four days before JT. Like JT, the magazine was financed by advertisements and also circulated to all congregation members. This magazine was, seemingly, most of all an attempt to make a profit, since it kept its journalistic aspirations and costs at a minimum by replicating a large part of its content from news pieces and stories from other sources—some about Jewish affairs and many about general Danish matters (see Margolinsky 1954, 5–6).
4. The paper builds on the findings from my unpublished PhD dissertation, in particular chapter 4, "The Jewish Journal," see Zuckerman 2016, 155–196. Several of the quotations in this paper also appear in the dissertation, but my analysis and focus in the present chapter are markedly different from those of the dissertation.

of nurturing a sheer silence about all things Jewish in a Danish context. As Frænkel, polemically, presented it in his editorial: "... the even fewer persons who have had something to say, were forced to keep quiet." The magazine was thus self-appointed to mend these lacks despite no perceived "common longing" for such an amelioration. The magazine, in other words, set out to challenge the Danish Jewish reticence and went, first of all, after its community leaders. In the present chapter, I explore the multiple ways in which JT, in the form of a community magazine, formed an opposition between itself and the Jewish leadership.[5]

The magazine, which was distributed for free to all members of the Danish Jewish unity congregation, comprising most of the Jewish community at the time, was primarily an object of dispute within the limited confinements of Danish Jewry. Though this small population was marginal in both European Jewish and Danish society at the time, the forging of JT is an apt case in point for discussing the implications of a challenge to communal authority from within, especially when the communal authority in question rests on a tacit assumption to refrain from appearing as an assertive and coherent collective. Hence, while this study focuses on the strategies of visibility and invisibility used in relation to communal affirmation among the Danish Jewish minority only, a similar interplay can be detected in most of European Jewish communities at the time as well as within other contemporary marginalized groups (Alexander 2006, 459–495; Penslar 2001, 197; Frankel 1992, 1–37).

While there were other avenues, occasions, and constellations through which criticism against the Jewish leadership was expressed, I argue in this chapter that JT formed a specific and pregnant medium that offered a means to manifest a profound contestation of the legitimacy and adequacy of the Danish Jewish leadership and its authority to rule over Jewish communal affairs. Louis Frænkel, the man who served as its editor and main journalist, overtly acknowledged this capacity. He explicitly attempted to advance all the magazine's potentialities in his quest for communal change and reforms. In a letter to the chairman of the Jewish community, Isak Glückstadt, who tried to halt the publication of the magazine, Frænkel defiantly wrote:

> By writing pamphlets or giving a lecture I do not get a hold on the Danish Jews; the pamphlets are not bought and therefore not read, and the lectures are only attended by those who already know the cause, while the greatest part [of the Danish Jews] are ignorant about and therefore uncomprehending of the very question. Only through my magazine, which I am able to send

5. In this paper my main objective is not to assess whether the claims of the magazine were truthful or not but rather to understand what and how claims were forged and the reactions it spurred.

> to everyone's doormat, can I get in touch with all those Danish Jews and at least bring them from a state of indifference to one of resistance, which is the first step towards understanding.[6]

As seen in this statement, which was written some weeks after the first publication, Frænkel clearly wanted the magazine to stir up the state of affairs within the community. In my analysis I show how the magazine mediated this contestation via its material design, outline, and article content. While the magazine never succeeded in toppling the community leadership, it nevertheless helped forge a different context through which Danish Jewish life could be experienced and understood. This alternative foundation would eventually undergird the transformation of Danish Jewish community life so that Jewishness ceased to be a stigma that could or should be concealed from the public eye.

Ruling through invisibility: Jewish communal authority

The complaint voiced by Frænkel and JT—that the Danish Jews were forced to keep quiet by the community leadership—can be related to historian David Sorkin's analysis of late eighteenth and early nineteenth century German Jewry and "why the nature of the most visible Jewry in modern Europe remained essentially invisible to its own members and to subsequent generations" (1987, 3). In his seminal study of the transformation of German Jewish community structures and culture from 1780–1840, Sorkin expounds the paradoxical and ironical process through which German Jews, in their eagerness to integrate into and incorporate features of the German majority culture into their form of Jewishness, developed their own distinct sub-culture. However, as Sorkin writes, "the German-Jewish sub-culture remained invisible to its members. German Jewry could not fully recognize the new kind of identity and the new form of community it had created" (Sorkin 1987, 3). Sorkin ascribes this phenomenon to the "incomplete emancipation" that never allowed German Jews a full and undistinguished membership into the emerging German nation. While the incorporation of the Danish Jews involved fewer limitations and thus might be considered more complete than the German, the issue of Danish Jewish visibility or invisibility was still notable and crucial in 1907 (Wagner 2001; see also Kjærsgaard 2013).

The space of the Danish Jewish community was, by the turn of the century, still defined fundamentally by stipulations laid down by the Royal Decree of March 29, 1814, generally referred to as "the Letter of Freedom," though amendments had been added when the Danish Constitution ("Grundloven")

6. Louis Frænkel to Isak Glückstadt, letter, April 30, 1907, file 27–28, Frænkel Papers, Rigsarkivet (Denmark; hereafter Frænkel Papers); my emphasis.

was created in 1849 (Lausten 2015, 122–124, 173–174). The decree announced that "[t]hose confessors of the Mosaic faith who were born in Our Kingdom, Denmark, or who have achieved permission to reside here, should enjoy the same opportunity as our other subjects, to earn a living by any legal means" (Lausten 2015, 123). In return, these "confessors" were now to follow only the civic laws of the country and not the Mosaic or "Rabbinic" laws and prescriptions. The Jews in Denmark were hence granted the same rights as other Danes on condition that they evaded or obfuscated their civic commitments to Judaism, Jewish law, and Jewish autonomy. In other words, like in many other European countries, they were granted equal rights *on condition* that they ceased to demand any rights as Jews (Wagner 2014, 10–24). Sociologist Jeffrey Alexander (2006) recaps the ambiguity of Jewish incorporation into European states:

> Only if Jews relegated their religious ideas and activities to the invisibility of private life would they be allowed to become fully enfranchised citizens, like every other members of the nation-state. ... The enlightened thinking that directed the formation of civil societies allowed that, in principle, the person of the Jews could be separated from Jewish qualities.
>
> (Alexander 2006, 464–465).

In Denmark this form of separation between, on the one hand, the Jew as a person and, on the other, Jewish qualities, played out in the sense that Danish Jews were generally accepted into prestigious jobs and circles, if they concurrently ceased to manifest, or at least agreed to downplay, any signs of Jewishness in the public sphere (Wagner 2001).

The Board of Representatives (hereafter, the Board) became an emblem of this accommodation of Jewish invisibility. The formal framework of the Board was a result of "The Letter of Freedom," which prescribed the creation of two communal bodies: one—the Board—was to deal with communal administration and oversee the community affairs as a whole; the other—the Council of the Synagogue—was to deal strictly with synagogue matters. Inspired by Enlightenment advocates, a somewhat paradoxical separation was drawn within the Jewish community between a supposedly secular and a religious leadership and, like in the Enlightenment-inspired state formation, the former was assigned to rule over the latter (Rothenberg 1964, 138–139).

By 1900, the Board had become the chief bastion for the separation of a public and a private form of Jewishness. The Board, which comprised seven members, all of whom had to be men over the age of 25 of independent means and property, were bi-annually elected by the leading male members of the community in an election where votes were openly disclosed and the candidates were largely agreed upon beforehand. The key criteria of qualification for Board membership seemed to have been one's social and economic standing in Danish society, whereas one's interests in Jewish matters as such appeared to be of little importance. In an interview from 1965, the long-standing member and later chairman of the Board, Supreme Court Attorney C.B. Henriques affirmatively summed up the motivation and attitude of the leading body of the Jewish congregation (including himself) around 1905:

> [The members of the Board] had obtained their seat not because they each were elected on a specific agenda, but because they were Jews and respected citizens in the larger society. This was their qualification for becoming members of the Board, and when they joined the Board, it was because they were Jews, not because they harboured any special interest for Judaism, for Jewish culture, religion, or history. But they were respected in Danish society, they held prominent positions, you elected them then exclusively for that reason, and they took part because they were Jews of old lineages in Denmark. (Pedersen 1964, 130).[7]

Henriques' elucidation of the qualifying parameters by which Board members were elected highlights the difference between how the Danish public sphere and the Jewish private sphere were being assessed by the Jewish community in general and the Board in particular. It was their accumulated respect and standing in Danish society that made them eligible for representing the Jewish community, whereas their interest in and knowledge of Jewish affairs were considered negligible for the task at hand.

Hence, in a rather ambivalent form of communal leadership, the Board spearheaded the Jewish community by refraining from overtly engaging in Jewish affairs and, vice versa, by refraining from eliciting and asserting Jewishness in the Danish public sphere. The Board was compelled by law to administer and represent the Jewish community, which it indeed did, conscientiously, through a politics of invisibility. It was this politics that the magazine tried to implode via its manifestation as a public medium for Jewish questions and debate.

7. Henriques was appointed Board member in 1905 and Chairman of the Board in 1930, a position he held until 1946. From the quote, it may seem that Henriques was distancing himself from the other Board members—describing them as "they" rather than "we," however, he in fact affirmed, one page later in the interview, his full sympathy with and understanding for the reasoning of the other Board members and aligned himself with their work. Moreover, Henriques' characterization of these representatives was perfectly fitting also for himself: he was of an old and respected Danish Jewish lineage and he had just been appointed Supreme Court Attorney when he got elected to the Board.

The approach to "authority" as it is presented in the introduction of the present book, namely as a dynamic, asymmetrical interrelation between people, places, and things, is useful for discerning the discourses that created the structures of silence and voice among the members of the Danish Jewish community. However, I will add to this conceptualization a more diachronic perspective that takes into account the historical reference points that were elicited in the community struggle and deployed to legitimize the asymmetric relations of authority in question.

As outlined in the introduction of the book, authority can, in the words of historian of religion Bruce Lincoln, be seen to ultimately pivot on

> the effect of a posited, perceived, or institutionally ascribed asymmetry between speaker and audience that permits certain speakers to command not just the attention but the confidence, respect, and trust of the audience, or ... to make audiences act as if this were so. (Lincoln 1994, 4)

This definition here underscores, firstly, that authority and authoritative relations can be identified as a willing obedience that is induced neither by the enforcement of violence and force, nor by explicit persuasion but by the latency of both (Lincoln 1994, 6). Secondly, rather than focussing on authority as an entity that one either has or has not, this approach foregrounds authority as an effect of asymmetrical relations and which enables some people to speak and act on behalf of others. In a Danish Jewish context, this could also be rephrased as an authoritative relation that could produce collective silence and public effacement. That is, when we look at the features of the communal authority ascribed to the Board, one of its main characteristics was its ability to dissuade the Jewish community from asserting itself publically as Jews, like the Board members themselves refrained from doing.

Lincoln emphasizes, moreover, the importance of material manifestations as active elements that partake in forging asymmetrical relations. Things, places and situations, Lincoln argues, can both authorize as well as be authorized to "confer authority on ... those whom the group permits to speak and that which they say within this setting" (Lincoln 1994, 9). Conferring authority through a material, spatial, and situational nexus rests to a large degree on the premise of being seen. A material manifestation of authority is per definition visible, audible or, at least, notable, though in some cases it is intentionally confined or secretive. In the Danish Jewish case, however, the wish for invisibility made material manifestations of Jewishness a delicate matter since material expressions inevitably elucidated a visible Jewishness. It is in this precarious context that one of the first communal magazines made its entrance, testing the boundaries and strength of the Board and its politics of invisibility.

While Lincoln looks primarily at authority through a synchronic perspective, that is, through a focus on existing authoritative relations, political philosopher Hannah Arendt (1968, 91–141) emphasizes the role of foundation and diachronic relations in establishing and legitimizing authority. Arendt argues that authoritarian power rests on a focal point outside and beyond the source of authority itself, most notably God, the nation, and/or the past, and that this focal point creates a foundation that legitimizes the power structures (Arendt 1968, 98–99). In her own words, "Authority, resting on a foundation in the past as its unshaken cornerstone, gave the world the permanence and durability which human beings need precisely because they are mortals" (Arendt 1968, 95). This approach to authority can help us reflect on how such reference points to the past can be used to legitimize or contest contemporary asymmetrical relations. In the case of JT, it seems particularly instructive to investigate how JT challenged the foundation on which the Danish Jewish leadership rested through forging and presenting a different foundation for Danish Jewish life.

Making Jewishness public

A Jewish congregational magazine had not been "a thing" which the communal leadership had attempted to establish prior to JT, nor did it become an object of appreciation by this body after it was launched. Against the backdrop outlined above, this seems logical. To establish a Danish-Jewish magazine meant fundamentally to strive to create some sort of affirmative Jewish public sphere—a wish that went diametrically against the agenda of the community leadership. Nevertheless, on April 5, 1907, *Jødisk Tidsskrift* was launched. It was published as a bi-weekly magazine that was written in Danish and distributed for free to all of the congregation's approximately 4,000 members. It was financed through advertisements that took up half of the magazine's eight pages; this meant that it was published without the supervision, permission, and financial support of the community leadership. Frænkel and his brother-in-law, Haakon Salomon, instigated, in other words, a magazine with the explicit aim of creating a medium that could make a Jewish public visible.

Louis Frænkel was a Danish-born Jew, a general physician with a clinic in Copenhagen, and the chairman of the Danish-Zionist Association ("Dansk Zionistforening"), which was established in 1903. The Zionist Association had in its first years organized lectures about Palestine and the Zionist cause for the Jewish community at large, and offered Danish classes to the new Jewish immigrants who were arriving from East Europe. Frænkel, however, was constantly looking for more venues and new forms through which to transmit what he saw as the most important pillars of Zionism, namely Jewish assertiveness, solidarity, and unity (see Zuckerman 2016). Thus, rather than working strictly within a Zionist framework or organisation, Frænkel tried to disseminate Zionist assumptions among as many people as possible—without necessarily disclosing or defining these assumptions as Zionist per se.

Just as the Zionist leader Theodor Herzl had paved the way for the establishment of the German Zionist magazine, *Die Welt*, in 1897 as a crucial stepping stone in the dissemination of Zionism to a broader constituency, Frænkel saw a similar potential for JT.[8] In a letter to the chairman of the Board, Isak Glückstadt, Frænkel wrote:

> (..) in the chief-editor position I saw a good opportunity to propagandize for the Zionist movement, which I consider the only solution to the Jewish question. (...) Only through my magazine, which I am able to send to everyone's doormat, can I get in touch with all those Danish Jews and at least bring them from a state of indifference to one of resistance, which is the first step towards recognition.[9]

Clearly, Frænkel saw the magazine as a medium for Zionist propaganda, but he also emphasized the importance of stirring up the Danish Jewish community. His aim was to reach out and prompt some reactions from the members of the Jewish community at large.

From April 5 1907, the Danish Jews thus began receiving a Jewish magazine every second week on their doorstep. The magazine itself, that is, its material form and appearance, made a significant impact on how it was received among some of the readers. It seems that even before the magazine's content was read, it was *noticed* and *seen* as a thing with embedded qualities, which some Danish Jews found undesirable—namely the specific qualities of the magazine that related to them as Jews. Isak Glückstadt voiced his concerns to Frænkel, and indicated that they were shared by many other congregation members, a few weeks after the magazine was launched:

> The fact is that it has caused me, and I am sure a big part of our peaceful congregation members, a lot of sorrows to see that the attention is drawn to us like a distinct community segregated from the rest of the population—or like a special caste that must have its own magazine.[10]

8. The weekly publication of *Die Welt* was initiated on June 4, 1897 in Vienna with Zionist leader Theodor Herzl as its founder, moneyman, and editor-in-chief. It survived until the outbreak of World War I and became the official journal of the Zionist Organisation. Herzl explicitly and affirmatively declared the weekly "ein Judenblatt" on the front page of the first issue: "Unsere Wochenschrift ist ein "Judenblatt," Wir nehmen dieses Wort, das ein Schimpf sein soll, und wollen daraus ein Wort der Ehre Machen." Frænkel would, ten years later, translate and quote these lines in JT. On Herzl and Die Welt, see Toury, 1980, 159–172.
9. Louis Frænkel to Isak Glückstadt, letter, April 30, 1907, file 27–28, Frænkel Papers.
10. Isak Glückstadt to Louis Frænkel, letter 25 April 1907, file 27, Frænkel Papers.

As is evident from Glückstadt's complaint, the problem was, initially, not the content of the articles, but the very production and distribution of a Jewish magazine. Glückstadt asserted that the magazine contributed to forging the Jews into a "special caste," that was segregated from the Danish population at large. The apparent logic of this argument was that in receiving this magazine on their doorstep, the Jews were singled out from their non-Jewish neighbours solely due to their affiliation with the congregation. They consequently feared that they would be negatively stigmatized by this difference.

Glückstadt, moreover, explicated that the very publication of a Jewish magazine, unlike other community, party, and even congregational magazines, could be perceived as a sign of civic subversion which the Jews should avoid at all cost:

> I have thought it over a great deal and I have talked with many about it and I am of the opinion that the distribution of that kind of community magazines in a country like ours can only hurt the position of the Jews. I am perfectly aware that other religious sects have their own magazines, but with Jews it is certainly different.[11]

Glückstadt concluded that the mere existence of this Jewish magazine would elicit the particularity of Jews and Jewish autonomy, which could potentially harm the Jews' status in the country. The position which Glückstadt here tried to defend was the continuation of the politics of invisibility. Glückstadt assessed the pros and cons of the magazine based on how the non-Jewish public would or could see it, and he reached the conclusion that the magazine evinced a Jewish presence in the public sphere which should be kept obscure.

The magazine, indeed, expressed anything but an evasive or apologetic Jewish character. In its very design and outline, it tried as much as possible to make Jewishness perfectly compatible with Danishness. This can be seen already in the font in which the magazine's name appeared on the cover. Frænkel, who was the graphic designer behind the font, had found a way to merge Danish and Hebrew letters so that the words *Jødisk Tidsskrift* appeared as a quasi-Hebrew word that even non-Hebrew literates could read (see Figure 9.1). Rather than simply write the name of the magazine with Latin letters and then describe the aspirations of the magazine in the articles, Frænkel stated some of the overall intensions through a visual and material expression. The magazine was to be a medium in which Hebrew and Danish, Jewishness and Danishness, were expressed together as equals, but not in the sense of equality posed by "the Letter of Freedom" and adopted by

11. Isak Glückstadt to Louis Frænkel, letter 25 April 1907, file 27, Frænkel Papers.

Figure 9.1 The merging of Danish and Hebrew letters for the magazine *Jødisk Tidsskrift*. The Royal Danish Library, photo by author.

the Board in which Jewishness always had to be subsumed within the supposedly neutral category of Danishness. Rather, in this framework, Danish Jewishness was underscored as perfectly compatible with and still distinctive from Danishness at large.

The subtitle of the headline read: "Organ for Jewish Questions" and carried an intriguing double meaning. On the one hand, Jewish presence and life in Europe had increasingly been defined and problematized as a matter of "the Jewish question." This question alluded to an ambiguity and also often a reluctance or refusal in the non-Jewish majority to incorporate Jewish communities into the European nation-states. By 1907, Anti-Semites and Zionists alike had made "the Jewish question" one of their major points of departure for their political agendas: where the Jews should live and what the present and future qualities and potentials were, were issues at the centre of attention. Framing the magazine as a medium for these questions thus meant making it into a blatant bone of contention for the Board's politics of Jewish invisibility. It foregrounded the ambiguity of Jewish life as something that could and should be talked about in the open.

On the other hand, describing the magazine as "an organ for Jewish questions" (in the plural) could also simply mean that it was to be a medium in which Jewish interests at large could be voiced and opinions exchanged. In this sense, Jewish questions were to be understood as a matter of bringing forth everyday issues in a Jewish public sphere. However, also in this latter meaning the intention undermined the Board's politics. In particular, the assertion that the Jews had mundane interests and questions that needed expression in an organ of their own was, as the quotes above make clear, an unacceptable premise for the Board.

Nevertheless, it was precisely the identification and elicitation of mundane Jewish interests that enabled the magazine to run and to be freely distributed to all congregational members. Despite the Board's wariness of organizing the Danish Jews as a public and interrelated community and despite the fact that there had not existed a Jewish magazine in Denmark prior to JT, Haakon Salomon—Frænkel's brother-in-law—persuaded advertisers that specific Jewish consumption needs existed and that this market brimmed of opportunities (on early twentieth century Jewish consumption, see Reuveni and Roemer 2010; Reuveni 2010, 113–138). Historian Gideon Reuveni, who has examined Jewish consumption and advertisements in Weimar Germany, described this as a matter of "ethnic-niche marketing" that combined or associated "Jewish tradition with bourgeois values" and outlined and created herein a specific Jewish consumption and consumer (Reuveni 2010, 116–118, 122).[12] Thus, the four bi-weekly advertisement pages that enveloped the four pages of articles addressed and outlined for the first time publically the Jewish consumer as a distinct subgroup of the Danish market.

This new hybrid was forged in the advertisement pages of almost any JT issue. Figure 9.2 shows two pages from August 9, 1907 which indeed addressed the Jewishness of its readers through multiple avenues. Some advertisements specifically identified and targeted Jewish needs or desires. On the left hand page, below the emblematic headline of *Jødisk Tidsskrift*, the reader could find an advertisement from one of the biggest bread factories in Copenhagen, *Schulstad & Ludvigsen*. It promoted itself here as the only place in town that sold "authentic water bread," which was produced under the supervision of the Chief Rabbi. To verify or perhaps elevate this fact, a Star of David designed especially for *Schulstad & Ludvigsen,* stamped with the Rabbi's initials, appeared in the ad. Another example can be seen at the bottom of Figure 9.2 (right page), where an advertisement from Scandinavia Gramophone Limited invited people to come by its store in Copenhagen and hear Hebrew recordings sung by a cantor, Gershon Sirota, from Warsaw. While the ad did not limit the invitation to Jews, the interest in Jewish liturgical music, and, moreover, the listing in the ad of the songs in Hebrew, would chiefly have resonated with a Jewish informed or affiliated readership.

Other advertisements did not promote distinctively Jewish products or services as such, but targeted instead the sort of class consumption to

12. Reuveni breaks down the German-Jewish advertisements in the Weimar period into two categories: "(1) advertisements for products and services that a priori were aimed solely at the Jewish consumer public and (2) advertisement for products and services that were promoted to accord with the specific needs of the Jewish public, or at least attract their attention. Among the first type were uniquely Jewish products, such as religious articles, Haggadoth, matzoth, Hanukkah matzoth, Hanukkah candles, and so forth. But the second type of advertising presented a broader and far more diverse range of products and services," see Reuveni 2010, 122. The German Jewish population examined by Reuveni and its advertisement market were significantly bigger than the Danish ditto and could thus comprise an array of consumption choices more varied that the Danish ones.

Schulstad & Ludvigsens
Brødfabrik
1 August
Kaaber
langt under Prisen.
H. A. Colbergs Eftf.
Østergade 42
De forenede Kulimportører
Landbrugslotteriet.
Parfumerie BREINING
Parfumer og Toiletartikler
BRITANNIAS KUL varmer godt.
Til Kapitalanlæg
5 pCt. Indiaansbeviser
Triers billige Medicinudsalg.
Pilestræde 35.
FAMILIEN-PENSIONAT
Undertøj
Alle Slags Herreklæder
S. WARBURG
Fritz Christensen
Annoncer
Jacobsens Modemagasin
Vesterbrogade 48
DALGAARDS KAFFE
Telefon 7911 7912 8055
LAX
Styrt
Cycler
Albert Jørgensen
Salomon Nielsen
Peter Hansen
C. C. Drewsen
H. E. Holst's Eftf.
Albert Christensen
OSTE
C. HEILBUTH
27. Nørrebrogade 27.
JOHAN F. POULSEN,
Strandvej 187.
Stor Møbel-Udstilling
Stue og 1ste Sal
Brødr. Nielsen's Flytteforretning,
Josef Nachemsohn,
Kunst- og Antiquitetshandel,
Valdemar Jørgensen
Selskabet ADAM
Flytteforretning
BAADMOTORER
JØRGENSEN & MATHIASEN
DOMUS
Carl Bauers
Møbelindustri
Vesterbrogade 66
Nattevagt
Grammophon
Skandinavisk Grammophon Aktieselskab.
Manufaktur
F. C. DA
Jødisk Tid
R. COHN
Hund

Figure 9.2 Two pages of advertisements from *Jødisk Tidsskrift*, August 9, 1907. The Royal Danish Library, photo by author.

which the Jews were imagined to belong, namely bourgeois consumption. The pages above thus advertised robes, perfumes, jewellery, rare books, and gilded frames. Some of the advertising companies had discernibly Jewish family names like Heibluth, Trier, Nachemsohn, and Cohn, while many did not have or did not promote the product or service through this connotation. Whether the product was ascribed such Jewish connotations or senders or not, the advertisements were deliberately placed in an explicitly Jewish magazine and thus targeted Jewish addressees. The advertisements, in other words, helped to forge a space that can aptly be described as a Danish Jewish public sphere.

By highlighting the advertisement pages of the magazine, I do not presume that the advertisers had any explicitly political aims. By choosing to advertise in a Jewish magazine, they had identified it as medium through which to reach a profitable market niche, namely the Danish Jewish bourgeoisie. So, while the Board preferred to keep Danish Jewish existence under the radar, the advertisements elucidated this life by tempting the Jews to peep out and buy products and services that they deemed suitable for Jewish consumption. As Reuveni argues: "[C]onsumer culture not only provided new venues to imagine cultural belonging beyond existing domination of political and cultural differences, but also insinuated ways in which Jews were expected to practice their Jewishness" (Reuveni 2010, 115). On the advertisement pages, such consumption was, obviously, not presented as denigrating or stigmatizing Jewish behaviour, but rather as a liberal way of buying elements of Jewishness, bourgeoisie-ness, and Danishness. In other words, explicitly Jewish consumption was outlined as perfectly compatible with Danish Jewish life, yet also distinct and worth underscoring in its own right and through its own medium.

Thus before even reading the articles inside the magazine, the design, outline and distribution pattern of the magazine already manifested a sense of Jewish presence that was unapologetically visible and inherent in the material. The Hebrew-Danish hybrid letters that spelled "Jewish Magazine" emphasized this assertion. As a blatant contestation of the politics of invisibility, this new form of Jewish presence was to be seen, noticed, and felt first of all among the Jews themselves. Rather than worrying about the perception of the non-Jewish majority, the magazine indicated that the Jews indeed comprised a community with questions and answers of its own. Moreover, this material presence also made clear that these were matters that should not be evaded, as the Board hitherto had indicated, but instead be considered a central part of Jewish public life. Hence, prior to, or perhaps rather intersected with, an explicit criticism of the politics and the legitimacy of the Board, the magazine in itself constituted a bone of contention: the Jewish community experienced it as an object that distributed Jewishness in a way that made the community more salient in the Danish landscape. This, as also Glückstadt's letter reflected, fostered anxiety in the inner circle of the community leadership.

In the articles in the magazine, attempts to undermine and circumvent the authority and legitimacy of the community leadership were omnipresent. Some of these attempts were specific verbal assaults, others were more subtle texts that showed the futility of the current community politics, and, finally, many articles simply narrated Jewish life and particularity in a way that ran diametrically counter to that promoted and personified by the Board. Here, I wish to focus on one specific, cogent case of contestation which found expression in several articles and revolved around the journal's explicit support for the new Chief Rabbi, Tobias Lewenstein, and his attempt to annul the congregation's annual *Store Bededag* (Great Prayer Day)[13] sermon due to its non-Jewish nature. In this case, JT and Lewenstein explicitly tried to defy the leadership's desire to incorporate national and

13. This was—and still is—a national holiday celebrated by the Danish Church during the fourth week after Easter. I elaborate on the meaning of this day below.

even Christian elements into the synagogue liturgy by calling out what they saw as the Board's misconceived and basically inappropriate concerns for Danish sensitivity.

Cutting the *Circulus Vitiosus*

From its very first editorial, JT had launched an outrage against the congregation's lack of interest in Jewish matters—from literature and history to politics and social concerns. The editor, Louis Frænkel, denounced what he saw as the lack of "Jewish self-respect." Six months later, Frænkel noted:

> The [Danish] Jewish society, which in other areas is so rich on radicals, is, due to the aforementioned lack, still dominated by Absolutism to this very day in administrative concerns. With an organisation that is based on regulations, ordinances and agendas from the beginning of the previous century, we have in dull indifference seen progress disappear from our hands, and thus we have become even more indifferent. We have a circulus vitiosus that we can only mend by severing it. (JT, September 20, 1907)

The critique of the Danish-Jewish community, the Board, and the community structures were forthright and total: the community as a whole lacked self-respect, modernity, democracy, and vigour. The ascriptions of the labels "dull indifference" and "Absolutism" seemed to connote that the community had turned into a lifeless and outdated entity. Here, JT blatantly suggested "severing" the vicious circle and instead advocated an attempt to reshape a Jewish community with a different foundation altogether. Precisely how much this collided with the Board's agenda became evident in the concrete dispute over the hallowing of the Danish Christian holiday Great Prayer Day ("Store Bededag").

The dispute over Great Prayer Day represented the accumulation of the disagreements and tensions that had emerged between the new Chief Rabbi of Denmark, Tobias Lewenstein, and the Board. Prior to taking up the position in Denmark, Lewenstein had been the Orthodox Rabbi of The Hague. The Board had been on the lookout for a new chief rabbi ever since the Danish-born Rabbi David Simonsen had announced, in 1902, that he wished to retire from the position in order to dedicate himself fully to his other profession as an Oriental scholar. The Board thought that they had found in Lewenstein a candidate who could carry on the rather idiosyncratic constellation of Jewish theology to which the Danish Jewish unity congregation subscribed. The congregation was nominally Orthodox, but during the nineteenth century it had incorporated many reformed elements and wished to continue to practise a lenient approach to Orthodox Jewish theology. These issues, however, were never fully settled before the new Chief Rabbi arrived in Copenhagen on May 1, 1903, with the full intent of heading an Orthodox congregation.

On October 4, 1907, the heading of the JT's front page stated "Ordinary Prayer Day." The first lines read:

> It is probably only a few who know what kind of day Prayer Day really is; but it must be a comfort then to know that our Board of Representatives and the Council of the Synagogue also have not known anything about it until they were recently informed about it through the Ministry of Church.

Great Prayer Day was—and still is—a national holiday celebrated by the Danish Church on the fourth Friday after Easter. It was introduced in 1686 under the name "extraordinary, common prayer day" by Bishop Hans Bagger who had prescribed this day as an official day of prayer and fasting. In 1832, the Chief Rabbi Abraham Wolff (1801–1891) had introduced a parallel prayer day sermon in the synagogue so as "to demonstrate that Judaism was a Danish religion on an equal footing with Christianity" (Lausten 2015, 223). Hence, for almost a century the Jewish community had hallowed this day as a national hallmark that indicated just how compatible the synagogue and Judaism were with Christian Danish values and Danish society at large. The new Chief Rabbi decided, in stark contrast to his predecessors, to clarify and disentangle what could be considered "purely" national commitments and obligations from religious ones. While he was ready to support some Danish civic impact on the Jewish community, he wished to disavow any Christian influence as fundamentally incompatible with Jewish liturgy.

Lewenstein proceeded, in order to disclose the deeper meaning of this holiday, by contacting the Ministry of Church and Education ("Kultusministeriet"). The ministry informed him about the Christian status of this day, and JT turned the matter into a public Jewish affair. Though siding unanimously with the Rabbi, JT tried to inform the Jewish community about the details of the case, while constantly ridiculing the Board for what it alluded to as its lack of comprehension with regard to Jewish matters and, accordingly, its inability to govern. As seen in the quote above, the Board was presented as not having known about the "purely" religious content of the Great Prayer Day. Moreover, in the article, the Bishop was quoted as writing that "there probably... is no good reason for the Jewish community[14] to hallow this day, just as it, as far as he knows, has not been ordained to do so" (JT, October 4, 1907). In other words, Frænkel stressed the point that the congregation had never been forced to implement this particular sermon in the first place, and that the Ministry of Church did not demand the retention of the tradition.

14. In the Danish original it says *Mosaisk Troessamfund.*

More than simply sharing and foregrounding these details with the Danish Jewish community, JT presented the readers with rather unflattering motifs for why the Board continued to hallow this day despite its seeming groundlessness. It stated that the Board made its decision based on the "fear that outsiders who also did not know the origins of the day could blame us for separatism" (JT, October 4, 1907). Continuing along this line of thought, JT noted, patronizingly, that the Board "cannot act on the basis of all the misconceptions it can be ascribed." The author ended by advising "the gentlemen to keep the synagogue and its service exempt from their assimilation efforts; in this instance, this should be so much easier since they have the support of the Bishop and the Ministry of Church" (JT, October 4, 1907). As a kind of exposé, the article seemed to aim at eliciting some of the latent forces behind the Board's agenda, namely that the Jewish community leadership was driven by an excessive fear of Jewish identification and that it was, consequently, retracting the whole community into a state of self-effacement by attending to its Danish rather than its Jewish needs.

In another article titled "Homeopathy," JT offered a satirical and poorly disguised allegory which represented the positions and values of the Board and the Chief Rabbi in the increasingly heated situation. This article opened with the fairy tale structure of "Once upon a time in the far north there was a congregation in need of a priest." From these seemingly innocent lines, the writer went on to describe, mockingly, the undertaking of the presumably "seven wise men" who were to hire a new priest. While the seven members of the Board (the article does mention that the men formed a board) were described as feeble, confused, and in a sense not really comprehending what the priest they found was saying, the priest, in contrast, was portrayed as showing spine and integrity. The priest was depicted as fully understanding the situation that the congregation in the north was facing, and he was, moreover, praised as being true to the values of his call, his religion, and his people:

> Just think! The Priest kept sticking to Moses and all the Prophets; he did not even dismiss his relations to one Habakkuk[15] after he had arrived to the fine and modern city, and he adhered to some old books he had at home and not to the protocols of the Board of Representatives. (JT, September 6, 1907)

Juxtaposing "the old books" with the Board's protocols, the story clearly delineated two different foundations from which Jewish authority could derive its legitimacy. The Board was portrayed as detached from any ancient and integral foundation and as navigating according to contemporary protocols and in-fighting concerns. In contrast, the priest, presumably, operated according to consistent values rooted in his tradition and beliefs.

15. In the jargon of the time, the prophet's name of Habakkuk was also slang for an oddball.

The story/article as a whole suggested that these were the positions that comprised the core of the conflict and that the Board had utterly failed to include the opinions of the larger community in this dispute: "... and none of them thought of asking the congregation of its opinion. Thereto the seven men were too wise—or perhaps not wise enough. But then the congregation began speaking without being asked" (JT, September 6, 1907). Thus, in an allegorical and highly satirical form, JT offered the Danish Jews a set of images that supposedly illustrated what was really going on in the community: on the one hand, the heroic figure of the Chief Rabbi/priest who assertively stood up for Jewish values, traditions, and integrity, and, on the other, the perplexed Board of Representatives who chiefly cared about bureaucracy and appearances. The congregation at large was pictured as having to form an opinion of its own and voice it publically. Obviously, this was the (heroic) task that JT saw itself facilitating. Without directly mentioning its own role, the article underscored the fundamental necessity of a community magazine for keeping the congregation committed and true to its Jewish values.

The title and the sender of the article also offered a particular framing of the situation. The homeopathy indicated in the title was described in the article as an attempt to cure stupidity and wrongdoing with more stupidity and wrongdoing. It suggested that the Board, upon realizing that they had hired a rabbi who did not match their aspirations and wishes, tried to mend the situation by undermining the institution of the rabbinate even further. The pseudonym of the journalist who had signed the article was, in contrast, the Allopath. Whereas the Board was connoted with a dubious and allegedly misunderstood form of handling community affairs, the sender of the article represented the conventional and more rational way of ameliorating problems. Though the latter clearly sided with the Orthodox priest and his wishes to ground the Danish congregation more closely in Orthodox Jewish theology and liturgy, rather than in Danish and Christian concerns, the sender's concerns were highlighted as acceptable, rational, and progressive.

From the articles cited above, we see that the attempt to cut the vicious circle of the contemporary administration and its community politics to a large degree targeted the very legitimacy of the Board. JT outlined the dispute about the Chief Rabbi in a way that presented the Board as profoundly lacking a foundation in Judaism and Jewishness and that it was therefore inept at leading the community. Previously, Board members could cheerfully and even proudly subscribe to a lack of Jewishness on behalf of the congregation; but now JT—siding with the new Chief Rabbi—had turned this line of politics into a bone of contention. Ultimately, JT suggested that current Jewish leadership was guided by a fear of Jewish visibility, and that the Board of Representatives was unfit to lead and unfit to represent, embody and envision Danish Jewishness.

The visibility of Jewishness

Jødisk Tidsskrift ceased to exist by September 1908, after it had published 36 issues over a time period of one and a half years. If the founder's and editor's main aspiration had been to topple the Board and reform the community structures at once, the magazine should be considered a failure. The disagreement between the Board and the Rabbi eventually reached a point where the Board discharged the Chief Rabbi, who then filed a lawsuit against the Board that reached all the way to the Danish Supreme Court, where the dispute ended in 1910 with the Board having to give the now resigned Rabbi a massive pecuniary compensation for breach of contract (Lausten 2015, 223). The Board, however, managed to overcome this crisis by finally replacing Lewenstein with the more lenient Rabbi Max Schornstein and thus hold on to its authority to rule over community affairs. The Board continued to represent the Jewish community formally, to preside over the administration of its members, and, ultimately, to rule over what could be considered the acceptable theological foundation of the congregation. Thus, in some aspects the Board sustained its formal and emblematic platform for representing Danish Jewry through a politics of invisibility. Until the 1930s, the Board members continued to be appointed not by virtue of their relations and commitments to Judaism, but due to their accomplishments in Danish society. Though their Jewish affiliation was a fundamental premise for being selected to the Board, this fact was never verbalized: like the Board's politics, their Jewishness remained inherent yet covert.

Yet, the politics of invisibility was, like most relations of authority, intrinsically vulnerable and fragile, since it rested profoundly on the Danish Jews' trust in the Board's judgement of Danish society and the Jewish space herein. For a century, the Board had reckoned that the Danish Jews would be more safe and prosperous, if they followed the logics of assimilation. However, JT fundamentally contested this rationalization by resisting the politics of invisibility. It brought Jewishness to the public fore and in this forum insisted on the particularity of the Jewish community. Manifesting Jewishness in the public sphere blatantly contested not only the politics of the Board but also its very legitimacy to run and govern the community.

As I have shown in this chapter, the contestation that the magazine voiced was mediated in several concurrent ways. First of all, it posed a challenge to the contemporary perception of Jewish invisibility by means of its very materiality. The appearance and circulation of a self-declared and identifiable *Judenblatt* was in and of itself a hallmark of change, since its very materiality insisted on the existence of an unapologetically Jewish public life. Secondly, its economic model of Jewish niche-marketing forged a temporary sense of a particularly Jewish market segment, of Jewish consumption, and Jewish consumers. Again, in stark contrast to the Board's politics, the advertisements discussed here elicited a sense of a thriving Jewish community that was tied together by consumer desires and needs and thus also shared a collective imagination of Jewish belonging. Thirdly, I focussed on one explicit way in which the articles in JT contested the authority of the Board. These articles composed an image of the Board as essentially un-Jewish and pushed this assertion to indicate that the Board was inadequate to represent and govern the Jewish community.

As the analysis above has hopefully made clear, an understanding of the material nature of the magazine is essential for grasping the contestation of the community leadership that this Danish Jewish magazine voiced. In many ways, the presence and distribution of a Jewish magazine attests to and reverses Lincoln's notion of how things can confer authority to specific members of a group and thus grant them special rights to speak and be listened to. The magazine as a *thing* challenged, rather than conferred, a certain constellation of authority due to its amalgamation of Danishness and Jewishness in a public sphere. Unlike a lecture or a meeting which will affect a limited group of people ephemerally and not necessarily leave a trace outside the minds of the attendants, the material substance of the magazine made Jewish invisibility seem unfeasible and superfluous. The sheer materiality of the magazine continually manifested and alluded to the collective existence of Danish Jewry.

The magazine's material presence as well as the content of its articles represented repeated attempts at unsettling the foundation on which the Board's authority presumably rested. It formed the argument that a high social standing in Danish society and a notable rootedness in Danishness was not a sufficient foundation that could legitimize the current Jewish leadership. Instead it suggested an alternative foundation: Jewish authority should be derived from an assertive and knowledgeable expression of Jewishness. The magazine presented itself, along with Chief Rabbi Lewenstein, as a pioneer of such an endeavour.

The Board managed to hold its grounds in the first place, whereas the Chief Rabbi was fired and JT closed down, but the changes happening in the community at large soon proved that the Board's politics of invisibility was futile. From 1906 onwards, east European Jewish immigrants were beginning to arrive in Denmark by the thousands (Thing 2008). Until ca. 1907/8, the Board and its appointed immigrant committee was successful in relocating the immigrants to other countries by paying for further transportation. However, the number of Jewish immigrants began to exceed the resources available and soon East European Jewish life was visible in the streets of Copenhagen. With their presence in Denmark, the politics of Jewish invisibility gradually crumbled and a wider constituency of Jewishness was needed to administer, incorporate, and try to gather the Jews of Denmark under one banner. JT had already outlined this broader foundation during its short lifetime.

References

Alexander, Jeffrey C. 2006. *The Civil Sphere*. Oxford: Oxford University Press.

Arendt, Hannah. 1968. "What is Authority." In *Between Past and Future Eight Exercises in Political Thought*, 91–141. New York: The Viking Press.

Frankel, Jonathan. 1992. "Assimilation and the Jews in nineteenth-century Europe: towards a new historiography?" In *Assimilation and Community: The Jews in Nineteenth-Century Europe*, edited by by Johnathan Frankel and Steven J. Zipperstein, 1–37. Cambridge: Cambridge University Press.

Kjærsgaard, Kristoffer K. 2013. "Opfindelsen af jødiskhed, 1813–1849: Semitisk diskurs og produktionen af jødiskhed som andethed." Unpublished PhD thesis, Roskilde University.

Lausten, Martin S. 2015. *Jews and Christians in Denmark: From the Middle Ages to Recent Times, ca. 1100–1948*. Leiden: Brill.

Lincoln, Bruce. 1994. *Authority: Construction and Corrosion*. Chicago, IL: University of Chicago Press.

Margolinsky, Julius. 1954. *Fra "Nordlyset" til "Jødisk Samfund": Strejflys over jødisk Bladvirksomhed i Danmark gennem 140 Aar*. Copenhagen: Jødisk Samfund.

Pedersen, Alex H. 1964. *En Rettens Tjener: C.B. Henriques, 1870–1957*. Copenhagen: Berlingske.

Penslar, Derek J. 1991. *Zionism and Technocracy: The Engineering of Jewish Settlement in Palestine, 1870–1918*. Bloomington: Indiana University Press.

Reuveni, Gideon. 2010. "Advertising, Jewish ethnic marketing, and consumer ambivalence in Weimar Germany." In *Longing, Belonging, and the Making of Jewish Consumer Culture*, edited by Gideon Reuveni and Nils H. Roemer, 113–137. Leiden: Brill.

Reuveni, Gideon, and Nils H. Roemer, eds. 2010. *Longing, Belonging, and the Making of Jewish Consumer Culture*. Institute of Jewish Studies in Judaica, volume 11. Leiden: Brill.

Rothenberg, Fritz. 1964. "Forfatning og Forvaltning. Af kontorchef ved Det kgl. Bibliotek." In *Ved 150 Aars-Dagen for Anordningen af 29. Marts 1814*, edited by Julius Margolinsky and Poul Meyer, 133–158. Copenhagen: Det mosaiske Troessamfund og Danmark Logen.

Sorkin, David. 1987. *The Transformation of German Jewry, 1780–1840*. Oxford: Oxford University Press.

Thing, Morten. 2008. *De russiske jøder i København 1882–1943*. Copenhagen: Gyldendal.

Toury, Jacob. 1980. "Herzl's newspapers: The creation of Die Welt." *Studies in Zionism* 1: 159–172.

Wagner, Thorsten. 2001. "Fællesskabets nationalisering og jødespørgsmålet i en liberal kultur. Jøderne i Danmark mellem inklusion og eksklusion." In *Folk og Fællesskab: Træk af fællesskabstænkningen i mellemkrigstiden*, edited by Cecilie F.S. Banke, 47–61. Aarhus: Werks.

———. 2014. "Jødernes ligestilling – et europæisk perspektiv." In *Jøderne som frie borgere: Det Jødiske Samfund i Danmark*, edited by Bent Blüdnikow, 10–24. Copenhagen: Det Jødiske Samfund i Danmark.

Zuckerman, Maja G. 2016. "Broadening home: The emergence of Danish Zionism and its typological expansion of Danish Jewishness, 1897–1914." Unpublished PhD thesis, University of Southern Denmark.

About the author

Maja Gildin Zuckerman is the Jim Joseph Post-Doctoral Fellow at the Concentrate of Education and Jewish Studies at Stanford University and an Adjunct Professor at the Swig Program in Jewish Studies and Social Justice at University of San Francisco. She has a PhD in Contemporary Middle Eastern Studies from University of Southern Denmark and a MA in Sociology and Anthropology from Tel Aviv University.

— 10 —

The Multiple Faces of Mustafa Kemal Atatürk: Authority, Iconography, and Subjectivity in Modern Turkey

Dietrich Jung

This chapter asks the questions of how we can understand the authoritative role and iconographic presence of Atatürk in modern Turkish life and state formation. The chapter argues that in the formation of the modern Turkish republic we can observe historical processes of the transformation of charismatic authority into the political legitimacy structures of a modern state. From a Weberian perspective, the legitimacy of Atatürk's early rule rested predominantly on his personal qualities as a "national hero" and military leader. In order to transform Atatürk's charismatic authority into a lasting order of rule, however, it had to be routinized through traditional and/or legal means. This routinization of charismatic authority took place by the mediation of a broad variety of material artifacts incarnating elements of Ataturk's charismatic personality. The chapter claims that in modern Turkish state formation Atatürk's charismatic authority has gradually been transformed into the abstract authority of corporate actors and related state institutions. At the same time, Atatürk has assumed a key role in the modern subjectivation of the Turkish people as citizens of the republican state. In these interdependent processes of modern state and subjectivity formation, the iconographic manifestation of Atatürk's symbolic power in Turkish everyday life has played and still plays an essential part. In the visualized omnipresence of Atatürk we can see the materialized expression of both the rationalized authority of modern Turkish state institutions and the central point of reference for the self-hermeneutics of the Kemalist modern Turkish subject. In Michel Foucault's terms, we can observe a complex dispositive of discourses, social practices, institutions and artifacts that together make the authority structure of the Turkish republic. The iconographic presence of Atatürk is the material dimension of an authority structure, which reminds us of Bentham's panopticon and thereby of the crucial development of the execution of state power from means of domination to technologies of the self.

Introduction: Under the gaze of Atatürk

In the academic year 1997–1998, I was a guest lecturer at Bilkent University in Ankara. During my stay in Turkey, I lived under the almost constant "surveillance" of Mustafa Kemal, later named "Father of the Turks"—Atatürk.[1] The iconic founder of Turkey's republican state has not only been omnipresent in the political narratives of modern Turkish history. In a multiplicity of ways, Atatürk has intervened in many aspects of Turkish everyday life. Public buildings and places welcome you with the stern gaze of the first republican president. In the images of Atatürk you see at the same time the elder statesman, the rigid bureaucrat, the disciplined military officer, the enlightened teacher, and the urban bohemian enjoying a "Western" style of life. Even in private homes you can find pictures of Atatürk, often matching the self-representation of their tenants or owners. Professional associations hold congresses flagged with the Turkish flag and with paintings of Atatürk who easily assumes the appearance of a medical doctor, a farmer, an engineer, a teacher or a lawyer. In short, during my stay in Ankara, I could not escape daily encounters with Turkey's iconic "father of the state". How can we understand this key role and iconographic presence of Atatürk in modern Turkish life? How did the paradigmatic iconoclast turn into an icon himself? What do my observations tell us about the relationship between authority and subjectivity in Turkey?

In borrowing its conceptual tools selectively from Max Weber and Michel Foucault, this chapter attempts to answer these questions in a theoretically guided description of modern Turkish state formation. I will argue that in the formation of the modern Turkish republic we can observe key, historical processes of the transformation of charismatic authority into the political legitimacy structures of a modern state. From a Weberian perspective, the legitimacy of Atatürk's early rule rested predominantly on his personal qualities as a "national hero" and military leader. In order to transform Atatürk's charismatic authority into a lasting order of rule, however, it had to be routinized through traditional and/or legal means (Weber 1972, 143). This routinization of charismatic authority took place via the mediation of a broad variety of material artifacts incarnating elements of Ataturk's charisma.

In theoretical terms, I fuse this Weberian thesis of the routinization of charismatic authority with Foucault's concept of modern governmentality, in particular the combination of governmental technologies of domination

1. In 1934, the Grand National Assembly passed a law, giving Mustafa Kemal the surname Atatürk. It also reserved this name exclusively for him, making its adoption by anybody else illegal (Kucukan 2010, 967). Throughout this text, I will mostly apply the given surname Atatürk instead of Mustafa Kemal. However, in terms of political ideology, I still retain the term Kemalism instead of Atatürkism.

with technologies of the self. The chapter claims that in modern Turkish state formation, Atatürk's charismatic authority was gradually transformed into the abstract authority of corporate actors and related state institutions. At the same time, Atatürk has assumed a key role in the modern subjectivation of Turkish people as citizens of the republican state. In these interdependent processes of modern state and subjectivity formation, the iconographic manifestation of Atatürk's symbolic power in Turkish everyday life has played and still plays an essential part. In the visualized omnipresence of Atatürk we can see the materialized expression of both the rationalized authority of modern Turkish state institutions and the central point of reference for the self-hermeneutics of the Kemalist modern Turkish subject. In Michel Foucault's terms, we can observe a complex dispositive of discourses, social practices, institutions and artifacts that together make the authority structure of the Turkish republic.

Applying a Foucauldian perspective, I will interpret the iconographic omnipresence of Atatürk as the material dimension of a modern political authority structure in an analogy to Bentham's panopticon. Following J. Bentham, Michel Foucault described the panopticon as a "marvelous machine which, [...] produces homogeneous effects of power." In abstracting from a prison's architecture, Foucault identified the panopticon with a "political technology" (Foucault 1977, 200–207). The prison's central surveillance tower induces a mental state of conscious and permanent visibility among the inmates, without them being able to verify the presence of a guard in the tower. In this way, real surveillance turns into self-surveillance, a technology of domination transforms into a technology of the self. Governing through this technology, modern political authorities can avoid the direct use of coercive means to a greater extent. Political authority becomes an inherent feature of the everyday life of the population, materialized in symbolic forms and executed in spontaneous ways without any noise. The political technology of the panopticon creates a society that is broadly infiltrated by open and hidden disciplinary mechanisms (Foucault 1977; Jung 2006). In the example of Turkey, this "silent" exercise of political authority materialized in the continuous symbolic presence of Atatürk in political and in everyday life. In Turkey, "Atatürk has been watching you!"

Coming back to Max Weber, his concept of authority is perfectly in line with the general contention of this volume that addresses authority as a relational concept fundamentally dependent on materiality and media for its maintenance. In his sociology of domination (*Herrschaft*), Max Weber distinguished between to diametrically opposed ideal types of domination. He defined the first type on the basis of economic interests. This type is represented in its most pure form by a monopolistic market position. The second type, and this is where authority comes into play, is based on mere obedience. In its pure form this type is entirely independent of all interest. Historical forms of domination, then, appear on a continuum between these outer poles (Weber 1972, 542). In his conceptual definition, Weber reserves his concept of domination solely for the second type, that is to say domination based on a stable set of rules which both rulers and ruled consider to be legitimate. Authority, therefore, rests on a power structure in which the social conduct of the ruled is characterized by a certain degree of internalization of the manifested will of the ruler (1968b, 946).

In my own reading, this move from the coercive execution of domination to its manifestation in the unquestioned symbolic representations of everyday life corresponds to Foucault's transition from technologies of domination to technologies of the self. Authority does not refer to the external means of domination, but it characterizes the inner justification of the relationship between rulers and ruled. Authority relates to a reservoir of symbolic power within which the self-hermeneutics of modern subjects are embedded. According to Weber, authority appears in three ideal types of legitimacy: charismatic, traditional, and legal legitimacy. Each type rests on different symbolic representations referring to the personal qualities of the ruler, the sanctity of immemorial traditions, or the legality of enacted rules (Weber 1968a, 215). Again historical forms of domination relate to these types in idiosyncratic and rather contingent ways. In their pure forms, these types of authority only serve as heuristic means. In Weber's words: "All ruling powers, profane and religious, political and apolitical, may be considered as variations of, or approximations to, certain pure types" (1991, 294).[2]

I will elaborate more on my conceptual frame of reference in the different sections of the chapter. Thereby, the argument will unfold in a chronological order. The first section will begin with the breakdown of the Ottoman Empire and the troublesome and very precarious establishment of the Turkish Republic. Here we can observe the formation of new political institutions still under Atatürk's direct charismatic leadership. Then I move to the consolidation of the republican regime in the early years of the Turkish Republic. This section focuses on the transfer of Atatürk's charismatic authority to a set of political institutions based on legal authority.

2. In methodological terms, I closely follow the assumptions of Max Weber. According to him, we apply ideal types only as heuristic instruments. They do not copy historical reality in a descriptive way, but they refer to it in their quality of concepts of research. They represent sociological constructs which are logically acccentuated concepts abstracted from concrete and significant historical phenomena. Their ideal status, therefore, does not express any normative stance or portray social reality in a direct way (Weber 1904, 85–95).

Moreover, it analyses the role of his iconoclast cultural revolution in this transfer of political legitimacy and in the formation of modern Turkish subjects. The third section, then, deals with the "incarnation" of Atatürk's authority in two republican institutions: first in the Republican Peoples Party (RPP) and second in the Turkish military which inherited Atatürk's authority in the post-Second World War period. This shift augmented the symbolic role of Atatürk as an icon of republican history in order to justify the relatively autonomous political role of the military within a system of electoral democracy. The fourth section deals with the personality cult around Atatürk and the panoptic situation it has produced. The chapter will then conclude with some tentative reflections on the current transformation of political authority in Turkey.

From empire to national state: Atatürk and the foundation of the Turkish Republic

On 12 November 1914, the Ottoman Empire declared war on the Entente powers France, Great Britain, and Russia. The Ottoman empire's entry into the First World War on the side of Germany and Austria-Hungary was the decisive step towards its eventual collapse in the early 1920s. Ever since the end of the eighteenth century, the Ottoman Empire had increasingly been drawn into the imperial power struggles of Europe. The Ottomans became something like the sixth player in the European Pentarchy of Austria-Hungary, France, Germany, Great Britain, and Russia. Given this inherent role in the European power struggle, the Ottoman involvement in the First World War was most likely unavoidable. However, it was not entirely certain which side the ruling Committee of Union and Progress (CUP) would join. Soon after the Ottoman Minister of War, Enver Pasha, made this fateful decision, the empire found itself surrounded by multiple fronts. Lacking the economic, military, and communicational means to fight a major war, the First World War ended in a total disaster for the Ottoman state (Zürcher 1993, 117). The only remarkable military success was the defense of the Dardanelles between April 1915 and January 1916. On the Gallipoli peninsula, the joint Ottoman-German forces successfully repelled the Entente's naval assault and prevented allied control over the Straits. Together with the Prussian officer Liman von Sanders, Atatürk, then a 34 year-old officer in the Ottoman army, earned the credits for this successful military campaign.

Officially, Ottoman participation in the First World War ended with the truce of Mudros on 31 October 1918. One day after Sultan Mehmet VI had signed the unconditional capitulation of the empire, the CUP leadership fled Istanbul aboard a German submarine (Zürcher 1993, 139). Beginning with the Young Turk Revolution (1908), the CUP increasingly undermined the political authority of the royal institutions of the empire. After a *coup d'état* in January 1913, the CUP "triumvirate" of Enver, Talal, and Cemal Pasha governed the country in close alliance with the army in a dictatorial manner. They instigated a radical nationalist reform program leaving the palace with mere formal responsibilities (Kazancigil 1981; Zürcher 1984). The CUP leaders having left Istanbul, political authority returned, formally, to the Ottoman sultan and the bureaucrats of the Sublime Porte. In fact, however, the reign of Mehmed VI (1918–1922) was at the mercy of the victorious war allies. Having signed the treaty of Sèvres (1920), Mehmed VI further eroded the political legitimacy of monarchical rule. At the conference of Sèvres, the war allies partitioned the territories of the Ottoman Empire, leaving only minor parts of Anatolia, with Istanbul as the capital, for the Turks. At the same time, troops led by the Turkish Nationalist Movement fought against Greek occupation forces in Western Anatolia. Due to the territorial claims of Russia, Britain, France, Italy, Armenia, and Greece, Turkey was at the brink of disappearing from the political map (Jung 2003).

The Turkish War of Independence (1919–1922) began with the Greek occupation of Izmir in May 1919. Concomitantly with the advance of Greek troops in Western Anatolia, Atatürk landed in the Black Sea Coastal town of Samsun. Appointed as inspector-general of the ninth Ottoman army, Atatürk soon cut his ties to the Supreme Porte in Istanbul and organized the nationalist resistance in Anatolia. Under his leadership, the nationalist movement was able to profit from the diverging interests among the War allies. In bilateral negotiations they played them off against each other and could concentrate their forces on the front along with the Greek occupational forces. In August 1922, Turkish troops stopped the Greek army at the Sakarya river north of Eskisehir and subsequently pushed them back to the coast. On 11 October 1922, Ismet (Inönü) Pasha signed the armistice of Mudanya that ended the Turkish War of Independence. This treaty handed eastern Thrace over to Turkey and formally confirmed Turkish sovereignty over the Straits. Between November 1922 and July 1923, a Turkish delegation under Ismet Inönü negotiated with the Entente at Lausanne. In light of the military victory of the Turks under Atatürk's leadership, the war allies accepted Turkish demands for self-determination. In July 1923, the treaty of Lausanne abolished the never implemented clauses of Sèvres and acknowledged the sovereignty of the Turkish Republic as an independent state. The Turkish War of Independence offered the nationalist movement and Mustafa Kemal the historical opportunity to seize political authority from the Ottoman rulers and to establish a republican regime in Ankara.

On 29 October 1923, the Grand National Assembly in Ankara proclaimed the Turkish Republic and elected Atatürk the first president of the modern Turkish national state (Jung and Piccoli 2001, 59 and 65).

The son of a customs officer, Atatürk, was born in Salonika in 1881. The reformed Ottoman military and its new schooling system were the institutions of his personal advancement. After graduation from the Staff College in Istanbul in 1905, he was a founding member of the nationalist Committee of Union and Progress in Salonika and he joined the Young Turk Revolution in 1908 (Macfie 1994, 34). Mustafa Kemal was a typical representative of the new Ottoman military bureaucracy and an ardent supporter of Turkish nationalism. The officers, bureaucrats and professionals behind the CUP based their aspirations to rule on the organizational and cognitive knowledge of their modern, Western style education (Mardin 1971, 201). However, why did this social background allow Mustafa Kemal to lead? For centuries, political authority in the Ottoman Empire rested on a symbolic order that to a large extent resembled Max Weber's type of traditional legitimacy. Weber defined this form of authority as "an established belief in the sanctity of immemorial traditions and the legitimacy of those exercising authority under them" (Weber 1968a, 215). Dynastic descent combined with Islamic legitimacy was the core source of political authority in the Ottoman Empire. In the stratified Ottoman society, the young military officer was certainly not a legitimate head of state. Atatürk had to justify his political leadership by new means in sharp contradiction to the established symbolic order of authority in the Ottoman Empire.

The nationalist movement under Mustafa Kemal seized power in the course of the death struggle of the Ottoman Empire. The victorious military campaigns against Greek occupational forces together with the successful negotiations in Lausanne turned Atatürk into a war hero in the otherwise very bleak context of Ottoman defeat. He was able to escape the Ottoman defeat as a highly respected officer, aloof from both the Supreme Porte in Istanbul and the leadership of the CUP. In the years immediately following the First World War, his mission to salvage the Turkish state became the core source of his authority. With his reputation as a war hero and as the "savior of the nation," Atatürk's claim to leadership was almost sacrosanct (Zürcher 1991, 41). In the very foundational phase of the Turkish national state, the political legitimacy of Atatürk rested largely in this "heroism" and in his individual "exemplary character." In close approximation to Weber's ideal type, he based his right to rule on charismatic authority: "The charismatic leader gains and maintains authority solely by proving his strength in life" (Weber 1991, 249). The worldwide veneration of Atatürk after his death

(1938) clearly showed that his charisma not only captivated the Turks, but his personality impressed people and political leaders far beyond the borders of the newly founded republican Turkish state (Dumont 1983). Mainly relating to times of severe social crises, however, charismatic authority is of a highly extraordinary nature. Weber reminds us that charismatic authority is not a stabilizing but a revolutionary force. Solely based on the virtues of the charismatic leader, Atatürk's authority could have remained a transitory phenomenon. In order to stabilize it into a firm social and political order, the charisma of the leader has to be routinized. This is to say, forms of charismatic legitimacy have to be institutionalized in structures of traditional or legal domination (Weber 1968a, 244–268). The following section will discuss this process of the routinization of Atatürk's charismatic authority during the foundational phase of the Turkish Republic. In this way, it will show the ways in which the establishment, transformation and contestation of political authority is closely linked to the mediation by material artifacts and related symbolic moves.

From charismatic to legal authority: Establishing Republican rule

After the signature of the treaty of Lausanne, the internal differences among the various wings of the Turkish national movement came more visibly to the fore. Having secured the territorial integrity of the Turkish state, its different forces lost their central common denominator. Many in this loose alliance of army officers, bureaucrats, professionals, merchants, as well as landlords and younger clerics still saw their struggle as a means to eventually restore Ottoman rule (Ahmad 1993, 52). Moreover, during the War of Independence, the National Movement itself employed Islamic language as a major means of cohesion and mobilization (Heper 1981, 350). The majority of Turkey's rural population apparently perceived the War of Independence not primarily as a national triumph of republican forces. For them, Atatürk's military success was, rather, a proof of the divine superiority of Islam over the infidels (Stirling 1958, 400). In this situation, Atatürk and the republican wing of the national movement had to defend their claim to power against different competitors. In particular, they had to fight the legitimating forces of the traditional Ottoman order that was based on dynastic and religious sources of authority. The republican avant-garde was neither a part of the genealogical line of Ottoman rulers, nor could it draw its political legitimacy from the religious institutions of the traditional empire. In the context of a struggle for domestic legitimacy and international recognition, the transformation of Atatürk's charismatic authority had to follow the new, specifically modern trajectory toward legal legitimacy. He consequently pursued this course with the formation of the Turkish Republic and his iconoclast "cultural revolution".

The first step in this direction was the constitutional enactment proclaimed by the oppositional national movement during the War of Independence in January 1921 in Ankara. This document replaced the Ottoman principle of divine sovereignty with the sovereignty of the Turkish nation. Concurrently with the beginning of the negotiations in Lausanne, then, Atatürk removed the Ottoman Sultanate in November 1922, renouncing the political authority of this centuries-long Ottoman institution. In March 1924, the abolition of the Islamic Caliphate followed and Ankara banned the Ottoman dynasty from residing in the Turkish Republic. Only one month later, in April 1924, the Grand National Assembly adopted a new republican constitution transforming the patrimonial Islamic empire into a secular national state. However, the role of Islam did not find an abrupt end. Instead, the republican elite were forcing its slow demise. Therefore, the constitution of 1924 retained Islam as the Turkish state religion. This provision was deleted along with other references to Islam with the constitutional amendments in April 1928. In February 1937, finally, secularism was given constitutional status as one of the core principles of the Kemalist Turkish republic (Jung 2006, 134).

These successive steps of the institutionalization of legal authority were accompanied by an iconoclast cultural revolution. Together with the abolition of the Caliphate, the new regime dissolved the religious courts, the Islamic schools, the juridical function of the Sheikh al-Islam, and the ministries of religious affairs and pious foundations. Moreover, it established the principle of coeducation of boys and girls. This process of the deliberate de- and reconstruction of social institutions continued with the enforcement of the so-called hat-law (1925), prohibiting the *fez*—the traditional red headgear of Ottoman bureaucrats. In 1926, then, Ankara introduced the Gregorian calendar and two years later the Latin alphabet and Western numerals. In 1934, the regime granted active and passive suffrage to women and prohibited the pilgrimage to Mecca. In 1935, it replaced the Muslim Friday by the Sunday as the official day of public rest (Jung and Piccoli 2001, 60). Finally, the six Kemalist principles—nationalism, stateism, revolutionism, populism, republicanism, and secularism – achieved constitutional status in February 1937 (Ahmad, 1993, 63). In this way, the institutional implementation of legal authority was mediated by a conscious reconstruction of the symbolic order of society. When Atatürk passed away on 10 November 1938, the political legitimacy of the republican government, at least in formal terms, was firmly built on the structures of legal authority.

The charismatic authority of Atatürk had been transformed into a political system based on the "belief in the legality of enacted rules and the right of those elevated to authority under such rules to issue commands" (Weber 1968a, 215).

Closely connected to this institutional and cultural transformation of society, the early Turkish Republic saw the willful construction of new Turkish subject positions by the republican elite. Two processes in particular combined the establishment of legal political authority with the formation of modern Turkish subjects. First of all, the regime provided a set of new prescriptive cultural types for individual identity construction in the Turkish population at large. This took place in the form of symbolic measures such as the compulsory adoption of surnames, the introduction of dress laws, the opening of public beaches for women, or by carrying out the first Miss Turkey contest in 1929 (Ahmad 1993, 87). In this implementation of new technologies of domination, Atatürk himself played a central role. He bolstered this cultural transformation in presenting himself to the public in Western-style clothes, socializing with women, and drinking alcoholic beverages. In short, Atatürk himself became the modern "model of Turkishness" (Rosita 2015). In addition, the regime started to make Atatürk omnipresent by erecting statues of the president in the centres of Turkish towns. In 1926, the first statue of Atatürk was unveiled in Istanbul. Then statues in Ankara, Kayseri, Samsun, and many provincial towns were to follow (Zürcher 2012).

Second, Atatürk founded two cultural institutions and entrusted them with the task of Turkish collective and individual identity construction. In 1931, he opened the Turkish History Society (1931) with the purpose of writing a Turkish national history based on the idea of an ancient Turkish civilization. According to this "Turkish Historical Thesis," Turkic people left Central Asia and founded ancient empires such as those of the Sumerians and the Hittites, making them the historical predecessors of the Anatolian Turks. Historical analysis showed the inventive character of this deliberate construction with its "overemphasis on Central Asian roots" (Alici 1996). In 1932, the establishment of the Turkish Linguistic Society complemented these nation-building tasks of the Turkish History Society. In line with the Turkish Historical Thesis, the Society invented the Sun Language theory. This theory declared Turkish to be an ancient "pure" language foundational for many, if not all, languages to come (Zürcher 1993, 198–199). Under the personal leadership of President Atatürk, these institutions manufactured a standardized national culture. Transmitted through the state's educational system, this national culture aimed at producing social cohesion among the ethnically and religiously fragmented population of Anatolia, as well as political legitimacy for the newly established institutions of the Kemalist state. In sum, the early republic saw the implementation of new social technologies of domination and the formation of authoritative reference points for new technologies of the self.

In the early Turkish republic, a consciously designed project of state and identity formation was thus set in place. This transformative process in Turkish society was facilitated by new material media and nationalist narratives. The republican elite did not only aim at establishing new political institutions, but the new rulers also tried to underpin their political authority with the deliberate construction of a whole symbolic cosmos defining what it meant to be a modern Turk. In this sense, Turkey's cultural revolution was both a paradigmatic phase for the "invention of traditions" (Hobsbawm and Ranger 1983) and, concomitantly, for the introduction of methods of modern governmentality in Turkish history. In stark contrast to the Ottoman Empire, the Turkish Republic attempted seriously to manage the individual and the Turkish populace in general. The modern Turkish state and its individuals thus entered into a relationship of mutual constitution. In the initial phase of this relationship, technologies of domination largely characterized the governmentality of the Turkish republic. Legitimated by the charismatic authority of Atatürk, state agencies provided the new prescriptive standard codes of conduct and monitored their implementation (cf. Foucault 1990, 25). After the death of Atatürk, the Republican People's Party assumed a key role in this coercive governance of the early Turkish republic. It was the first institution incorporating the charismatic authority of Atatürk in its institutional logic. It was later succeeded by the Turkish armed forces.

From the Republican People's Party to the Turkish Military: Institutional incarnations of Atatürk's charismatic authority

Atatürk founded the Republican People's Party (RPP) in the summer of 1923. Within a few years, the party developed into the core instrument of the Kemalist elite's governance from above. In this development, they used internal security threats in the establishment and justification of the power monopoly of the RPP. In March 1925, Ankara promulgated the "Law on the Maintenance of Order." This emergency law allowed Atatürk to enforce his policies using the armed forces and specific courts, the so-called independence tribunals (Lewis 1961, 270). Initially, the emergency status was justified by the Kurdish insurrection in Eastern Anatolia. On 13 February 1925, the Nakshibandi Sheikh Said called his followers to a "holy war" against Ankara. The rebel forces were able to put the mountainous area north of the town of Diyarbakir under their temporary control. However, the better equipped and trained government troops and loyal Kurdish units soon crushed the insurrection and captured Sheikh Said on 27 April 1925. Together with him, 47 religious and tribal leaders of the rebellion were executed on 4 September 1925 (Bruinessen 1992, 291). After the rebellion, the Law on the Maintenance of Law and Order remained in place for four more years, offering the regime a legal platform to crack down on political opposition, silence critical journalists, and rush through its cultural reforms.

The short life of the Progressive Republican Party (PRP), a political alternative to the RPP, is a good example of these coercive moves with which the regime in Ankara eliminated forces of opposition during the years of emergency rule. The party was officially founded in November 1924 by a number of "able, disgruntled and still very influential former associates of Mustafa Kemal" (Frey 1965, 324). Knowing about the widespread dissatisfaction with his government, Atatürk at first did not intervene against the formation of this opposition party. On the contrary, he even removed his heavily criticized Prime Minister Inönü from his position. In June 1925, however, he seized the opportunity of the Sheikh Said rebellion and used the emergency law against the PRP. An Independence Tribunal accused leading members of the party of supporting the insurrection and the party branches were subsequently closed down (Zürcher 1993, 176–180). The final stroke against the PRP came with the so-called Izmir plot. On 15 June 1926, state security officers reported an assassination attempt against Atatürk, who was on his way to visit Izmir. In show trials in July and August 1926, a number of prison and death sentences were passed on the alleged plotters and politicians of the PRP based on weak evidence. The end of the PRP and the Izmir plot mark the ascendance of the RPP to more than twenty years of single party rule (Jung and Piccoli 2001, 71–72).

Between 1938 and 1946, Ismet Inönü governed Turkey with an iron hand. Deprived of the charismatic legitimacy of its founding father, political authority in Turkey rested with the republican institutions and the RPP. Yet, the elitist and iconoclastic reforms had not yet penetrated Turkish society at large (Heper 1998). While the new regime enjoyed legitimacy among parts of the urban population and the Kemalist military-bureaucratic elite, for large parts of the Turkish population the legally defined authority of the republican state was enforced by coercive means. Until the end of the Second World War, Inönü predominantly governed the country through the RPP. The Kemalist party was the central instrument in the regime's technologies of domination. Animated by a revolutionary and corporatist spirit, the cadres of the RPP infiltrated all sectors of Turkish society. Political opposition was only possible within and not against the RPP. Whoever opposed Ankara's policies was soon confronted with the state's means of physical force. In a tactically clever move, Atatürk assumed political control over the military in the foundational phase of the republic. In 1923, the Assembly passed a law according to which military officers must resign from the army if they were aspiring to a political office. This law entailed that those officers who embraced Kemalist policies were represented by the RPP and could stay in office without losing political representation. Officers in opposition to Atatürk, however, had to leave the military in order to pursue their political interests. Consequently, the Turkish army was gradually cleansed of non-Kemalist officers and put under the control of the president and his vanguard party (Ahmad 1993, 57).

This "Kemalization" of the Turkish armed forces facilitated single-party rule after Atatürk's death. Moreover, it prepared the military for becoming the natural heir to Atatürk's charismatic authority as soon as the hegemonic position of the RPP would disappear. This happened immediately after the Second World War with Inönü's decision to introduce multi-party politics in 1946.[3] The following pages will show how the Turkish military institutionalized the charismatic authority of Atatürk in its own favour as a necessary framework before we move to a discussion of the role of iconographic media under the political supremacy of the Turkish armed forces.

In the general elections of 14 May 1950, the RPP received a devastating bill for its autocratic rule at the ballot. With 408 against 69 seats, the newly founded Democratic Party (DP) achieved a landslide victory in appealing to hitherto neglected parts of the Turkish population (Ahmad 1993, 108–109; Zürcher 1993, 231). In the ten years of Democratic rule, the DP represented the Turkish social periphery, that is to say the peasants, lower middle-class urban dwellers, and the petty bourgeoisie. Excluded from political participation under single-party rule, these parts of the population made the DP the political vehicle for voicing their aspirations.

The DP leadership tried to underpin its political role in two crucial ways, marking a clear break with the ideological heritage of the Kemalist founder of the state. On the one hand, the DP increasingly utilized religious symbols in their appeal to peripheral voters. Islam could offer a unifying dimension to Turkey's "peripheral code" (Mardin 1973). Under DP rule many new mosques were built, holy tombs reopened, new religious schools founded, and faculties of divinity established at Turkish universities (Jung 2006, 136).

3. The reasons for this decision are still debated, but it certainly had a strong international component. In the rising Cold War, Turkey could no longer maintain its political neutrality in the international realm. Inönü's decision to join the "Western camp" therefore implied a shift in the political structures of the Turkish Republic.

On the other hand, in sharp contrast to the Kemalist military-bureaucratic elite, the DP politicians underlined their civilian profile. They were the first political leaders in the Turkish republic "who had not won their spurs in the military" (Harris 1970, 441). During the DP era (1950–1960), retired officers and state officials suffered a dramatic decline in parliamentary representation. Moreover, the successive DP governments hardly veiled their contempt for the officer corps and tried to subordinate the military to direct civilian control. At the same time, the American military aid program under the Truman Doctrine strengthened the self-image of the Turkish officer corps to be a vanguard force in the modernization of the country. In particular those young Turkish officers who enjoyed technical and military training in the West embraced the inherited image of the Turkish army as a defender of Atatürk's reforms (Harris 1965a, 66). Therefore it did not come as surprise that these young officers were the driving force behind the military intervention on 27 May 1960.

The military coup of 1960 became the foundation stone for more than 40 years of the relative autonomy of the army in Turkish politics. Moreover, it set the precedent for a series of future military interventions. In 1971, 1980, and 1997, the Turkish military brought civilian governments down, justifying its involvement in Turkish politics by drawing on the legacy of Atatürk's charismatic authority. The military took over the claim to leadership previously associated with the RPP. The decline of the Kemalist party was accompanied by the rise of the Turkish armed forces as an autonomous political force in Turkish society. In this way, Atatürk's charisma had moved from the Republican People's Party to the military. The relative autonomy of the Turkish military mainly rested on three pillars. First of all, it was institutionalized in subsequent Turkish constitutions, drawing on the legitimacy of a founding institution of the Turkish republic. Second, the Turkish armed forces became an important, partly self-sufficient, economic player. Thirdly, the army underpinned its political role by turning the iconoclast Atatürk into an icon himself. During the political supremacy of the Turkish armed forces, the cult around Atatürk developed into unprecedented forms via the use of iconographic media forms.

The Kemalist panopticon: Atatürk is watching you!

In institutional terms, the National Security Council became the key institution through which the Turkish army exerted its political power. Introduced in the constitution of 1961, the National Security Council developed from an advisory board to the government into a political institution that determined the major directions in Turkish politics. In particular, the new Turkish constitution of 1982 strengthened the position of the National Security Council in the aftermath of the military coup from September 1980. According to Article 118 of the constitution, the council met under the chairmanship of the president. The prime minister as well as the ministers of defence, foreign affairs, and the interior, represented the government, whereas the general chief of staff and the commanders of the air force, the army, the gendarmerie, and the navy were the representatives of the military. In addition, the Council's meetings were joined by the director of national intelligence and the secretary-general of the Council, who was himself a high-ranking officer responsible to the general chief of staff. In November 1983, a Law on the National Security Council defined its tasks as protecting the state against any foreign or domestic threats. Since then, the National Security Council has frequently issued policy recommendations in fields such as the economy, foreign policy, education, human rights, and the university administration. The council of ministers had to give priority to these recommendations, and for almost two decades they have obtained approval without exception (Jung and Piccoli 2001, 95).

The enormous political influence of the armed forces was further strengthened by the military's economic activities and its relatively autonomous education system. During the 1990s, the economic holdings of the Turkish army employed more than 40,000 people in businesses such as real estate, financing, manufacturing, tourism, and the retail trade. Furthermore, the military ran 55 joint ventures together with private companies, documenting the interlacement of interest among the political, the economic, and the military elite (Parla 1998). The separate education system of the army provided academic knowledge and military ethics based on Kemalist values. The teaching institutions raised the military cadets in a genealogical spirit, tracing a direct line from Atatürk to the role of the Turkish armed forces as the guardian and trustee of the republican state (Birand 1991, 23). After the Second World War, the military education system clearly played a central role in the routinization of Atatürk's charismatic authority. In its high schools and academies, the army created a military caste that stood apart from and above the rest of Turkish society (Karaosmanoglu 1993, 27). Although a military career did not lead to a wealthy future, it offered its officers absolute material security and constantly emphasized the soldier's moral superiority over against civil society. The young military cadets were socialized according to the role model of Atatürk.

The relative autonomy of the Turkish armed forces in the realms of politics, economy, and society in general was closely tied to the veneration of Atatürk and the concomitant defence of the secular nature of the Turkish

Republic. The military tried to bolster its political legitimacy with reference to the father of the nation. Therefore, an upsurge in the personality cult of Atatürk was visible after each military intervention (Zürcher 2012). The will of the founding father of the state was symbolically represented by his iconographic omnipresence in the public sphere, and the Turkish military positioned itself as the key institution in interpreting his will. In particular after the military intervention of 1980, the junta imposed the materially visible veneration of Atatürk on the people. Under the new regime, busts and statues of Atatürk were erected throughout the country (Dündar 2016, 53). State employees distributed his portrayals among shopkeepers and other public businesses. The regime covered mountain slopes and public spaces with giant images of Atatürk and added his name to major construction projects such as dams, bridges, or airports. In doing so, the military junta was basically in line with ways of depicting Atatürk established since the early years of the republic. He appeared as a "supernatural human," as a "progenitor of the whole nation" (Özyürek 2004, 380). The press further underpinned this proliferation of iconographic media and material manifestations of Atatürk's lasting authority in praising the unveiling and inauguration of each and every monument. In the immediate aftermath of the coup, newspaper articles helped to justify the military's bid for political power with reference to these material manifestations of the veneration of Atatürk. They published articles about students sculpting busts of Atatürk, or ordinary citizens "who could not afford to have a bust, but instead clean existing busts" (Dündar 2016, 53).

Looking at the use of media and materiality in the personality cult around Atatürk from a sociological point of view, his virtual omnipresence has had different effects. Since its inception in the early republic, the personality cult provided a political means for national integration and the execution of the corporate claims of Kemalist ideology in republican state building. The image of Atatürk transcended all ethnic, social, religious, and regional factions of Turkish society. Moreover, the multidimensional personality of Atatürk—the military officer, the statesman, the bureaucrat, the teacher, and the secular intellectual—reflected the self-representation of the major social forces that once constituted the core of the Kemalist bloc. The material interests and personal identity constructions of the major social forces were inseparably nested in the institutional manifestations of the republican Turkish state. Recalling Weber's two diametrically opposed ideal types of domination, the Kemalist elite was in control of the means of legitimacy through authority and of economic interest. In addition, for this stratum of Turkish society, Atatürk—in one of his many appearances—was one of the central types for individual subjectivity formation. Emulating the founding father became a part of the Kemalist technologies of the self.

Yet the founder of the Turkish state was not only the focal point of the personal interest and self-representation of these forces. Even more important, the personality cult around Atatürk turned into a central means of justification of their claim to power. It came to represent a symbolic, disciplinary mechanism in the panoptic character of Turkish politics, in which Atatürk's omnipresence symbolically expressed the function of permanent surveillance. While initially a visible means of Kemalist state domination, his gaze increasingly turned into a silent mechanism of self-discipline and political self-restraint among the Turks. Especially the changes in the personality cult during the 1990s, which saw the emergence of a new market of Atatürk paraphernalia, indicates a gradual shift in this mechanism, which led from technologies of domination to technologies of the self.

In the course of the 1990s, the "human side" of Atatürk increasingly entered the personality cult of the leader. A whole market of new Atatürk paraphernalia appeared displaying a version of Atatürk relevant for every trade: "Atatürk seated at a table for use in restaurants and bars, several poses of Atatürk drinking coffee for coffee shops, a dancing Atatürk for nightclubs, and even Atatürk with cats and dogs for veterinarians" (Özyürek 2004, 374). It was this mixed omnipresence of Atatürk, the almost supernatural political leader and the Atatürk of all trades, whom I met when working as a guest lecturer at Bilkent University. Esra Özyürek convincingly argued that this "privatization" of Atatürk was a reaction to the construction of a market-based liberal economy in Turkey as well as to the emergence of a competing market of Islamic paraphernalia in the country. Putting these economic and symbolic factors together, we can see how, in the 1990s, Turkey experienced a commodity-based form of identity politics, which rested on the structures of a global consumer culture (Özyürek 2004, 377).

In addition to this, however, the privatization of Atatürk also shows how the disciplinary mechanism moved into Turkish homes. At least for those supporting the secularist camp of Turkish politics, purchasing Atatürk paraphernalia became a means to express consent with the republican political institutions; Atatürk on mugs and T-shirts became political statements of their owners. They became expressions of a political authority struggle in which the cultural pre-eminence and the vested interest of Turkey's Kemalist elite was—to a greater extent—challenged by a Turkish "counter-elite" drawing from the rich symbolic reservoir of Islamic traditions (Göle 1997). While suppressed by the state elite for some decades, the symbolic language of Islam has nevertheless remained a major source for individual identity construction for many Turks. The opposition to Atatürk during the early republic and the DP under Menderes drew from this symbolic language of Islam. The governing Justice and Development Party (AKP), founded in 2001, stands in the tradition of this Islamic political wing and has made successful use of the ideological power of Islam. By drawing on very different symbolic reservoirs, the two opposing political camps, simplistically described as secularist and Islamist political wings, have been able to rely, in their political struggle, on the self-hermeneutics and subject positions of their respective supporters.

Conclusions: The legacy of Atatürk contested

Taking the perspective of the materiality of political authority structures, the ongoing power struggle in Turkish politics is symbolized in the architecture of the Turkish capital. Taking in the view of Turkey's capital from the Ankara Hisar, the historical Citadel, you will see two architectural landmarks representing Turkey's two political wings. On your right hand side, we have the Anitkabir, the classicist mausoleum of Mustafa Kemal Atatürk, completed in 1953. Moving to the left, your eyes will stop at the huge building of the Kocatepe Mosque, the largest mosque in Ankara, built in the 1960s in a neo-Ottoman style. While the monumental building of the Anitkabir contains the sarcophagi of Atatürk and his successor Ismet Inönü, the Kocatepe Mosque offers room for more than 20,000 believers. Together with its republican museum and elite soldiers parading the site, Anitkabir represents the material expression of the political narrative of Turkey's Kemalist state elite. With its reminiscences of Ottoman grandeur and a supermarket in its basement, Kocatepe Mosque, instead, symbolizes major features of the populist economic, social, and foreign policies of the incumbent AKP government and President Erdogan. The Kemalist understanding of the legacy of Atatürk's authority, elitist policies of laicist, state-centred and rather inward-looking nationalism, have been successfully contested by an economically neo-liberal, but politically increasingly authoritarian brand of Islamic nationalism with neo-Ottoman imperial connotations. In this contestation, both sides have drawn heavily on iconographic artefacts symbolizing the two major competing political narratives and forms of subjectivities that have characterized the modern path of Turkish state formation.

This chapter has argued that this path, the transformation from the Ottoman empire to the modern Turkish national state, was accompanied by the strong mediation of political authority through material symbolic artifacts and iconography. In particular, the cult around Mustafa Kemal Atatürk was instrumental in Turkish nation- and state-building. Without this mediating function of Atatürk, the ethnic, linguistic, religious and social mosaic of Anatolia would hardly have been integrated in the new political form of a republican state after the First World War. In the early republic (1923–1945), Kemalist iconoclasm helped along the transfer of the charismatic authority of Turkey's foundational figure Atatürk into the hands of his political representative, the Republican Peoples Party (RPP), and the newly built republican institutions. I framed this process in Weberian terms as the routinization of Atatürk's charismatic authority; or, in other words, as a translation into a rationalized form of legal domination.[4] After the Second World War, Atatürk's institutionalized charisma was seized by the Turkish military after the electoral defeats of the RPP. Again, this seizure of political authority was strongly underpinned by an enhanced use of Atatürk as an icon of the legitimate representation of state power by the military.

On 15 July 2016, a part of the Turkish armed forces attempted to topple the incumbent AKP government and President Recep Tayyip Erdogan. The military coup failed and met with unified opposition from Turkey's political parties and the Turkish population at large. While the details of this failed coup are still unclear, it has seemingly accelerated and supported the ongoing transformation of Turkish politics, moving its symbolic representation from Anitkabir to Kocatepe Mosque. Apparently, the Turkish military has largely lost its political legitimacy once justified by means of the cult around Atatürk. Interestingly, however, the Turkish AKP government's response to the coup showed striking parallels to the country's early republican history. President Erdogan's move against the media, the oppositional parties, and parts of the state bureaucracy remind us of similar measures undertaken by Atatürk in consolidating his power in the aftermath of the Sheikh Said rebellion and the so-called Izmir plot. While relying on religious, political discourse, Erdogan nevertheless acts in ways quite similar to the convinced secularist Atatürk, when he seized power in the 1920s. There are also visible tendencies of a new cultural revolution, gradually replacing the symbols of laicist Kemalism by an Islamic Turkish nationalism of sorts. In this sense, we can observe both change and continuity in current Turkish politics by focusing on the role of materiality and media. To be sure, history does not repeat itself and the monopolization of power by the AKP under Erdogan has not yet reached the level of Turkish single-party rule under the RPP. Moreover, while being visible to a lesser degree, Atatürk's omnipresence still prevails. Whether the charismatic leadership of President Erdogan will

4. This transformation was certainly accompanied by force and also facilitated by a number of social practices and power configurations that are not captured by Weber's concept of legal domination. I demonstrated this in chapter four of *Turkey at the Crossroads* (Jung and Piccoli 2001).

be able to replace the charisma of Turkey's founding father remains to be seen. Yet it seems as if the Islamic wing of the Turkish national movement, for decades suppressed by the Kemalist state elite, has gained the political lead. Observing the materiality and media of Erdogan's rule will be a key analytical instrument of our understanding of the political direction in which Turkey will move.

References

Ahmad, F. 1996 [1993]. *The Making of Modern Turkey.* London: Routledge.

Alici, D. M. 1996. "The role of culture, history and language in Turkish national identity building: An overemphasis on Central Asian roots." *Central Asian Survey* 15(2): 217–231.

Birand, M. A. 1991. *Shirts of Steel: An Anatomy of the Turkish Armed Forces.* London: I.B. Tauris.

Bruinessen van, M. 1992. *Agha, Shaikh and State: The Social and Political Structures of Kurdistan.* London: ZED books.

Dumont, P. 1983. *Mustafa Kemal, invente la Turquie moderne.* Bruxelles: Ed. Complexe.

Dündar, Lale. 2016. "A tribute to art or ideology: The news coverage of Ataturk statues in Turkish press after the coup of 12 September 1980." *Art-Sanat/Histart* 15: 41–54. Special Issue.

Foucault, M. 1977. *Discipline and Punish. The Birth of the Prison.* London: Penguin.

———. 1990. *The Use of Pleasure.* New York: Vintage Books.

Frey, F.W. 1965. *The Turkish Political Elite.* Cambridge, MA: MIT Press.

Göle, N. 1997. "Secularism and Islamism in Turkey: The making of elites and counter-elites." *Middle Eastern Journal* 51(1): 46–58.

Harris, G.S. 1965a. "The role of the military in Turkish politics, Part 1." *Middle East Journal* 19(1): 54–66.

———. 1970. "The causes of the 1960 revolution in Turkey." *Middle East Journal* 24(4): 438–454.

Heper, M. 1981. "Islam, polity and society in Turkey: A Middle Eastern perspective." *Middle East Journal* 35(3): 346–363.

———. 1998. *Ismet Inönü. The Making of a Turkish Statesman*, Leiden: Brill.

Hobsbawm, E. and T. O. Ranger, eds. 1983. *The Invention of Tradition.* Cambridge: Cambridge University Press.

Jung, D. 2003. "The Sèvres syndrome: Turkish foreign policy and its historical legacies." In *American Diplomacy.* http://www.unc.edu/depts/diplomat/archives_roll/2003_07-09/jung_sevres/jung_sevres.html

———. 2006. "'Secularism': A key to Turkish politics." *Intellectual Discourse* 14(2): 129–154.

Jung, D. and W. Piccoli. 2001. *Turkey at the Crossroads: Ottoman Legacies and a Greater Middle East*, London: Zed books.

Karaosmanoglu, A. 1993. "Officers: Westernization and Democracy." In *Turkey and the West: Changing Political and Cultural Identities*, edited by Metin Heper, Heinz Kramer, and Ayse Oncu, , 19–33. London: I.B. Tauris.

Kazancigil, A. 1981. "The Ottoman-Turkish state and Kemalism." In *Atatürk: the Founder of a Modern State*, edited by A. Kazancigil and E. Özbudun, 37–56. London: C. Hurst.

Lewis, B. 1968 [1961]. *The Emergence of Modern Turkey.* Oxford: Oxford University Press.

Macfie, A. L. 1994. *Atatürk.* New York: Longman.

Mardin, S. 1971. "Ideology and religion in the Turkish revolution." *International Journal of Middle East Studies* 2(3): 197–211.

———. 1973. "Center-periphery relations: A key to Turkish politics?" *Daedalus* 102(1): 168–190.

Özyürek, Esra. 2004. "Miniaturizing Atatürk: Privatization of state imagery and ideology in Turkey." *American Ethnologist* 31(3): 374–391.

Parla, T. 1998. "Mercantile militarism in Turkey 1998: 1960–1998." *New Perspectives on Turkey* 19: 29–52.

Rosita, Suzan M. 2015. "The silent nation: Identity formation and the everyday life in post-genocidal Turkey 1923–1953." Unpublished PhD thesis, European University Institute, Florence.

Stirling, A. P. 1958. "Religious change in republican Turkey." *Middle East Journal* 12(4): 395–408.

Weber, M. 1904. "'Objectivity' in social science and social polity." In *The Methodology of the Social Sciences.* Translated and edited by Edward A. Shils and Henry A. Finch, 49–112. New York: The Free Press.

———. 1968a. *Economy and Society: An Outline of Interpretive Sociology*, edited by Guenther Roth and Claus Wittich, volume I. New York: Bedminister Press.

———. 1968b. *Economy and Society: An Outline of Interpretive Sociology*, edited by Guenther Roth and Claus Wittich, volume III. New York: Bedminister Press.

———. 1972. *Wirtschaft und Gesellschaft. Grundriss der verstehenden Soziologie.* Studienausgabe, Tübingen: J.C.B. Mohr (Paul Siebeck).

———. 1991. *From Max Weber: Essays in Sociology*, edited, with an introduction by H. H. Gerth and C.Wright Mills, with a new preface by Bryan S. Turner. London: Routledge.

Wehler, H.-U. 1989. *Deutsche Gesellschaftsgeschichte, Bd. 1: Vom Feudalismus des Alten Reiches bis zur defensiven Modernisierung der Reformära 1700-1815*, Munich: C.H. Beck.

Zürcher, E. J. 1984. *The Unionist Factor: The Role of the Committee of Union and Progress in the Turkish National Movement, 1905-1926*, Leiden: Brill.

———. 1991. *Political Opposition in the Early Turkish Republic. The Progressive Republican Party 1924-1925.* Leiden: Brill.

———. 1998 [1993]. *Turkey: A Modern History.* London: I.B.Tauris

———. 2012. "In the name of the father, the teacher, and the hero: The Atatürk personality cult in Turkey." In *Political Leadership, Nations and Charisma*, edited by Vivian Ibrahim and Margret Wunsch, 129–142. London: Routledge.

About the author

Dietrich Jung is Professor and Director of the Center for Contemporary Middle East Studies, University of Southern Denmark. He holds an MA in Political Science and Islamic Studies, as well as a PhD from the Faculty of Philosophy and Social Sciences, University of Hamburg, Germany, and has large field experience in the Muslim world. His most recent books are *Orientalists, Islamists and the Global Public Sphere: A Genealogy of the Modern Essentialist Image of Islam* (Equinox 2011); *The Politics of Modern Muslim Subjectivities: Islam, Youth and Social Activism in the Middle East*, together with Marie Juul Petersen and Sara Lei Sparre (Palgrave 2014); *Muslim History and Social Theory: A Global Sociology of Modernity* (Palgrave 2017).

— 11 —

A Tradition in Need of How-To Books: The Revitalization of Traditional Rituals and Lifestyle among Smārta Brahmins of South India

MIKAEL AKTOR

The authority of South India's smārta Brahmins has long been under pressure. The challenges have not only come historically from the anti-Brahmin sentiments of the South Indian political environment. Globalization and "Westernization" are addressed as more acute challenges. Due to these developments, the traditional ritual knowledge and lifestyle have almost died out. So today, *smārta* leaders attempt to revitalize traditional "values" and render them authoritative. Traditional values may be articulated as certain ideas and attitudes, but they are first of all revitalized through bodily and material practices in rituals and habits of dress, food and lifestyle. Smārta leaders organize sessions where people are taught some of these rituals, followed up by how-to books that explain both the ritual details and how to dress and cook in a traditional fashion. The present chapter examines the recent popularization of the almost extinct *smārta pañcāyatanapūjā*, a worship of five gods in the form of five aniconic stones from five different places of South Asia ranging from Northern Nepal to Tamil Nadu in the South. The popularization of this tradition uses various media—from how-to book literature, television, and the internet to the commoditization of ritual utensils. Weakened authority is strengthened through the *pañcāyatanapūjā*, where the five stones represent the Hindu South Asia as an integrated geographical and religious unit. The material presented in this chapter is used to discuss the interplay of authority, materiality and media with contemporary identity politics.

Introduction

The Hindu priestly class, the Brāhmaṇas (also known as Brahmins or Brahmans),[1] has dominated the transmission and dissemination of classi-

1. In this chapter I use the form "Brahmin" except in quotes or mentioning where the form "Brahman" has been used.

cal Hindu culture throughout the South Asian subcontinent from north to south. As masters and guardians of the Sanskrit language (Pollock 2006), they composed not only the Hindu scriptures that articulate the Hindu ritual orthopraxy but, importantly, also the socio-religious legal texts that defined and promoted the hierarchical social ideology of the caste system (Aktor 2018.)

According to these law texts (*dharmaśāstra*), society forms a system of embedded hierarchical relations. As the Brahmins had a monopoly on teaching the Vedas, which were regarded as texts that emerged directly from the creation of the world and therefore not of human origin, and as they also had a monopoly on officiating at sacrifices, they regarded themselves as the highest of the four social classes of the Hindu society. Together with the warrior and the farming classes (the Kṣatriyas and Vaiśyas), they constituted the "Twice-Born" who were entitled to Vedic initiation, regarded as a second birth, which gave them the rights to study the Vedas and to use Vedic mantras at rituals. Below these upper classes, the Śūdra class, consisting of artisans, workers and servants, was considered "Once-Born," with no rights to initiation or Vedic study and sacrifice. The same held for women of all classes; they were not initiated into the recitation of the Vedas. The visible mark of this division is the sacred thread which is received at initiation and therefore only worn by boys and men from the three upper classes.

The system of the four classes (*varṇas*) as known from these texts is not a mere reflection of an already existing social reality. Rather:

> It is clear that the *varṇa* system was not an objective and disinterested classification of ancient Indian society. It was from the start an ideologically driven enterprise designed to place the Brāhmaṇa at the top of a pyramidal social hierarchy, supporting the claim to power of the Kṣatriya class and in a special way reducing the Śūdras and other lower classes to a marginal and oppressed status (Olivelle 2018, 18.)

This disdain for the low classes, this "poetics of contempt" (Vajpeyi 2010, 158), is characteristic of much of the *dharmaśāstra* literature, and often with an economic twist as in this ruling in one of the most influential of these texts, the Law Code of Manu (*Mānavadharmaśāstra*), probably from the second century CE: "Even a capable Śūdra must not accumulate wealth; for when a Śūdra becomes wealthy, he harasses Brahmins" (*MDh* 10.129 in Olivelle 2005, 214).[2]

The elevated position of the Brahmin class was explained by the Brahmin authors in glorifying eulogies:

2. Some groups of Śūdra artisans managed to improve their economic status via increased trade and urbanization, a process that was further reinforced by the royal building projects during the Gupta dynasty (third–sixth century CE) (Sharma 1990, 263–264).

> For when a Brahmin is born, a pre-eminent birth takes place on earth—a ruler of all creatures to guard the storehouse of Laws. This whole world—whatever there is on earth—is the property of the Brahmin. Because of his eminence and high birth, the Brahmin has a clear right to this whole world. The Brahmin eats only what belongs to him, wears what belongs to him, and gives what belongs to him; it is by the kindness of the Brahmin that other people eat. (*MDh* 1.99–101 in Olivelle 2005, 91–92)[3]

Smārta Brahmins in south India

South India, the non-Indo-Aryan, Dravidian speaking part of the subcontinent,[4] was only gradually influenced by the Sanskritic ideas and culture of the Brahmins. By the seventh century, Brahmin influence on the religious life of the elites was substantial. The magnificent Tamil temple complexes visited by millions of pilgrims every year are evidence of this development. However, the Tamil classification system of social stratification is different from that of the North. In contrast to the system of four social classes, the social structure of the South only accepted two of the classical class categories, Brahmins and Śūdras.

Below the castes belonging to the four classes in the North and the two in the South, the castes regarded as the lowest in the caste system formed a separate section. These were the castes that performed, and still perform, unskilled labour and who work in occupations that were regarded as "polluting" by the Brahmin authors of the normative texts. These occupations typically involved the handling of materials from dead animals, or work connected with cremation, latrines, and renovation. In the classical law books, people from these castes were regarded as "untouchable" (Sanskrit: *aspṛśya*, see Aktor 2010). The notion of untouchability was further cemented by the colonial administration when the commissioner of the 1901 Census of India, Sir Herbert Risley, introduced "Asprishya Shudra" as a demographic category (Charsley 1996, 1–3).

During the same period, an anti-caste movement started to gain strength in Tamil Nadu, and as a result Tamil legislators decided, in 1914, to name this lowest section of society Adi Dravidas, "Original Dravidians." The name-change was intended as a protest against the derogatory, anglicized word

3. The sacrificial, priestly thinking behind this praise is the idea that all kinds of prosperity are based on the regular rains and good harvests that are the outcome of the sacrifice: "An oblation duly consigned to the fire reaches the sun; from the sun comes rain; from rain, food; and from food, offspring" (*MDh* 3.76 in Olivelle 2005, 112).

4. Today, South India is divided into five states: Telangana and Andhra Pradesh (language: Telugu), Karnataka (language: Kannada), Kerala (language: Malayalam), and Tamil Nadu (language: Tamil). These main languages all belong to the Dravidian language family unlike the Indo-Aryan main languages of North India.

"Pariah" that was formed from the Tamil designation of the Paṟaiyar drummer caste that was among the so-called "Untouchable castes." Behind this change of name, which stressed a specific South Indian, "Dravidian" ethnicity, lay not only an anti-caste protest but also an ethnic protest against the North Indian self-proclaimed Sanskritic supremacy that had been promoted by Brahmins for several centuries. Today, however, the commonly accepted all-Indian term for this section of society is "Dalit," a Marathi word that means "downtrodden" or "broken." This designation was first introduced by the Maharashtrian social reformer Jotirao Govindrao Phule (1827–1890) and applied as self-designation by Dalit activists in their campaign for social rights that gained momentum from the 1970s onwards (Begrich and Randeria 2014).

As a result of this development, Tamil society is divided into three sections, "Brahmans," "Non-Brahmans" (the new designation in Tamil Nadu for the Śūdras), and "Dalits" (Fuller and Narasimhan 2014, 7). The caste society is a pyramid structure with a very narrow top and a huge bottom. In Tamil Nadu, estimations suggest that the Brahmin castes only make up somewhere between two and two and a half percent of the population (Fuller and Narasimhan 2014, 5; infoelections.com 2016). They are divided into two broad sections, Smārtas and Śrī Vaiṣṇavas. The latter are worshippers of Viṣṇu, whereas the Smārtas worship several Hindu gods on an equal footing, but in particular five: Śiva, Viṣṇu, Sūrya, Gaṇeśa and Devī.[5]

Smārtism arose in continuation and as a consequence of the decline of the Gupta dynasty in the sixth century. The Gupta dynasty (320–550 CE) is seen as the "golden age" of classical Hindu culture. Its disintegration resulted in sectarian fragmentations, in particular an antagonism between Śiva and Viṣṇu worshippers. To prevent sectarian tendencies, the Smārtas promoted a worship of the five gods together based on the ideas of Advaita Vedānta (the non-dualist Hindu philosophy) that all gods are ultimately manifestations of the one Brahman, the absolute, undifferentiated, all-pervading divine principle (Jackson 2012).[6] In this Smārta context, the five gods are mentioned collectively as Pañcāyatana ("Five Abodes" or "Five Altars") and their worship as Pañcāyatana Pūjā. The worship is typically performed

5. In Hindu mythology, Śiva represents the cosmological destructions that precede the cyclical recreations of the universe. He is associated with asceticism but he is also married to Pārvatī, one of the many manifestations of Devī, the "Goddess." Viṣṇu represents the preservation of the universe and of social norms (*dharma*). Sūrya is the Sun god. Gaṇeśa, god of success and happiness, is the elephant-headed son of Śiva and Pārvatī. Devī is the Goddess, the female divine principle or energy (*śakti*).

6. The word "Brahman," apart from being a name for the priestly class (like "Brahmin"), is also the name of the abstract, undifferentiated divine principle, especially known from the Upaniṣads and the Advaita Vedānata philosophy.

with small statuettes of the five gods placed on a metal tray, or it is performed with aniconic representations of the gods in the form of five different stones from various locations in South Asia. In the aniconic form, the worship of the five gods, which had almost died out, has been re-promoted and revitalized in recent years, in particular among the Smārta Brahmins of Chennai, the capital of Tamil Nadu. Thus, on 15 August 2014, the Indian Independence Day, a ceremony took place in Chennai whereby 108 married couples of Smārta Brahmins were initiated into this worship in front of the Indian national flag. This particular type of worship has been the subject of my research for the last three to four years. I have described the ritual in detail elsewhere (Aktor 2016), but in this chapter I wish to focus more on the social and historical context of this revival which seems to be part of a broader re-traditionalization of Brahmin culture and values in Tamil Nadu.

The anti-Brahmin movements in Tamil Nadu

The Tamil terminology that divides society into three groups, the Brahmins, the Non-Brahmins, and the Adi Dravidas (or Dalits), is a result of the anti-caste and especially the anti-Brahmin movements that became influential in the first part of the twentieth century. The "Śūdra" and the "Pariah" categories which both were perceived as derogatory were replaced by the "Non-Brahmin" and the "Adi Dravida" designations respectively. In 1916, a group of Non-Brahmin leaders gathered in order to organize the publication of newspapers in local languages that could "voice non-Brahman grievances," and soon they issued a *Non-Brahmin Manifesto* in two newspapers. One of these was the *New India* published by Annie Besant, president of the non-American branch of the Theosophical Society, whose headquarters were, and are still, located in Chennai (then: Madras) (Irschick 1969, 47–48).[7]

The *Non-Brahmin Manifesto* (quoted in full in Irschick 1969, 358–367) first of all calls for a more proportionate political, juridical, and cultural representation of Non-Brahmins in the society of British India. At that time, like today, the demographic share of Brahmins compared to Non-Brahmins was minimal but their public influence was immense. This, the *Manifesto* maintains, is not due to any inborn mental superiority of Brahmins, as claimed in classical Brahminical texts such as Manu's Code of Law, but due to tradition and religious propaganda:

7. Annie Besant did not support the non-Brahman movement, and the Movement was distrustful of Annie Besant. As a Theosophist she was involved in the construction of the Neo-Hinduism that was brought to Europe and America via translations of primarily Brahmin Sanskrit literature such as the Upaniṣads, the Bhavadgītā, Purāṇas and the Law Code of Manu. Her campaign for Indian "Home Rule" was met with skepticism by Non-Brahmins who feared a disproportionately insignificant political representation of Non-Brahmins compared to Brahmins (see Irschick 1969, 44–45).

> Old established traditions, the position of the Brahmins as the highest and the most sacred of the Hindu castes, the nature of their ancient calling, and the steady inculcation of the belief, both by written texts and oral teaching, that they are so many divinely ordained intermediaries without whose active intervention and blessing the soul cannot obtain salvation and their consequent freedom from manual toil—all these helped them to adapt themselves easily to the new conditions under British Rule, as under previous epochs, in larger numbers and far more successfully than the other castes and communities. [...] In a variety of ways and in different walks of life non-Brahmins will now be found unostentatiously and yet effectively contributing to the moral and material progress of this Presidency. But they and their brethren have so far been groping helplessly in the background, because of the subtle and manifold ways in which political power and official influences are often exercised by the Brahmin caste.
>
> (*The Non-Brahmin Manifesto* in Irschick 1969, 362–363)

In 1917, a year after the publication of the *Non-Brahmin Manifesto*, members of the same group founded The Justice Party. It won the elections to the Madras Legislative Council in 1920 and succeeded in introducing a reservation policy that secured a more proportionate recruitment among the different castes. In 1925, the great Tamil social reformer, E. V. Ramasamy (1879–1973), founded the Self-Respect Movement. It was later transformed into the Dravida Kazhagam (DK), the "Dravidian Federation," the aim of which was not only to eradicate caste and "untouchability," but also to establish a separate Dravidian Nation for the Tamil-speaking area of South India. It was an activist movement with a militant anti-Brahmin agenda. During the 1950s–1970s, its activities included campaigns where members forcibly cut off the topknots and sacred threads of male Brahmins, two traditional and visible markers of Brahmin identity. Apart from these two elements, the traditional dress code of the Brahmins included a long white cloth (*veṣṭi*) tied around the waist and fastened behind between the legs. The upper part of the body would be naked in order to make the sacred thread, which is worn over the left shoulder and under the right arm, visible. The secular national ideology that influenced public life in India during the first decades after the independence and the campaigns of the anti-Brahmin movement prompted the Brahmins to leave these traditional hair and dress styles behind, especially in the urban areas (Fuller and Narasimhan 2014, 10–13).

The Dravidian Federation (DK) was later replaced by the Dravidian Progress Federation (DMK), from which the All-India Anna Dravidian Progress Federation (AIADMK) broke away in 1972. Although the latter party cannot be characterized as outright "anti-Brahmin" like its predecessors, it has kept up a Dravidian rhetoric based on the divide between Brahmins and Non-Brahmins.

Apart from the first twenty years after Indian independence in 1947, Tamil Nadu has been headed by chief ministers from either DMK or AIADMK. Fuller and Narasimhan note that during their shifting periods of governance the two parties have expanded the reservation system greatly, "so that Brahmans are vastly outnumbered by non-Brahmans at all levels of the government service and public sector" (Fuller and Narasimhan 2014, 10). The dominance of non-Brahmin values in Tamil public life is also reflected in the low support in Tamil Nadu to the Hindu nationalist Bharatiya Janata Party (BJP), which only won 2.86 percent of the votes at the latest elections in 2016. In contrast, BJP won the majority (39.7 percent) in the northern state of Uttar Pradesh during the latest election in that state.

The political developments in Tamil Nadu form part of the background for the relative marginalization of traditional Brahmin values and lifestyle in that state compared to states in North India. The much less distinctly defined set of cultural and social changes that traditionalist Brahmins in Tamil Nadu label "Westernization" form another part of the background. This label is most often pasted on the younger generation and often framed as a critique of young people's ways of dressing, speaking, and behaving. It sums up some of the diverse effects of modernization, secularization, and globalization on the lifestyle and life choices of the young generation, but with a twist. It is a critique, not of modernization as such, but of adopting values and lifestyles associated with "the West" or "Western culture." As such, it emphasizes the uniqueness and autonomy of the Indian civilization in relation to the West. Historically, the rhetoric is linked to the experiences of Western colonialism and post-World-War-II dominance.

Traditionalism as a safeguard against Westernization

The revival of the Pañcāyatana Pūjā that I studied in Chennai in 2014 was started and promoted by Sarma Sastrigal. He is a religious authority figure with a large group of followers among Smārta Brahmins in Chennai, as well as on Facebook, where he is followed by more than seven thousand persons. He organized the ceremony in which 108 married couples of Smārta Brahmins were initiated into the performance of this specific worship. All couples had been selected carefully beforehand from a larger group of candidates through a process of personal interviews, etc.[8]

For Sarma Sastrigal, however, the promotion of the Pañcāyatana Pūjā is only part of a larger agenda of revitalizing traditional Brahmin values and lifestyle in Tamil Nadu, an agenda that has been articulated more fully in his book *The Great Hindu Tradition* (Sastrigal 2011). The book is organized

8. All details can be found in Aktor 2016.

as a Hindu how-to book with instructions for traditional dress, rituals, and the use of modern communication devices—like the cell phone—in manners acceptable from the point of view of traditional religious values. The need for how-to books is, while symptomatic of the situation, paradoxical. *Traditionally*, a traditional lifestyle in dress, manners, and rituals would be passed on from generation to generation through close family ties. Thus, for instance, the five stones used in the Pañcāyatana Pūjā are meant to be handed down from father to son together with the knowledge of their worship. They are not supposed to be bought in a shop as is customary today, and their proper use is not supposed to be learned from a written manual in a book or on the internet. Traditional patterns have, however, weakened due to a stronger global occupational and cultural integration brought on by modernization. Traditions are no longer tied to the family as a matter of course, and the family is no longer a guarantee of their transmission. While religious identity is still mediated through the material forms of certain lifestyles, the authority of transmission is no longer located exclusively in the family.

Instead, transmission processes are mediatized in a broader and more open framework, via how-to-manuals for instance, and the task has changed from one of maintenance of traditional identity to a rebuilding of lost group identities or the construction of new ones. Interestingly, the contemporary traditionalism among Smārta Brahmins is thus not anti-modern (Fuller and Narasimhan 2014, 16, 219–221). It embraces modern communication media and techniques, but it negotiates the scope of their use and especially the content that they make available. Priests answer their cell phones as much as others, even during temple service, but at the same time they are confronted with new problems:

Veda mantra as ring tone?

Qn: Can I have a Veda mantra as my Ring tone in my mobile?

Ans: No. It is not advisable. Instead please choose some sloka for this purpose. (Sastrigal 2011, 152)[9]

For this segment of Brahmins, the Vedas still stand out as the foundation of Brahmin exclusivism. The Vedas, regardless of what is grasped of their content, constitute the basis of their claim to sacredness, and must not be trivialized by worldly talks. It is different with verses (*ślokas*) from the epics and Purāṇas because these texts are regarded as universally open

9. "Veda mantra" in this connection typically refers to a recitation of one or more verses from hymns in the Rig Veda, for instance the Gāyatrī mantra (RV 3.62.10) which is part of the Hindu early morning service (*saṃdhyā*) and many other rituals.

to all. Ironically, however, these Brahmin readers have to be taught what is meant by "Vedas":

Veda and Vedanta

Qn: I would like to know the precise meaning of the words Veda and Vedanta.

Ans: Vedanta is a part of Veda. As you know, the Vedas are four: Rig, Yajur, Sama and Atharvana. The main text of each of the Vedas is known as its Samhita. Besides Samhita, the Veda has two other sections: Brahmana and Aaranyaka. Brahmana contains the basic mantras, and lists the Vedic karmas [rituals] and the procedure of each of the karmas. Aaranyaka is concerned with the philosophy and the fundamental meaning of each mantra in the Samhita and each Vedic karma described in Brahmana. Known as 'Gnana kanda', the final section of Aaranyaka comprises the Upanishads. (Sastrigal 2011, 148)[10]

"Westernization" is seen as an influence from popular globalized mass media which has to be restricted:

Valentine's day

Qn: What are your views on celebrating Valentine's Day?

Ans: The very concept of Valentine's day is absurd. Young minds have been polluted and misguided into making this barbaric practice an acceptable one. Elders object to it primarily because it propagates permissive behavior that is alien to our culture. (Sastrigal 2011, 142)

Similarly on birthday parties:

Qn: Celebrating birthday parties has these days become a way of life. What do you feel about this?

Ans: Generally in our tradition, there is no place for individual birthday celebrations. [...] However, if you feel that you should celebrate the birthday please do not follow the Western culture in doing so. You can go to a temple [...] and devote yourself to prayer for your well-being. Especially the practice of blowing out candles is reprehensible to our Dharma. We believe in lighting lamps to celebrate something, not putting them out. (Sastrigal 2011, 120)

Another way of negotiating modernity is to project its scientific, technical and cultural advances into the ancient past of the indigenous tradition. In October 2014 during my field work in Chennai, Prime Minister Narendra

10. The term *vedānta*, "the end of the Vedas," denotes the Upaniṣads but also what was considered the central teachings of these texts and the later Hindu philosophical interpretations of them. This is also referred to in the quote as "Gnana kanda" (*jñānakāṇḍa*), the knowledge part of the Vedas as distinct from the ritual part, the *karmakāṇḍa*.

Modi became notorious for claiming, in a public speech, that the mythology of the elephant-headed Gaṇeśa is an indication that a technique of plastic surgery was known in ancient India, and that the story in the Sanskrit epic Mahābhārata about the hero Karṇa who, according to the narrative, was born outside the womb from the ear of his virgin mother, means that "genetic science was present at that time" (Rahman 2014). One of my Smārta Brahmin informants who had returned to India after a career in the USA as a nuclear physicist made similar claims. He was also firmly convinced that *all* modern languages have developed from Sanskrit and that Greek philosophers like Aristotle and Socrates were really Indians, since names that sound similar to these Greek names can be found in the Mahābhārata. This search for an "autochtonous ordering" of the present (Klimkeit 1981, 314), whereby foreign ideas or inventions are re-framed as rooted in one's own soil, has been a recognizable trope of the discourse *vis à vis* influence from Western thinking since the reform movements during the eighteenth and nineteenth century, not only within Hinduism, but equally within Islam and Buddhism.

The materiality of traditionalism

In the Indian context that I have studied, "traditionalism" refers on its rhetorical surface to a holding on to a dwindling body of traditional and inherited customs, rituals, and values; customs, rituals, and values that are now revitalized and promoted as a form of resistance, not to modernization, but to "Westernization." "Westernization" is typically understood as consisting of a mixture of Western materialism, consumerism, and lack of respect for social norms. Traditionalist Brahmins criticize the way their fellow-Indians have imitated and adopted Western habits, and they "wish that traditional Brahman customs had not been so overwhelmed by modern change and non-Brahman tastes" (Fuller and Narasimhan 2014, 14). They frequently lament the young generation's attraction to things "Western" in terms of clothing, food, entertainment, family structures, etc., as well as their neglect of traditional knowledge. As a traveler in India I have overheard many such conversations between adults (typically teachers) who put all kinds of present calamities down to the young people's lack of knowledge of Sanskrit, *dharma* (social norms), religion, etc.

As is well-recognized, traditionalism must be understood dialectically as "a product of modernity and a characteristically modern ideological orientation toward tradition and traditions" (Fuller 2003, 162). In his discussion of this relationship between modernity and traditionalism, Fuller (2003, 160–167) supports S. N. Eisenstadt's characterization that traditionalism should not be confused with a simple upkeep of a tradition. "Rather, it denotes an ideological mode and stance oriented against the new symbols; it espouses certain parts of the older tradition as the only legitimate symbols of the traditional order and upholds them against 'new' trends" (Eisenstadt 1973, 22, quoted in Fuller 2003, 160). This is why we need to be more specific about the nature of these "new symbols" that traditionalists, in the Indian context, are oriented against. Fuller suggests that in this context the promise of equality in the Indian Constitution is an important defining factor in the transition to modernity and one with far-reaching historical consequences: "In modern India, therefore, equality is not just a secondary or residual social fact; it is progressively displacing traditional hierarchy as a compelling value" (Fuller 2003, 161). The fundamental agenda of the *Non-Brahmin Manifesto* from 1916 was exactly to point out the disproportionate privileges of the relative small Brahmin section of society at that time. In Tamil politics, the situation has changed radically since then, and the Brahmin community has lost any defining influence on state politics, job recruitment, education, etc. In addition, it has lost the prerogative to define the common values and norms for Indian society at large, what Ronald Inden has called the "enunciative function" (Inden 1992, 573). This situation conflicts with Brahmin self-perceptions since it is a function to which Brahmins have felt entitled during the long pre-colonial history of India.

The notion of "traditionalism" is understood differently in different academic contexts. In its relative unproblematic relationship with modernization and scientific progress, the Brahmin traditionalism in Tamil Nadu, for example, is different from the traditionalist heritage in the West studied by Mark Sedgwick (2004). One key difference is that traditionalism in the Indian context is not a dream of a lost spiritual knowledge. According to Sedgwick, the Western traditionalist movement understands tradition as "belief and practice transmitted from time immemorial—or rather belief and practices that *should* have been transmitted but was lost to the West during the last half of the second millennium A.D." (Sedgwick 2004, 21). The Western traditionalist movement sought spirituality in ancient gnostic texts as well as in "the Wisdom of the East." Their view on religion was *perennialist*; i.e., they believed that "all religions shared a common origin in a single perennial (or primeval or primordial) religion that had subsequently taken a variety of forms, including Zoroastrian, Pharaonic, Platonic, and Christian" (Sedgwick 2004, 24). Perennialism has its origin in the Renaissance, but was revitalized by the modern traditionalist movement during the late nineteenth and early twentieth century in a cultural exchange with Asian intellectuals. Classical Oriental texts were translated into Western languages and influenced the intellectual climate in Western countries. Seen through this perennialist filter, the Vedānta philosophy with its emphasis on a monistic teaching of unity between an abstract, undifferentiated divine principle (*brahman*) and the human "Self" (*ātman*) was understood as the very essence of Hinduism. The synthesis that blended these old ideas with the contemporary colonial experience of religious diversity—in the teaching that all religions are really paths to the same goal—was, however, what made this "Neo-Vedānta" (or "Vedanta-Perennialism," Sedgwick 2004, 24) quite different from medieval Vedānta theology.

According to Sedgwick (2004, 40–41), Western Theosophists, like Henry Steel Olcott who operated in India in the late nineteenth and early twentieth century, had an important impact on the process by which the neo-Vedānta became part of Western traditionalism. The non-Brahmin movement distanced itself from the Theosophist version of Vedānta, which built on Brahminical ideas and values (see fn. 7 above), whereas intellectual Brahmins readily took part in this joint venture project between Western and Indian intellectuals.

Today, traditionalist Smārta Brahmins in Chennai still subscribe, in parts, to the neo-Vedānta, at least to its symbols,[11] but their attitude is quite different from the ideals of Western traditionalism as described by Sedgwick. They are not looking for a lost spirituality. Instead, they strive to preserve an identity, that is, an identity as well as a traditional authority based on Hindu religious practices. These practices are not lost but have come under pressure due to specific developments in Tamil Nadu. Their attempt to preserve religious identity and traditional authority is mediated in material forms. In this context, I draw on a notion of materiality as a perspective on human practices that stresses human interactions, through the senses, with the surroundings, places, objects, and their uses. David Morgan argues that it is inadequate to regard religion primarily as a matter of belief, or rather, belief takes place *as* time and *as* space via the many activities involved in religious practice, including the objects and places with which, and at which, such practices unfold—and including the production processes and networks that make these practices possible (Morgan 2010, 4-5). Thus, contemporary authority construction and traditionalism in South India sim-

11. Those I interviewed in Chennai may not make a clear historical distinction between medieval Vedānta and neo-Vedānta, but I noticed that the Pūjā room of one of my informants, besides some drawings of the eighth century Vedānta philosopher Śaṅkara, was decorated with the photos of Ramakrishna, Sharada Devi and Vivekananda, the three icons of neo-Vedānta. Swami Vivekananda deliberately transformed the devotional and Tantric religiosity of his guru, the Bengali saint Ramakrishna (1836-1886), into a rationalized, philosophical neo-Vedānta message about the unity of all religious paths in the one goal of realizing the Absolute.

ply cannot be understood in depth, if we disregard the forms of media and materiality involved.

Sarma Sastrigal's book (2011) is instructive with regard to how traditionalism and traditional authority is materialized. It gives instructions about rituals and their utensils, such as the use of the specific stones in the Pañcāyatana Pūjā (116), the use of the beads (*rudrākṣa*) from the Utrasum Bead Tree that are associated with the worship of Śiva (133), the leaves of Holy Basil (*tulasī*) used in the worship of Viṣṇu (126), the ritually purifying ring of sacred straw (*pavitra*) worn around the ring finger of the right hand during rituals (172), and much more. Readers are also educated about traditional clothing, hair styles, and ear piercings. Special attention is given to the traditional Tamil dress of the husband and wife, the *pañcakacchā* and the *madisar* respectively. The *pañcakacchā* is a special way of binding the male lower garment, the *veṣṭi*. There is a whole sociology of the male lower garment in South India. Colors (white for Brahmins and in formal contexts; ochre for monks but now also a fashion among family men; patterned for working class men), size (bigger for formal purposes), and folding—as a skirt (informal), or not, all these aspects signal status and context:

> **Qn:** Can grahastas (married men) wear veshti in kaavi (brownish yellow / orange colour)?
>
> **Ans:** No. *Kaavi vastra* is meant for Sanyasa ashram [the life of monks and nuns]. It should not be worn by grahastas. Even while observing some vrata [votive observance], kaavi to be avoided. If there is a need for a colour vastram [cloth], one can use a colour other than kaavi. (Sastrigal 2011, 137)

Today, the *pañcakacchā* has mostly disappeared as part of normal everyday dress. But that should be changed, according to this guide:

> **Qn.** Please elaborate on special dresses like madisar and panchakachcham that we have to wear on religious occasions.
>
> **Ans.** There is an error—though it is understandable—in your question. Madisar and panchakachcham are NOT special dresses! We are supposed to be wearing these daily. And there was a time when these were being worn as a way of life. They have now become rare through the ravages of time. (Sastrigal 2011, 97)

To mend the situation, the book spends eight illustrated pages to instruct readers how to bind the *veṣṭi* in the *pañcakacchā* manner ("Pancha kachcham in *visuals*," Sastrigal 2011, 51–58).[12]

12. Similar instructions can easily be found on the internet. A Google search on "panchakachcham" or "madisar" will produce several illustrated web pages and video demonstrations.

The authority of traditionalism

If authority is a kind of speech act exerting a force on its hearers, as Bruce Lincoln suggests, and if it depends on a "theatrical array" of "stage devices" in the form of dress, spaces, images, and other material paraphernalia (Lincoln 1994, 2–5), how does it function in the traditionalist communication expressed by Sarma Sastrigal and other Smārta Brahmins in words, appearances, and performances, and what is the target audience? How is authority distributed among the different agents that are part of the promotion of Brahmin traditionalism, and how do different forms of media and materiality play into contemporary constructions of authority and identity?

The target group of a book like *The Great Hindu Tradition* is first of all the group of Smārta Brahmins in Tamil Nadu; it is written by a leader within the community who teaches his less traditionally trained fellow members how to cultivate a traditional Smārta Brahmin identity. Identity markers, however, are two-sided. They are meant to promote self-assuredness, self-respect, and pride internally in the group but also to make clear and visible statements targeted at the surrounding society. The identity markers are meant to signal that the leaders are the heirs to the tradition that has steered India in terms of politics, social structure, culture, and religion through thousands of years; accordingly, they deserve respect and their authority is needed in society if it is to survive in a globalized world.

"Tradition" is a typical status phenomenon that is articulated by professional groups such as a priestly class or a class of intellectuals. But in line with the development through which these social classes become institutionalized, they acquire the means to execute power, to be *in* authority (Lincoln 1994, 3–9). For religious institutions, this can involve an ethical conflict, which may prompt such institutions to hide their use of power. The internal authority structure within the group of traditionalist Tamil Smārta Brahmins is not limited to the relationship between religious entrepreneurs like Sarma Sastrigal and a large group of less knowledgeable lay Brahmins. Sastrigal's authority is further supported by a weighty religious institution, the Kāñcī Maṭha (Kāñcī Kāmakoṭī Pīṭham). This is one of two South Indian monastic seats of the Daśanāmī order of the Advaita Vedānta school, which forms the doctrinal foundation for *smārta* theology (for more information about the order, see Dazey 2012). The ceremony in 2014, revitalizing the Pañcāyatana Pūjā, was carefully coordinated with the Maṭha, whose two junior and senior pontiffs (*śaṅkarācāryas*) had blessed the 108 wooden boxes, each containing the Pañcāyatana sets of five stones to be handed over to the 108 married couples of Smārta Brahmins at the ceremony. On Facebook, Sarma Sastrigal later posted photographs of the letters in which the pontiffs officially blessed his book *The Great Hindu Tradition* (Sarma Sastrigal on Facebook 12 February 2017).[13]

Kāñcī Maṭha and its two pontiffs represent the highest level of religious authority among Smārta Brahmins, supported both by strong economic resources and powerful social networks. In the surrounding non-Brahmin society, however, its authority is far from undisputed. According to media theorist Stig Hjarvard, "if power is understood as the ability to influence actions and thoughts, authority occurs when the power of an entity [...] is recognized as effective and legitimate" (Hjarvard 2016, 11). This means that if the use of power by a religious institution is no longer accepted as legitimate, say, its authority will decline.

The Kāñcī Maṭha is a good case. The authority of this institution was severely jeopardized when a former accountant at the Maṭha, Sankararaman Anantakrishnasharma, was murdered in 2004 by a group of men, some of whom had been in contact with the senior pontiff. The accountant had openly accused the Maṭha of a long-running misuse of money and the pontiffs of sexual relations with several women over the years. A large sum of money was transferred from the bank account of the Maṭha and received by the pontiff's contact among the murderers.

The case was heavily politicized from the start. Tamil Nadu's Chief Minister and leader of the Dravidian AIADMK, J. Jayalalithaa, ordered that the senior pontiff should be arrested and held for interrogation. She did this in accordance with the non-Brahmin ideology of the AIAMDK and its voters, despite the fact that she herself was a Brahmin by birth and had been a devotee of the Maṭha. Appeals were made by the pontiffs to the Supreme Court of India, suggesting that they would not be given a fair trial in Tamil Nadu due to the Dravidian and more or less anti-Brahmin ideology of the leading political parties DMK and AIAMDK. As a result, the case was moved to the neighboring union territory Puducherry (formerly Pondicherry). The victim's widow and other key witnesses gave statements that supported the accusations against the group of men that had been arrested for the murder and against the senior pontiff as responsible for ordering the killing. Years later, during the legal proceedings, however, these key witnesses retracted their former statements and were all declared hostile by the judges. Allegations were made that this happened under political pressure from the rival DMK party which wanted to put the AIAMDK chief minister in an unfavorable light, in a case into which she had invested her personal political prestige. By declaring the witnesses hostile, the court would be in

13. https://www.facebook.com/Sarmasasthrigal/posts/1414259698696463. Sarma Sastrigal's timeline on Facebook is public.

a position to acquit the accused. Whatever the actual circumstances, the Puducherry court eventually acquitted all of the accused in the case, including the pontiffs of Kāñcī Maṭha, in 2013 due to lack of evidence (Jesudasan and Nadarajan 2013).

In an interview with Sheela Bhatt from the news media *Rediff.com* in 2004 when the case had opened, Supreme Court advocate Kavi Tejpal Singh Tulsi, who represented the Tamil Nadu government in the case against the accused, defended Jayalalithaa's order to arrest the pontiffs:

> Tulsi: What is Jayalalithaa's fault? Is it that she has allowed the law to take its own course? Is she not supposed to? Perhaps not. Because for them a Brahmin is above the law!
>
> Bhatt: How can you entirely delink the case against the Shankaracharya from Dravidian politics in Tamil Nadu?
>
> Tulsi: It is true that Dravidian politics is anti-Brahmin. But Jayalalithaa has not got this murder engineered.
>
> Bhatt: The prosecution's case suits her politics...
>
> Tulsi: Let it suit her, but it suits constitutionalism too. It suits the majesty of law. It suits the concept of *equality* of all before the eyes of the law. May you ever be so high, but the law is above you. (Bhatt 2004)[14]

Compare this to the analysis of another news media from the same year:

> Within the state [Tamil Nadu], the seer [the senior pontiff] has found no support from political parties. The Dravida Munnetra Kazhagam (DMK), which had planned an agitation in connection with the murder case to demand the arrest of the 'real culprits,' cancelled its programme following the arrest. [...] The only support the seer has received in the state has come from the BJP and the Sangh Parivar [the Hindu Nationalist organizations], whose influence in the state is inconsequential. BJP's national General Secretary L. Ganesan condemned the arrest and demanded the Shankaracharya's immediate release. The Vishwa Hindu Parishad (VHP), Hindu Munnani, and the RSS also condemned the arrest. The hartal called by the VHP to protest the arrest failed to evoke any response, proving that public at large have not been affected by the turn of events. (Kumar 2004).[15]

14. Italics added. Compare Fuller's remarks about the constitutional promise of equality as the essential symbol of modernity in the Indian context.

15. The Viśva Hindū Pariṣad (VHP, The World Hindu Council) was founded in 1964 by RSS leader Madhav Sadashiv Golwalkar and journalist Shivram Shankar Apte in order to oppose the challenges from Christianity, Islam, and Communism on a global level. It works internationally to strengthen Hindu nationalist courses such as active opposition to conversion to Christianity and Islam, the banning of cow slaughter, and the building of a temple for the god Rāma in Ayodhya at the spot where the sixteenth century Babri Mosque was located until it was demolished in 1992 by Hindu nationalists with support from VHP. The Hindu Munnani (Hindu Front) is a Hindu militant nationalist organization located and operating in Tamil Nadu subscribing to some of the same courses as

The general political leanings among the traditionalist Smārta Brahmins in Chennai, also articulated by Sarma Sastrigal, is to support the BJP and the Sangh Parivar organizations. Sastrigal tells his readers about his own relationship with the RSS:

Qn: Can we have a brief sketch of Sri Golwalkar?

Ans: Sri Golwalkar [...] became the chief of RSS after the demise of its founder Dr K B Hedgewar in 1940. [...] I had the fortune of interacting with this great soul several times from 1964 to 1975 when I was actively associated with RSS, and receiving his blessings. I recollect the occasion when both the Acharyas of Kanchi, Sri Sri Maha Swamigal and Sri Sri Jayendra Saraswati Swamigal addressed and blessed the cadres at a training camp of RSS in Hyderabad in the year 1964. Guruji [Golwalkar] was indeed a glorious personality. (Sastrigal 2011, 157)[16]

As mentioned, the BJP support in Tamil Nadu is only 2.86 percent, but within a large area of the inner southern suburbs of Chennai, the demography is radically different from the rest of the state. In this area, the Brahmin residents make up somewhere between one half and two thirds of the population and therefore form a critical mass "as a cohesive, relatively homogeneous, subcultural group" (Fuller and Narasimhan 2014, 157). We may therefore expect the amount of BJP votes to have been somewhat higher in that area than in the rest of the state, although not so high as to threaten the AIADMK majority in the area. After all, only a portion of the Brahmin population in the area can be described as "Smārta traditionalists," and as shown here, their attempt to construct authority emerge in a contested setting.

The mediatization of traditionalism

Hinduism has been kept alive during the centuries through an extraordinarily rich body of mythological and hagiographical narratives transmitted from generation to generation through a multiplicity of media—oral and written forms of storytelling, imagery,[17] music, ritual, drama, and dance.

the VHP and the other organizations in the Sangh Parivar group. Rāṣṭriya Svayaṃsevak Saṅgh (RSS, The National Volunteer Organization) founded in 1925 is the militant branch of the Hindu nationalist movements in India. It has been banned thrice since independence: in 1948 after one of its members shot Mahatma Gandhi, during Indira Gandhi's emergency in 1975-1977, and after the demolition of the Babri Mosque in 1992. It is especially active in its mobilization of the Indian youth. On Hindu nationalism in Tamil Nadu, see also Fuller 2003, 130–142.

16. "Sri" (*śrī*) like the Hindi suffix "-jī" and the Tamil suffix "-gal" are typical Indian expressions of respect. When "Sri" is doubled it is intensified. "Sri Sri Maha Swamigal" is the late pontiff of the Kāñcī Maṭha, Chandrasekharendra Saraswati (1907-1994). Jayendra Saraswati is the present senior pontiff.

17. For the strong visuality of Hinduism, especially as expressed through three-dimensional

Popular prints, television, film, and comic books are modern mass media that have been instrumental in popularizing and standardizing this old narrative culture, but also functioned as instruments for the communication of new messages. The historical processes of the struggle for independence and post-independence nation-building efforts have produced their own narratives, and new syntheses of ancient mythology and modern secularist and nationalist ideologies have emerged and found expression in new media.[18] From this perspective, the mixture of religious revitalization and nationalism in Sarma Sastrigal's book and his staging of the Pāñcāyatana Pūjā initiation on Independence Day and in front of the national flag is not in itself surprising, but the role played by contemporary media is certainly worthy of more discussion.

Television productions with religious content, such as drama series based on mythological narratives, have a relatively large audience in India. This is also addressed by *The Great Hindu Tradition*:

> **Qn:** We see a number of programs these days on TV related to religion, Godliness and Bhakti [devotion]. Are these good?
>
> **Ans:** Certainly—it is worth seeing such programs to refine our religious beliefs. But there is an inherent danger here—we might get lulled into a sense of complacence and stop doing our nitya pujas [daily worship] and visiting temples. For example, the mere passive watching of a person chanting Vishnu Sahasranama ["The Thousand Names of Viṣṇu," a Sanskrit hymn] on TV is not equal to chanting it ourselves. (Sastrigal 2011, 135)

Stig Hjarvard's mediatization theory was developed with a view to the contemporary Scandinavian context. Nevertheless, it is quite clear that in India too we see the double-sidedness of the process of mediatization pointed out by Hjarvard (Hjarvard 2012, 24–26). In India, the media also have their own logic according to which they focus on gaining the attention of the audience, and religious and other messages will be subordinated to this aim. Religion is only one among other areas of communication in Indian mass media. In addition, religious institutions here too develop their own media platforms on television and the internet (Hjarvard 2016, 10). One such TV-station is the *Swasthictv.com* which has sent live TV from various events in the Smārta

images and image worship, see the brilliant *Lives of Indian Images* by Richard Davis (1997).

18. God posters and other forms of popular prints that started to be produced during colonization and are still important media of a contemporary religious and national aesthetics, have been examined in their historical context by Christopher Pinney (2004); the ubiquitous comic book series Amar Chitra Katha with stories from the mythology as well as from the religious and national hagiography has been studied by John Stratton Hawley (1995) among others.

Brahmin community, including Sarma Sastrigal's Pañcāyatana Initiation ceremony. Altogether, all parts of the Smārta traditionalist network are mediatized through modern mass media. The Kāñcī Maṭha has its own website, and the TV-station, the Maṭha, and Sarma Sastrigal all have parallel profiles on Facebook, which has become the platform that brings it all together. This includes many individual lay persons (with their own Facebook profiles) not only from India, but also among Hindu converts from Western countries and academic researchers like myself, who find this new kind of religious networking interesting. In this sense, their Facebook usage is an example of a significant process: Social network media like Facebook "rely on sociable forms of communication typical of small groups in face to face contexts, yet social network media transform and re-embed such communicative forms into larger networks of mediated 'friendships'" (Hjarvard 2016, 9).

Thus, the structure of authority within the community of traditionalist Smārta Brahmins is enlarged and amplified but still kept together through a mediatized practice in which all the elements of the structure take part. Yet, the larger question of how mediatization affects religious authority remains. According to Hjarvard, the effects of mediatization are individualization and a more consumer-oriented approach to the religious field. In as much as the authority of religious leaders is often questioned and critiqued in news media, religious institutions have to conform to media formats, rather than the other way around, and a proliferation of new voices in the religious field is facilitated by new media forms (Hjarvard 2016, 15). The new forms of media today are factors which are likely to contribute to a multiplication and potential renegotiation of traditional authority roles. Media theory makes a distinction between *mediation* and *mediatization*:

> Media and communication research has primarily been occupied with the study of "mediation," that is, the use of media for communicative practices, whereas the study of "mediatization" is concerned with the long-term influence of media on cultural and social structures and agency. (Hjarvard 2016, 9)

Traditional elements such as material ritual objects, books, and pamphlets with instructions and hymns, forms of clothing, and body practices are all media for the communication of traditional values, norms, and identity. Communication via modern media platforms like television and internet, however, influence the forms of participation and agency within the community. Therefore, the ascription of authority is now a mutual process of individual and collective practices.

> [Media] allow users to ascribe authority on an individual and voluntary basis. The process of building authority in the media is nevertheless a collective practice in the sense that participation by others becomes a token of author-

ity: the accumulated actions of reading, watching, liking, following, sharing, and commenting become indexes of the popularity of the media or communicator in question and his or her ability to articulate the sentiments and perceptions of a given community of people (Hjarvard 2016, 14).

In this sense, modern mediatization processes seem to reach beyond the classical Weberian forms of authority, the *charismatic*, the *traditional*, and the *rational*, which "concern the legitimacy of leaders to act on behalf of a collectivity and the ability to get subordinates to act in compliance with the person in authority [...] This does not apply to the same extent in the case of modern mediated communication. The use of mass media and social network media is predominantly a voluntary activity" that allows users "to ascribe authority on an individual and voluntary basis" (Hjarvard 2016, 13–14). Clearly, the use of modern media among traditionalist Smārta Brahmins is an example of how these media have become an indispensable part of "doing religion" under modern circumstances (Hjarvard 2016, 9) and of how authority claims are subject to constant negotiations in a more open religious field.

The commodification of traditionalism

An additional node in the Smārta traditionalist network in Chennai is the shop Giri Trading, which also has its own website with international internet sale and a parallel Facebook profile. The shop sells all kinds of items for worship—books, pamphlets, CDs, Pūjā remedies, images, posters, dress—in short, everything "FOR ALL YOUR DIVINE NEEDS," as the shop's slogan tells us.

"Traditionally," the set of five different stones that are worshiped in the Pañcāyatana Pūjā was passed on from an older family member to the younger and was never to be bought or sold. "Traditionally" each of the five stones should be collected at a certain specific location in South Asia. Together, these locations encompassed the whole South Asian subcontinent from northern Nepal to a town near Thanjavur in the present Tamil Nadu. "Traditionally," four of the five stones were also supposed to be as unprocessed as when they were collected from their natural locations in the landscape, because they were regarded as direct manifestations of the divinities they make present, and therefore not in need of any further processing or sacralization. I have never been able to find textual, normative evidence in classical Pūjā manuals for these traditions, but they flow around as oral instructions and can also be found on the internet today.[19]

19. See for instance the talks of the late pontiff of Kāñcī, Chandrasekharendra Saraswati that have been translated in written form and put on the internet by Ananandji Varadarajan

The point is—hence the quotation marks in the above—that whatever may have been the normative practice in earlier generations before the ritual was more or less forgotten, new generations now participating in its revitalization have to set aside these rules. Most people will have to buy the stones in a shop like Giri Trading, rather than receive them from an elder; the stones in the shop are not collected at the traditionally prescribed locations, but are obtained from professional distributers from wherever it is feasible; and some of them can no longer be found in their previous natural condition but are produced mechanically (for details, see Aktor 2015, 25–31 and 2016, 9–22). Do these modern changes devaluate the religious significance of the stones? No. Instead, modern commodification processes from collection and distribution to payment at the cash desk in the shop (or digitally on the internet) have taken over the old structures and made the ritual survive in a new context. The notion of commodification encompasses all these processes from collection to payment. In the words of Vineeta Sinha:

> The term "commodification" is not used pejoratively but refers to a complex process of treating something as an object of commerce and exchange in a marketplace. Such a focus warrants a discussion of production and distribution mechanisms and consumption patterns with respect to *pūjā* items, for example. Focusing on consumption of ritual objects is a necessary component of the larger story. (Sinha 2012, 644)

Commodification is not a profanation. The idea that the market *per se* trivializes or inhibits the sacred potential of ritual objects is not confirmed, neither historically nor by contemporary use (Sinha 2012, 643). What matters is the treatment of the objects by the customer when the items are brought home. I was told that while the Pañcāyatana stones are not in need of any specific sacralization ritual like those performed for man-made images, their "lives" are nevertheless dependent on regular worship by the user. Lack of worship brings the stones into a stage of withering. The transformation from an item for sale in a shop to an object of actual worship is a transition from a neutral to a charged state. Interestingly, this is in line with ancient and medieval rules in the Hindu legal literature (*dharmaśāstra*) about buying food from persons who are supposed to be polluting. According to these rules, pollution is generally transferred from person to person through touch, as well as via things handed from one person to another. But this rule is suspended for food items on sale. In that state they are neutral until they are appropriated by the customer, at which point they are associated with the personal state of the new owner (Aktor 2008, 141–143).

on his blog *Advaitham - By Lt. Col KTSV Sarma* (http://advaitham.blogspot.dk/2006/09/deivathin-kural-series-57.html).

Once bought and used, however, "Hindu religious objects acquire the status of being non-exchangeable." At that stage they are "not recyclable, and thus cannot circulate again in the marketplace" (Sinha 2011, 193).

While commodification is not in itself a profanation, merchandizing seems to differ depending on the context. On field work in Varanasi, I walked around in a t-shirt with an abstract but recognizable representation of Gaṇeśa. This funny-looking elephant-headed god is a frequent subject on t-shirts, bags, and other Hindu merchandize targeted at tourists. Later, I learned that my Gaṇeśa t-shirt was frowned at by pious Hindus who do not like their gods to be taken lightly as mere decoration. Sinha (2012, 647) mentions the Italian designer Roberto Cavelli who produced designer bikinis with a depiction of the god Rāma and Lacey Footwear "featuring the *om* sign on shoes" as creating both anger and indignation. These reactions are not so much about the images – Gaṇeśa, Rāma or the *om* sign – but more about the deliberately profane contexts they are set in by the producers: tourist souvenir, bikinis, and sandals. Religious merchandize sold at pilgrimage sites is one thing, and another is merchandize targeted at non-religious consumer markets like fashion or international tourism. These distinctions are not always clear, however, which is the reason why the merchandization of religious motives tend to trigger these debates about the limits of respectful handling of religious objects. Like other media forms, the internet has also changed the scope of commodification possibilities. Some internet shops, for instance, host blogs or discussion fora where customers can exchange experiences and knowledge. The internet as a new bazaar "has clearly surfaced not only as a powerful new marketplace in the trade of *pūjā* items but also as a critical teaching and learning platform" (Sinha 2012, 645).

Conclusion

I started my study of stones used in Hindu worship with a primarily theoretical interest in the contrast between the eloquence of Hindu mythology and the tacit quality of the unprocessed stones. Lying there in the landscape, these stones attract our attention but do not seem to tell us anything specific. And yet, they have been overlaid with layers of mythological and theological knowledge through their use in the Smārta Pañcāyatana Pūjā ritual. As such they have served as "exograms," brain-external memory stores of religious knowledge (Bednarik 2017). I did not find much information about the ritual, which seemed to have mostly died out in most parts of India—except for Tamil Nadu where it was revitalized among a group of Smārta Brahmins. Globalization has its benefits: via a Swedish colleague I met a Swedish convert to Hinduism who had been initiated into the Pūjā by a Tamil master. He knew about the group around Sarma Sastrigal in

Chennai. Doing field work in the city, however, I was puzzled by the strong traditionalist attitudes that were expressed both in interviews and in the many lifestyle choices that make the group stand out from their surroundings, and how it was combined with the use of a range of modern media forms. While I understand the pride of belonging to a tradition as rich as the Indian and the wish to preserve its cultural richness against the uniform effects of globalization, the irrationalities involved in claiming that all languages in the world originate from Sanskrit or that advanced techniques of aviation, genetic engineering, or plastic surgery were fully developed in ancient India, seem unnecessary for articulating the love of one's tradition. Neither is the support of militant Hindu nationalist groups like the RSS. This led me to investigate what lay behind this special kind of Tamil traditionalism and its claims to authority, and of the role played by the use of contemporary media forms.

In this chapter, I have tried to point to some elements in the Indian context that might deepen our understanding of these contemporary developments. The political history of Tamil Nadu, with its strong resistance to Brahmin supremacy, is certainly one factor. Key parts of Brahmin identity revolve around the ideas that Brahmins embody the highest spiritual knowledge, and that they are therefore entrusted with the authority to guide the rest of society, and to provide guidelines on its social structure. These ideas were passed on through the classical texts in Sanskrit discussed at the beginning of this chapter. Since the independence, Brahmin authority has been contested by the promises of equality laid down in the Constitution as well as by the non-Brahmin movements in South India. It seems that the call for self-respect, which was originally a means of uplift for the lower castes in the pre-independence era anti-caste campaigns, has now been appropriated by these high-caste Brahmins in their struggle for renewed social and political recognition. In a globalized Indian society, traditionalism also appropriates modern media communication and commodification networks in order to strengthen internal authority structures, as well as to spell out the traditionalist life style in material and bodily ways. This means, however, that South Indian traditionalism and traditional forms of religious authority are now articulated on mediatized, voluntarist, and individualizing terms.

References

Aktor, Mikael. 2008. *Ritualisation and Segregation: The Untouchability Complex in Indian Dharma Literature with Special Reference to Parāśarasmṛti and Parāśaramādhavīya.* Torino: Corpus Iuris Sancriticum / Cesmeo.

———. 2010. "Untouchability." In *Brill's Encyclopedia of Hinduism*, vol.2 ("Texts, Rituals, Arts, Concepts"), edited by Knut A. Jacobsen, Helene Basu, Angelika Malinar, and Vasudha Narayanan, 876–881. Leiden: Brill.

———. 2015. "The *śivaliṅga* between artifact and nature." In *Objects of Worship in South Asian Religions: Forms, Practices, and Meanings*, edited by Knut A. Jacobsen, Mikael Aktor and Kristina Myrvold, 14–34. Abingdon: Routledge.

———. 2016. "Five stones—four rivers—one town: The Hindu *Pañcāyatanapūjā*." In *Soulless Matter, Seats of Energy: Metals, Gems and Minerals in South Asian Traditions*, edited by Fabrizio M. Ferrari and Thomas W. P. Dähnhardt, 3–27. Sheffield: Equinox.

———. 2018. "Social classes: *varṇa*." In *Hindu Law: A New History of Dharmaśāstra*, edited by Patrick Olivelle and Donald R. Davis, Jr., 60–77. Oxford: Oxford University Press.

Bednarik, Robert G. 2017. "Aniconism and the origins of palaeoart." *Religion* 47(3): 353–365.

Begrich, Richard and Shalini Randeria. 2014. "Dalit Critiques of Hinduism." In *Brill's Encyclopedia of Hinduism*. Edited by Knut A. Jacobsen, Helene Basu, Angelika Malinar, and Vasudha Narayanan. http://referenceworks.brillonline.com/entries/brill-s-encyclopedia-of-hinduism/dalit-critiques-of-hinduism-COM_9000000156 .

Bhatt, Sheela. 2004. "'For them a Brahmin is above the law!'" *Rediff.com*, 1 December 2004 at http://in.rediff.com/news/2004/dec/01inter.htm

Charsley, Simon. 1996. "'Untouchable': What is in a Name?" *The Journal of the Royal Anthropological Institute* 2(1): 1–23.

Davis, Richard H. 1997. *Lives of Indian Images*. Princeton, NJ: Princeton University Press.

Dazey, Wade. 2012. "Daśanāmīs." In *Brill's Encyclopedia of Hinduism*, edited by Knut A. Jacobsen, Helene Basu, Angelika Malinar, and Vasudha Narayanan.

Eisenstadt, S. N. 1973. "Post-traditional societies and the continuity and reconstruction of tradition." *Dædalus* 102(1): 1–27.

Fuller, C. J. 2003. *The Renewal of the Pristhood: Modernity and Traditionalism in a South Indian Temple*. Princeton, NJ: Princeton University Press.

Fuller, C. J. and Haripriya Narasimhan. 2014. *Tamil Brahmans: The Making of a Middle-Class Caste*. Chicago, IL: The University of Chicago Press.

Hawley, John Stratton. 1995. "The Saints Subdued: Domestic Virtue and National Integration in Amar Chitra Katha." In *Media and the Transformation of Religion in South Asia*, edited by Lawrence A. Babb and Susan S. Wadley, 107–134. Philadelphia: University of Pennsylvania Press.

Hjarvard, Stig. 2012. "Three forms of mediatized religion: Changing the public face of religion." In *Mediatization and Religion: Nordic Perspectives*, edited by Stig Hjarvard and Mia Lövheim, 21–44. Gothenburg: Nordicom.

———. 2016. "Mediatization and the changing authority of religion." *Media, Culture & Society* 38(1): 8–17.

Inden, Ronald. 1992. "Changes in the Vedic priesthood." In *Ritual, State and History in South Asia: Essays in Honour of J. C. Heesterman*, edited by A. W. van den Hoek, D.H.A. Kolff, and M. S. Oort, 556–577. Leiden: Brill.

Infoelections.com. 2016. "Tamil Nadu latest caste/religion wise population demographics." http://infoelections.com/infoelection/index.php/tn/7434-caste-religion-wise-population-in-tamil-nadu.html

Irschick, Eugene F. 1969. *Politics and Social Conflict in South India: The Non-Brahman Movement and Tamil Seperatism, 1916–1929*. Mumbai: Oxford University Press.

Jackson, William J. 2012. "Smārta." In *Brill's Encyclopedia of Hinduism*. Edited by Knut A. Jacobsen, Helene Basu, Angelika Malinar, Vasudha Narayanan.

Jesudasan, Dennis S. and S. Nadarajan. 2013. "Sankararaman Murder: Kanchi Seers, Others Acquitted." *Outlook* 27 November 2013 at http://www.outlookindia.com/newswire/story/sankararaman-murder-kanchi-seers-others-acquitted/818765

Klimkeit, Hans-Joachim. 1981. *Der politische Hinduismus: Indische Denker zwischen religiöser Reform und politischem Erwachen*. Wiesbaden: Otto Harrassowitz.

Kumar, P. C. Vinoj. 2014. "The seer's fall from grace." *Tehelka.com*, 27 November 2004 at http://www.tehelka.com/2004/11/the-seers-fall-from-grace/

Lincoln, Bruce. 1994. *Authority: Construction and Corrosion*. Chicago, IL: University of Chicago Press.

Morgan, David. 2010. "Introduction: The matter of belief." In *Religion and Material Culture*, edited by David Margan, 1–17. London: Routledge.

Olivelle, Patrick. 2005. *Manu's Code of Law: A Critical Edition and Translation of the Mānava-Dharmaśāstra*. Oxford: Oxford University Press.

———. 2018. "Social and literary history of Dharmaśāstra: The foundational texts." In *Hindu Law: A New History of Dharmaśāstra*, edited by Patrick Olivelle and Donald R. Davis, Jr., 15–29. Oxford: Oxford University Press.

Pinney, Christopher. 2004. *Photos of the Gods: The Printed Image and Political Struggle in India*. London: Reaktion Books.

Pollock, Sheldon. 2006. *The Language of the Gods in the World of Men: Sanskrit, Culture, and Power in Premodern India*. Berkeley: University of California Press.

Rahman, Maseeh. 2014. "Indian prime minister claims genetic science existed in ancient times." *The Guardian* 28 October 2014. https://www.theguardian.com/world/2014/oct/28/indian-prime-minister-genetic-science-existed-ancient-times

Sastrigal, Sri Sarma. 2011. *The Great Hindu Tradition: An Insight into Vedic Principles, Sastras and Heritage*. Second ed. Privately published. Printed in Chennai.

Sedgwick, Mark. 2004. *Against the Modern World: Traditionalism and the Secret Intellectual History of the Twentieth Century*. Oxford: Oxford University Press.

Sharma, Ram Sharan. 1990 [1958]. *Śūdras in Ancient India: A Social History of the Lower Order Down to circa A.D. 600*. Third edition. Delhi: Motilal Banarsidass.

Sinha, Vineeta. 2011. *Religion and Commodification: "Merchandizing" Diasporic Hinduism*. New York: Routledge.

———. 2012. "Commodification." In *Brill's Encyclopedia of Hinduism*, vol. 4 ("Historical Perspectives, Poets, Teachers, and Saints, Relation to other Religions and Traditions, Hinduism and Contemporary Issues"), edited by Knut A. Jacobsen, Helene Basu, Angelika Malinar, and Vasudha Narayanan, 641–649. Leiden: Brill.

Vajpeyi, Ananya. 2010. "Śūdradharrna and legal treatments of caste." In *Hinduism and Law: An Introduction*, edited by Timothy Lubin, Donald R. Davis, Jr. and Jayanth K. Krishnan, 154–166. Cambridge: Cambridge University Press.

About the author

Mikael Aktor is Associate Professor of the Study of Religions at the University of Southern Denmark. His research has been divided between studies of the South Asian precolonial Law Books (*dharmaśāstra*), with special regard to the rules of untouchability, and fieldwork studies of contemporary Hindu material culture.

Indices

Name Index

Italic text is used for titles of texts. *Italic* numbers are used for illustrations.

Subject Index

Italic text is used for titles of texts. *Italic* numbers are used for illustrations. Placenames are given their current country.